BEYOND THE BAY

A Collection of Recipes

The Junior Service League of Panama City, Florida

The purpose of the Junior Service League shall be to foster interest among its members in the social, economic, cultural, and civic conditions in their community and to make effective their volunteer service. The proceeds from the sale of *Beyond the Bay* will be used for community projects sponsored by The Junior Service League.

| First Printing | September, 1985 | 10,000 copies |
| Second Printing | June, 1986 | 10,000 copies |

Published by
The Junior Service League of Panama City, Inc.
P.O. Box 404
Panama City, Florida 32402

Library of Congress Catalog Card Number 85-080022
ISBN 0-9615014-1-3

Printed in the United States of America
WIMMER BROTHERS
P.O. Box 18408
Memphis, Tennessee 38181-0408

BEYOND the BAY

INTRODUCTION

The Junior Service League of Panama City proudly presents *Beyond the Bay*, a companion edition to our acclaimed *Bay Leaves*, first published in 1975.

While much has changed in the decade since 1975, much has stayed the same, particularly in the quiet backwaters of towns such as Panama City, where gracious living and entertaining is still a way of life.

It was this that the League set about to capture in *Bay Leaves*, and we're happy to add to the heritage with this exquisite new edition, *Beyond the Bay*. This book, however, goes one step further by expanding its horizons "beyond the Bay" to Panama City's other major body of water—the shimmering Gulf of Mexico and the luxury condominiums indicative of today's faster-paced lifestyles that line its shores.

Unifying these themes of Bay and Gulf, old and new, are eight lovely illustrations by local artist Paul Brent, specially commissioned for *Beyond the Bay*. These watercolors bring home to the reader the incredible natural beauty of Bay County, which draws visitors back again and again. From the moss-dripping magnolias and flamboyant day lilies of Bunkers Cove to the sugar-white beaches of the Gulf, proudly presided over by rare brown pelicans, Panama City abounds in Southern style and grace - as do the recipes of *Beyond the Bay*.

To your culinary enjoyment and the endeavors which this book will support, we dedicate *Beyond the Bay*.

BEYOND the BAY

COMMITTEE

Ruth Pilcher Lark, *Chairman*
Nell Mathis Ennis, *Co-chairman*
Amy Wilson Armstrong
Georgia Greenwell Dake
Jann Wyckoff Daughdrill
Anda Boyd Gagnet
Judy Elms Hughes
Linda Armstrong Johnson
Inez Gray McCloy
Carol Dresser Mizell
Laura Alfred Presley
Robin Steinbrecher Ross
Amy Baker Scott
Billie Kelly Smith
Janice Wynn Strickland
Bettina Mead Youd

TABLE OF CONTENTS

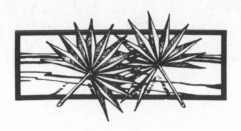

ABOUT THE ARTIST

The illustrations for *Beyond the Bay* are the creation of local artist Paul Brent and reflect the grace and style of Panama City the same way as our recipes do.

Paul Brent is a member of the National Watercolor Society and has exhibited his work in museums and galleries throughout the United States. His paintings have been selected for numerous corporate and private collections, including Disney World, Ameri-First Federal and Winsor-Newton. When asked about his work for *Beyond The Bay,* he explained, "I hoped to convey to the person using this book what our area is like visually. I accomplished this through a series of images that conjure up sights and smells of Bay County to make the use of this cookbook a total experience."

The artist has lived in Bay county since 1969 and is married to the former Lana Jane Lewis, a native of Panama City. Both the Brents enjoy cooking and serving the regional specialties in their home.

APPETIZERS
& BEVERAGES

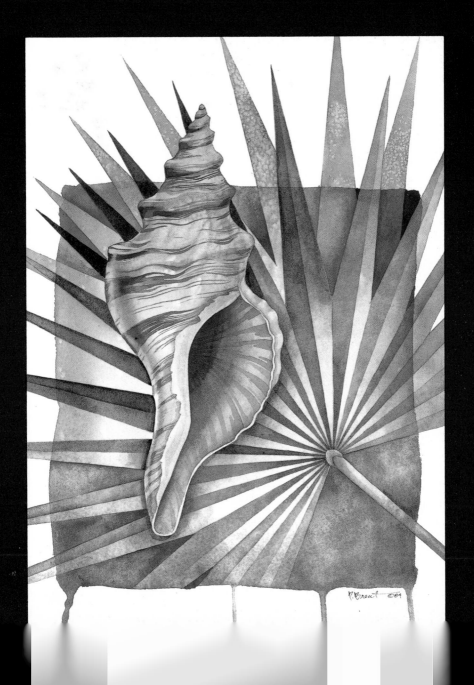

Horse Conch and Palmetto—The horse conch is the area's largest mollusk, sometimes growing over 18 inches in length. The palmetto, a native shrub, lines Bay County's shores.

APPETIZERS

COUNTRY PÂTÉ

4 to 6 bay leaves
6 slices bacon, divided
4 tablespoons butter or margarine, divided
1 cup chopped parsley, divided
½ cup chopped green onions
½ cup chopped onions
3 cloves garlic, minced
2 shallots, minced
2 pounds mild Italian sausage

1¼ cups beer, divided
1 teaspoon fennel
1 pound ground veal or very lean ground beef
2 cups herb seasoned stuffing mix
2 large eggs, lightly beaten
Salt and pepper to taste
½ cup chopped walnuts

Line a paté mold or 9x5x3-inch loaf pan with bay leaves in a decorative pattern then cover length of pan with 3 strips bacon; set aside. Half fill a roasting pan with water and put in a 350°F. oven. Melt 3 tablespoons butter in a large skillet. Sauté ½ cup parsley, onions, garlic and shallots about 2 minutes. Remove to a large bowl. Slit sausage and remove casing; sauté and separate sausage and ¼ cup beer until meat starts to lose pink color. Stir in fennel and add to parsley-onion mixture. In same skillet melt remaining 1 tablespoon butter and sauté veal adding ¼ cup beer; add to onion-sausage mixture. Sauté remaining bacon in same skillet for 2 minutes. Blend in stuffing mix and remaining ¼ cup beer. Combine with onion-sausage mixture; allow to cool slightly. Add remaining parsley, eggs, salt and pepper to taste. (Country Paté is not a smooth texture but at this time you may run mixture through food processor just to mix well; do not over process.) Add nuts and carefully pack into prepared pan. (Excess may be placed in custard cups for individual paté.) Wrap entire pan in heavy duty aluminum foil; place in roasting pan and bake 1 hour at 350°F. Remove from oven and place weights (canned goods or books) on top of paté for 3-4 hours. Refrigerate. To serve remove foil and loosen sides of pan, pat excess fat with paper towel. Serve with French bread, cornichons and mushrooms. Serves 20-25.

Note: This may be made 3-4 days in advance and frozen until ready to use.

Marsha Lewis (Mrs. E. Clay, III)

CHAFING DISH BEEF BOURGUIGNON

12 (½-inch thick) slices beef
fillet, cubed
½ cup clarified butter
½ teaspoon paprika
Salt to taste
2 beef bouillon cubes

Juice of 1 lemon (about 2
tablespoons)
¼ cup burgundy
2-3 medium fresh garlic cloves,
minced

Brown beef quickly over very high heat in clarified butter. Remove steak from pan. Add remaining ingredients, lower heat and cook until thickened. Combine beef and sauce in chafing dish over low heat so the fillet will remain rare.

Betty Steinbrecher (Mrs. Raymond)

MUSHROOM AND SAUSAGE STRUDEL

2 pounds sweet Italian sausage
2 pounds fresh mushrooms
¼ cup minced shallots or green
onions
16 tablespoons butter or margarine
2 tablespoons vegetable oil
Salt and pepper to taste

2 8-ounce packages cream cheese
8 sheets strudel dough (16x22
inches), available at gourmet
stores
¾ cup or more melted butter
or margarine
Breadcrumbs

Remove sausage meat from casing and cook and crumble until no longer pink. Mince mushrooms and squeeze dry. Sauté with shallots in butter and oil over moderately high heat, stirring frequently. Cook until pieces separate and liquid has evaporated. Season to taste with salt and pepper. Combine with sausage and blend in cream cheese. Spread a sheet of strudel dough on a damp towel, narrow end toward you. Brush with melted butter and sprinkle on breadcrumbs. Repeat with second and third sheets but do not crumb the fourth sheet. Put half the sausage-mushroom mixture on narrower edge of strudel dough leaving a 2-inch border at sides; fold in sides. Using edge of towel roll jelly-roll fashion. Put strudel on buttered baking sheet and brush with melted butter. Repeat with remaining strudel sheets and sausage-mushroom mixture. Bake at 400°F. about 20 minutes until brown. Cut with shears if possible. If not to be served that day, cover tightly and freeze. Leave at room temperature for a while the day of serving then reheat in oven.

Ann Aldrich Logue

MUSHROOM SPREAD

4 slices bacon
8-ounces (about 3 cups) fresh
 mushrooms, chopped
1 medium onion, finely chopped
1 garlic clove, minced
2 tablespoons all-purpose flour
¼ teaspoon salt

Dash of pepper
1 8-ounce package cream cheese,
 cubed
2 teaspoons Worcestershire sauce
1 teaspoon soy sauce
½ cup sour cream

Cook bacon until crisp; drain, reserving 2 tablespoons of drippings. Crumble bacon and set aside. Cook mushrooms, onion and garlic in drippings until tender and most of the liquid has evaporated. Stir in flour, salt and pepper. Add cream cheese, Worcestershire and soy sauce. Heat and stir until cheese is melted. Stir in sour cream and crumbled bacon. Heat thoroughly but do not allow it to boil. Serve warm. Makes about 2½ cups.

Laurie Combs (Mrs. Sam)

MUSHROOM PÂTÉ

1 pound mushrooms
1 large onion, finely chopped
2 tablespoons butter or margarine
3 tablespoons lemon juice

2 teaspoons Worcestershire sauce
½ teaspoon salt
½ teaspoon pepper
¼ cup mayonnaise

Clean and trim mushrooms; set aside. Sauté onion briefly in butter. Process mushrooms until finely chopped. Add to onion. Mix in all remaining ingredients except mayonnaise. Cook over medium high heat until mixture dries but does not brown. Place mixture in bowl and cool. When cool, stir in mayonnaise. Pack into small souffle dish or crock; chill thoroughly. Serve with crackers or Melba toast.

Hannelore Holland (Mrs. William)

STUFFED RAW CABBAGE

1 large cabbage head
½ medium onion
1 pound fresh shrimp or crabmeat,
    cleaned and peeled, and cooked
2 3-ounce packages cream cheese,
    softened

½ cup mayonnaise
Salt and pepper
Red pepper
Worcestershire sauce

Hollow out large cabbage reserving cabbage removed from center. In a food processor blend reserved cabbage, onion, and shrimp. Mix in cream cheese together with mayonnaise, salt and pepper, red pepper and Worcestershire to taste. Put mixture into hollowed cabbage head. Oil large cabbage leaves to put underneath-to make it look like a flower. Serve with crackers.

Jan Fensom (Mrs. James B.)

VEGETABLE SANDWICH FILLING

4 firm tomatoes
2 small onions
2 small cucumbers
1 green pepper
1 tablespoon unflavored gelatin

2 carrots, grated
1 cup mayonnaise
½ teaspoon salt
2 tablespoons Worcestershire sauce

Grind tomatoes, onions, cucumbers and pepper in food processor. Drain vegetables, reserving 3 tablespoons juice. Sprinkle gelatin over vegetable juice and dissolve over hot water. Combine vegetables, grated carrots and gelatin mixture. Add mayonnaise and seasonings. Refrigerate overnight to congeal, stirring occasionally. Spread on bread that has been lightly spread with soft margarine to prevent sogginess. Makes about 3 cups.

Note: May be made up to 8 hours ahead if stacked only two sandwiches high.

Mary Louise Reese (Mrs. William)

MARINATED CAULIFLOWER

1 medium cauliflower

Wash and break into flowerets; set aside.

Marinade

1½ cups vegetable oil
½ cup cider vinegar
1 teaspoon prepared mustard
2 teaspoons salt
½ teaspoon Worcestershire sauce

½ teaspoon red pepper
½ teaspoon pepper
1 teaspoon sugar
1 minced garlic clove
Dash of hot pepper sauce

Place all ingredients in a covered dish or large jar, shake until well mixed. Pour over cauliflower. Marinate several hours, turning occasionally to keep cauliflower coated with dressing. Drain before serving.

Ann Bane (Mrs. Curtis)

ITALIAN OLIVES

1 8-ounce jar green olives,
  drained
1 cup black olives, drained
  and pitted
2 4-ounce cans mushrooms,
  drained

3 medium onions, sliced into rings
1 14-ounce can artichoke bottoms,
  quartered
3 large garlic cloves, crushed

In a medium serving bowl layer green and black olives, mushrooms, onion rings and artichokes. Put garlic on alternating layers. Pour marinade over top.

Marinade

⅓ cup tarragon vinegar
⅔ cup olive oil
¼ teaspoon tarragon

1½ teaspoons basil
¼ teaspoon crushed oregano

Mix ingredients well and pour over salad. Refrigerate 8 hours.

Mary Lane Smallwood (Mrs. Henry)

ARTICHOKES WITH CREAM CHEESE AND CAVIAR

1 8-ounce package cream cheese,
  softened
1 tablespoon sour cream
1 tablespoon mayonnaise
1 14-ounce can artichokes,
  drained and chopped

1 teaspoon grated onion
Salt and pepper to taste
Caviar

Blend softened cream cheese with sour cream and mayonnaise. Blend in artichokes and onion. Season with salt and pepper to taste. Mold into a ball, flatten and top with caviar. Serve with assorted crackers.

Note: This is served at the Blue Moon Inn, Montgomery, Alabama.

Rosamond Coleman (Mrs. William H.)

ARTICHOKE CHEESE DIP

1 8½-ounce can artichoke hearts,
  chopped
½ cup mayonnaise

1 cup shredded Cheddar cheese
Garlic powder

Combine artichoke hearts, mayonnaise and cheese in an oven-proof serving dish. Sprinkle with garlic powder. Bake at 350°F. for 20 minutes. Serve with corn chips.

Mildred Hooks (Mrs. A. V.)

ASPARAGUS CANAPÉS

1 8-ounce package cream cheese,
  softened
3 ounces blue cheese, at room
  temperature
1 egg

20 slices thin-sliced bread
  with crust
20 asparagus spears, drained
1 cup butter or margarine, melted

Combine cream cheese, blue cheese and egg; blend well. Spread on bread slices which you have rolled over with a rolling pin. Roll up one asparagus spear in each slice and secure with a toothpick. Dip in butter then freeze. When ready to serve, slice into 3 pieces and bake at 400°F. for 15 minutes.

Margaret Downer (Mrs. K. C.)

SPINACH DIP IN THE "ROUND"

1 10-ounce package frozen
chopped spinach, thawed,
drained and squeezed
1 2¾-ounce package vegetable
soup mix
1 8-ounce can water chestnuts,
chopped

6 green onions, chopped
1 cup mayonnaise
1½ cups sour cream
1 loaf round bread

Mix all ingredients together except bread. Chill overnight to combine flavors. Just before serving, scoop out large area in center of bread, cutting center into small squares. Spoon dip into center and arrange squares around bread ring. For extra cubes cut a loaf of French bread into cubes if necessary. Serves 25.

Judy Davidson (Mrs. John)

MUSTARD CREAM PUFFS

½ cup water
¼ teaspoon salt
¼ cup butter

½ cup all-purpose flour
2 eggs

Bring water to a boil; add salt, butter and flour all at once. Add eggs 1 at a time, beating after each addition. Drop by spoonfuls on ungreased miniature muffin tin. Bake at 400°F. for 20 minutes. Cool then slice through middle.

Filling

½ cup cream
1 teaspoon sugar
1 tablespoon Dijon mustard

Chopped radishes
Parsley (optional)

Beat cream with sugar and add mustard. Place a teaspoon or so of filling on bottom half of puff, top with chopped radishes and/or parsley. Place top on puff. Makes about 20 puffs.

Mimi Bozarth (Mrs. John)

CAROLE'S SHREDDED HAM ROLLS

1 cup butter or margarine
3 tablespoons mustard
3 tablespoons poppy seed
1 medium onion, finely chopped
1 teaspoon Worcestershire sauce

3 (20 per package) packages
  party rolls
1 pound shredded boiled ham
½ pound sliced Swiss cheese

Combine butter, mustard, poppy seed, onion and Worcestershire in a small saucepan and heat until butter melts. Split each package of rolls horizontally without breaking apart into individual rolls. Spread tops and bottoms of split rolls with butter mixture. Place a layer of ham and a layer of cheese on bottom layer of rolls. Replace roll tops and place in baking pan. Bake, uncovered, at 400°F. for 10 minutes. Cut apart with sharp knife. Makes 60 small ham rolls.

Jane Keller (Mrs. Joe)

CHAFING DISH FRUIT

1 1-pound can apricot halves,
  drained and juice reserved
1 1-pound can peach halves,
  drained and juice reserved
1 1-pound can pear halves,
  drained and juice reserved
1 1-pound can pineapple slices,
  drained and juice reserved

Juice of 2 oranges
Grated rind of 1 orange
Grated rind of 1 lemon
1 6-ounce package pitted
  dates, cut in half

Combine ⅔ cup syrup of each of the fruits in a saucepan. Add orange juice and grated rinds; simmer uncovered until reduced by half. Taste the syrup, if it is too sweet, stir in the juice of half a lemon. Transfer to top of double boiler, add drained fruit and dates and cook for 15 minutes. When ready to serve, transfer to a chafing dish and serve hot. Serves 8-10.

Note: Serve with cookies for a nice "sweet" alternative at a cocktail party or perfect for a coffee or afternoon tea.

Carol Crisp (Mrs. Donald)

CINNAMON TOASTED PECANS

½ cup sugar
¼ teaspoon salt
2 teaspoons cinnamon
1 teaspoon nutmeg

2 tablespoons water
1 egg white
2 cups pecan halves

Combine sugar, salt and spices and mix well. Add water to egg white beating until frothy. Stir pecans into egg mixture until well coated. Combine with sugar mixture; spread over buttered cookie sheet. Bake at 350°F. for 30 minutes, stirring every 10 minutes. Watch carefully. Stir once after removing from oven.

Lorena Surber (Mrs. Emmett)

SESAME SEED CRACKERS

2 cups unsifted all-purpose
  flour
1 teaspoon salt
Dash of cayenne pepper

¾ cup shortening or margarine
Ice water (approximately ¼ cup)
1 cup roasted sesame seed
Additional salt

Mix dry ingredients, cut in shortening and add enough ice water to make a dough the consistency of pie pastry. Add sesame seed. Roll thin; cut into small round wafers. Place in baking pan and bake at 300°F. for 15-20 minutes. While hot, sprinkle with salt before removing from pan. These may be kept in a covered tin or cracker jar and crisped in a slow, warm oven before serving.

Helen Kruse (Mrs. Foster)

BACON FAVORITES

2 pounds thick sliced lean
  bacon
1 cup firmly packed brown
  sugar

1 teaspoon dry mustard

Cut the bacon in half. Lay the strips in a single layer on a baking sheet. Sprinkle with sugar then mustard. Bake at 250°F. for about 45 minutes or until very crisp. Makes about 60 pieces.

Raymond Steinbrecher

CHEESY-ONION SPREAD

1 cup chopped onion
1 cup shredded sharp cheese

1 cup mayonnaise

Mix all together and heat at 350°F. for 30 minutes. Serve with thinly sliced sourdough rolls, lightly buttered and toasted. May be doubled or tripled easily.

Nancy Harris (Mrs. David)

SPANAKOPETES

5 tablespoons olive oil
2 medium onions, finely chopped
2 10-ounce packages frozen
  chopped spinach, thawed
  and thoroughly drained
1 pound feta cheese
12-ounces cottage cheese
½ cup chopped parsley

2 teaspoons dried dill weed
1 teaspoon salt
¼ teaspoon pepper
6 eggs, beaten
½ cup corn flake crumbs
1 pound phyllo sheets, thawed
2 cups butter or margarine,
  melted

Heat oil and sauté onions until wilted. Add spinach and simmer until moisture evaporates. Crumble feta cheese in a bowl. Blend in cottage cheese, parsley, dill, salt and pepper. Add eggs, spinach mixture and corn flake crumbs; blend thoroughly. Remove phyllo from refrigerator. Cut sheets into thirds; wrap two-thirds in a towel and refrigerate until needed. Wrap ⅓ in dampened towel. Remove 3 sheets at a time to work with. Brush sheets with melted butter. Fold in the 2 long sides towards the middle, making a strip about 2-inches wide and 11-inches long. Brush again with butter. Place 1 tablespoon of spinach mixture in a bottom corner of strip. Fold pastry over to form a right angle with side edge. Continue folding over from side to side until end of strip. Brush finished triangle with butter. Repeat process until all pastry and filling have been used. Place finished triangles on baking sheet. Bake at 425°F. for 25 minutes, turning once. Cool 5 minutes before serving.

Patty Sikes (Mrs. Lamar)

DEEP-FRIED MOZZARELLA WITH CREOLE SAUCE

½ pound mozzarella cheese
Seasoned flour
2 eggs
1 cup milk
Cracker meal
3 medium onions, chopped
4 tablespoons bacon fat
10 ripe tomatoes, unpeeled and
  chopped

4 ribs celery, chopped
2 green peppers, chopped
1 tablespoon oregano
Salt and pepper
Hot sauce to taste
1 tablespoon chopped parsley
1 tablespoon liquid smoke

Cut mozzarella into bite-sized pieces about 1-inch square. Dip in flour then in eggs-beaten-with-milk-mixture. Next dip in cracker meal thoroughly coating each piece. Place pieces on a rack set over a baking sheet and refrigerate until needed (cheese may be breaded up to 3-4 hours in advance). In a large skillet cook onion in bacon fat until soft. Add tomatoes, 1 at a time, sautéeing over high heat. Add remaining ingredients and cook over high heat, stirring constantly, for 4-5 minutes. To serve, deep fry breaded mozzarella, a few pieces at a time, in very hot (400°F.) oil until golden brown. Drain on absorbent paper, then spoon hot Creole sauce over cheese and serve at once.

Note: This sauce may be refrigerated for several days or may be frozen. Reheat over low heat to serve.

The Editors

BLUE CHEESE MOUSSE

6 egg yolks
6 tablespoons light cream
1½ tablespoons unflavored
  gelatin

¼ cup cold water
¾ pound blue cheese
1½ cups heavy cream, whipped
3 egg whites, stiffly beaten

In a saucepan over low heat beat egg yolks with cream until creamy. Soften gelatin in cold water. Dissolve gelatin over hot water and add to eggs. Force blue cheese through sieve; add to gelatin mixture; cool. Fold in whipped cream and stiffly beaten egg whites. Pour into oiled mold and chill at least 2 hours. Garnish with watercress and serve with Melba rounds.

Betty Kirby (Mrs. T. J.)
Rochester, Minnesota

CHEESE AND CHUTNEY TOAST

1 pound bacon, cooked very
    crisp and well-drained
3 cups shredded sharp Cheddar
    cheese

1 8-ounce jar English chutney
1 loaf thinly sliced bread,
    crusts removed and
    slices cut into thirds

Finely mince cooked bacon; add to shredded cheese in medium bowl. Finely blend chutney in food processor and add to bacon and cheese. Mix by hand with spatula until well blended. Spread generous amount on bread strips covering top surface to edge. (Appetizers may be frozen at this point.) Bake at 400°F. 6-8 minutes until brown and bubbly. Caution: This burns easily.

Note: A food processor makes this preparation very easy but is not necessary.

Shirley Penewitt (Mrs. Paul)

CORDON BLEU BITES

Thin slices of ham, cut into
    1½-2-inch wide strips

Thin slices of Swiss cheese,
    cut into 1½-inch wide strips

Place a piece of cheese on ham and roll up securing with a toothpick; set aside.

Beer Batter

1⅓ cups all-purpose flour
1 teaspoon salt
¼ teaspoon pepper
1 tablespoon melted butter or
    vegetable oil

2 beaten egg yolks
¾ cup flat beer

Mix first 5 ingredients together. Gradually add beer and mix well. Batter should be thick, add more flour to thicken if necessary. Dip rolled ham and cheese into batter covering well. (The ends must be completely covered.) Deep fry in 375°F. oil until golden brown. Serve with mustard for dipping.

Carolyn Kruegar (Mrs. Keith)

SHRIMP SPREAD

¼ cup butter or margarine,
     softened
1 8-ounce package cream cheese
2 tablespoons mayonnaise
2 tablespoons lemon juice
Minced onion and celery
     to taste

3 dashes Worcestershire sauce
Salt, pepper and garlic salt
     to taste
2 7-ounce cans shrimp

Combine all ingredients in a mixing bowl and blend well.

Betty Ross (Mrs. Raymond)

PICKLED SHRIMP

Marinade

1⅓ cups vegetable oil
1 cup vinegar
½ cup catsup
1 tablespoon prepared mustard
1½-2 teaspoons hot pepper
     sauce
2 tablespoons Worcestershire
     sauce

3 tablespoons capers
3 cloves garlic, minced
½ teaspoon allspice
1 teaspoon celery seed
4 bay leaves
1 teaspoon salt
¼ teaspoon pepper

Combine ingredients for marinade; set aside.

6 cups cleaned, cooked shrimp
1 cup green pepper rings

2 cups onion rings

Toss together shrimp, pepper and onion in a large plastic bag, add marinade and refrigerate for several days, turning bag at least once a day. (Place plastic bag in another container just in case it leaks.)

Marsha Lewis (Mrs. E. Clay, III)

SHRIMP MOUSSE

3 cups shrimp, cleaned and
  cooked
1 cup sour cream
1 8-ounce package cream cheese
½ cup mayonnaise
Dash of hot pepper sauce
1 teaspoon salt
1½ teaspoons Worcestershire
  sauce
¼ cup green pepper, finely
  minced

¼ cup finely minced green onion
2 tablespoons finely minced
  pimento
¼ cup chili sauce
1 tablespoon unflavored gelatin
Juice of 1 lemon
⅛ cup cold water
Watercress for garnish

Chop shrimp (reserving some whole for garnish) and set aside. Mix together sour cream, cream cheese and mayonnaise. Add all seasonings. Dissolve gelatin in lemon juice and water. Heat in top of a double boiler for 5-10 minutes; cool. Gradually fold into cream cheese mixture. Add shrimp and blend well. Pour into mold and chill overnight. Garnish with reserved shrimp and watercress. Serve with Melba toast rounds.

Ruth Lark (Mrs. William E.)

ESCARGOTS A LA PROVENÇALE

4 dozen snails (canned)
1 cup butter or margarine,
  softened
8 cloves garlic, peeled and
  crushed
⅓ cup finely chopped fresh
  parsley

1 teaspoon salt
½ teaspoon white pepper
4 dozen snail shells (natural
  or ceramic)
4 snail plates (escargotiere)

Rinse snails with water and drain well; set aside. (Large snails may be cut in half without affecting appearance or taste.) Mix together next 5 ingredients. Place ½ teaspoon of mixture in the bottom of each shell. Push one snail into each shell. Finish by completely filling each shell with the butter mixture, being sure to make level with top of the shell. Place shells in snail dishes on a cookie sheet. Bake at 400°F. for 12 minutes or until butter bubbles. Serve hot in snail dishes.

Note: Special forks and tongs are used as a convenience but are not essential; small seafood forks work as well. This makes a wonderful party dish when served in a chafing dish with French bread for total consumption of the butter sauce.

Frances Carey (Mrs. Robert E.)

22

GREEK CRABMEAT PASTRIES

4 tablespoons butter or
   margarine
½ medium onion, minced
¼ pound mushrooms, chopped
1 pound fresh crabmeat
8 sprigs parsley, minced

15 sprigs dill, minced
1 pimento, finely chopped
Dash of hot pepper sauce
Salt and pepper to taste
½ pound filo sheets
1 cup clarified butter

Melt butter in heavy skillet. Add onion and cook over low heat until transparent. Stir in mushrooms and cook, stirring 3-5 minutes. Combine all remaining ingredients, except filo and clarified butter. Mix well and cook 3-5 minutes more. Remove from heat and set aside until dish reaches room temperature. Cut sheets of filo pastry in half. Refrigerate ½ of pastry, covered. Cover other ½ with a damp towel. Take 1 sheet at a time and using a feather brush coat sheet with clarified butter. Place 1 tablespoon of crabmeat mixture 1-inch from narrow edge of sheet. Fold the 1-inch margin over crabmeat. Butter folded pastry again on exposed parts and roll up like a rug. Place in baking dish. Continue same procedure with remaining pastry sheets. At this point pastries may be frozen. Defrost before using and bake at 425°F. for 20 minutes. Serve warm. Shrimp or lobster may be substituted. Makes about 72.

Dee Redding (Mrs. Ben)

PRETTY-EASY-CRABMEAT DIP

8-ounce cream cheese
8-ounce jar cocktail sauce

6-ounce can crabmeat
Dry parsley

Spread cream cheese on a plate. Cover with cocktail sauce. Top with crabmeat. Garnish with parsley flakes. Serve with crackers.

Bobby Nordan
Walnut Creek, California

CRAB DIP

1 pound fresh crabmeat, cleaned
½ cup mayonnaise
1 cup sour cream

1 .63-ounce package dry Italian
salad dressing mix
1 teaspoon mustard horseradish

Mix all ingredients together well. Serve with crackers.

Chris Abbott (Mrs. Bill)

CRABMEAT BITES

1 cup crabmeat
½ cup butter or margarine,
softened
1 container Rondele cheese

1½ teaspoons mayonnaise
1 12-ounce package English
muffins

Combine first 4 ingredients blending well. Split muffins in half; toast lightly and spread with cheese mixture. Cut each muffin half into quarters. May be served at room temperature or run under broiler at last minute to warm. Makes 4 dozen.

Judy Davidson (Mrs. John)

MOCK WEST INDIES SALAD

1 pound fish (Trigger fish,
Wahoo or Dolphin are
especially good)
Crab boil
Salt

1 large onion, chopped
3 ounces cider vinegar
4 ounces vegetable oil
4 ounces ice water
Pepper to taste

Cook fish in water with crab boil and salt. (Do not overcook so fish will have the texture of crabmeat.) Cool and flake. Layer the fish and chopped onion in a bowl. Pour over vinegar, oil then ice water. Add salt and pepper but do not stir. Marinate 2-24 hours; stir before serving. Add more salt or pepper to taste.

Note: It's very hard to tell the difference.

Rosamond Coleman (Mrs. William H.)

OYSTER COCKTAIL IN GRAPEFRUIT

3 chilled grapefruit, halved   3 dozen medium oysters

Cut the grapefruit into halves removing larger core than usual. Place 6 oysters in center cavity. Pour sauce over oysters. Serve well-chilled on beds of shaved ice garnished with foliage.

Cocktail Sauce

6 tablespoons catsup   2 drops hot pepper sauce
4 tablespoons lemon juice   Celery salt to taste
½ teaspoon Worcestershire sauce   Horseradish to taste

Combine all ingredients well and chill before pouring over oysters.

Ann Aldrich Logue

TUNA DIP

3 hard-cooked eggs, finely   3 dashes hot pepper sauce
  chopped   1 7-ounce can tuna, drained
2 tablespoons onion flakes   Salt and pepper to taste
1 teaspoon Worcestershire sauce   Mayonnaise

Combine ingredients with enough mayonnaise to make it creamy-not soupy. Serve with corn chips.

James I. Lark, Sr.

BRIE EN CROUTE

1 frozen individual patty shell   1 4½-ounce package brie cheese

Thaw patty shell without removing "top". Roll out with rolling pin until large enough to cover cheese. Carefully pull dough over top, sides and some of the bottom of the cheese, tucking in the pastry on the bottom. Put on a baking sheet and bake at 450°F. about 15 minutes until brown. Serve with crackers.

Karon Wakstein (Mrs. Gary)

CHILI CON QUESO

3 slices bacon
1 large onion, chopped
2 8-ounce packages old English
   process cheese

½ 16-ounce can tomatoes,
   drained
1 8-ounce can tomatoes and
   chilies with juice

Fry bacon and remove from pan. Sauté onion in bacon drippings. Add cheese, tomatoes, undrained tomatoes and chilies and crumbled bacon. Heat to melt. Serve in chafing dish with plain tortilla chips.

Ruthie Hunter (Mrs. Charles)

BLACK BEAN SOUP DIP

2 cups thick, cold black bean
   soup (use leftover soup)
1 cup sour cream
2 tablespoons mayonnaise
2 tablespoons lemon juice
1 small onion, finely chopped

¼ teaspoon hot pepper sauce
2 tablespoons olive oil
2 tablespoon dry sherry or
   cooking sherry
1 garlic clove, crushed

Combine all ingredients except garlic and pour into electric blender or food processor. Blend 1 minute. Pour into a bowl that has been rubbed with the unpeeled crushed garlic clove. Cover and refrigerate. Mix well before serving. Delicious with nacho-flavored or plain tortilla chips. Makes approximately 1 quart.

Dottie San Juan (Mrs. Edward F.)

COCKTAIL CHILI CON QUESO

1 16-ounce can tomatoes
1 cup chopped onions
¼ cup vegetable oil
1 teaspoon chili powder
½ teaspoon oregano
4 garlic cloves, crushed

1 4-ounce can green chilies,
   chopped
½ cup light cream or evaporated
   milk
1 pound American cheese, cubed
Salt to taste

Pour tomatoes into colander; drain well. Cook onion until limp in oil in large saucepan. Add tomatoes, chili powder, oregano and garlic. Cook until all is well blended. Stir in chilies and cream. Add cheese stirring constantly over low heat until cheese is melted. Add salt to taste. Serve in chafing dish with large corn chips. Serves 25 at cocktail party.

Note: Best prepared ahead of time to blend flavors.

Judy Davidson (Mrs. John)

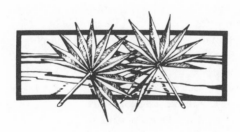

JULIE'S MEXICAN SNACK

1 8-ounce package cream
   cheese, softened
⅓ cup hot taco sauce
1 teaspoon milk
½ cup sour cream
1 tablespoon lemon juice

Chopped lettuce
Chopped onions
Chopped tomatoes
Chopped black olives
Lots of shredded cheese

Combine cream cheese, taco sauce, milk, sour cream and lemon juice and mound in center of a serving platter. Top with remaining ingredients and surround with taco or nacho-flavored tortilla chips.

Mrs. Charles Wooley

TOREADOR BEAN DIP

1 medium onion, minced
2 jalapeño peppers, finely
  minced
1 teaspoon cumin seed
1-2 tablespoons butter or
  margarine

2 11-ounce cans black bean
  soup
1-2 cups shredded sharp cheese

Cook onion, peppers and cumin seed in butter. Add soup, heat well and stir in cheese until melted. Serve hot with corn chips. This recipe is quite hot but wonderfully seasoned.

Libby Hertell

MEXICAN LAYERED DIP

2 large avocados
⅛ teaspoon garlic powder
⅛ teaspoon garlic salt
1 tablespoon lemon juice
2 tablespoons mayonnaise
1 8-ounce carton sour cream

2 8-ounce jars picante sauce
¾ cup chopped black or green
  olives
3 cups (about 3 medium) tomatoes,
  peeled and chopped
1½ cups shredded Cheddar cheese

Peel, seed and mash avocados; stir in garlic powder, garlic salt, lemon juice and mayonnaise. Spread evenly in a 12x8x2-inch dish. Carefully spread the sour cream over avocado mixture. Drain picante sauce well; spoon over sour cream. Top with layer of olives and tomatoes; sprinkle with cheese. Serve with large corn chips or plain tortilla chips. Makes about 6 cups.

Karen Green (Mrs. Hubert)

CHILE RELLENO DIP

2 large tomatoes, finely
  chopped
3-4 green onions, chopped
1 4-ounce can green chile
  peppers, diced
1½ teaspoons vinegar

3 tablespoons olive oil
1 4-ounce can pitted black olives,
  chopped
1 teaspoon garlic salt
Salt and pepper to taste

Combine all ingredients well and serve with plain tortilla chips.

Ruth Lark (Mrs. William E.)

BEVERAGES

STRAWBERRY PUNCH

3 6-ounce cans frozen orange
   juice concentrate, thawed
3 6-ounce cans frozen pink
   lemonade concentrate, thawed

2 10-ounce packages frozen
   strawberries, thawed
1 quart ginger ale, chilled

In a large container or punch bowl add orange juice and lemonade concentrates
diluting with cold water according to package directions; stir. Stir in thawed
strawberries; add ginger ale just before serving. Makes 32 cups.

Gwyn Hill (Mrs. Alvin)

FRESH MINT PUNCH

1 cup packed mint leaves and
   stems
1½ cups water
1 12-ounce can frozen lemonade
   concentrate, thawed

2 33.8-ounce bottles ginger ale,
   chilled
Mint for garnish
Strawberries for garnish

In a saucepan bruise mint, cover with water and bring to a boil. Remove from heat
and let stand for 20 minutes; strain. Combine with lemonade concentrate and
refrigerate until ready to use. To serve combine mint-lemonade mixture with
chilled ginger ale. Garnish with mint and strawberries. Makes ¾ gallon.

Marsha Lewis (Mrs. E. Clay, III)

PINEAPPLE SCHLEGEL

1 46-ounce can pineapple juice
½ cup firmly packed brown sugar
1 teaspoon whole allspice

½ teaspoon whole cloves
2 sticks cinnamon

Combine all ingredients, heat and serve in mugs.

Jane Keller (Mrs. Joe)

WEDDING PUNCH

6 cups sugar
5 quarts water, divided
4 3-ounce packages lemon
flavored gelatin
1 6-ounce can frozen lemonade
concentrate, thawed

1 6-ounce can frozen orange
juice concentrate, thawed
2 46-ounce cans pineapple
juice
1½ ounces almond extract

In a large pot make a syrup of sugar and 1 quart water. While hot, stir in gelatin until dissolved; cool. When cool add juices, remaining water and almond extract. Recipe may be halved easily. Serves 100.

Lillie Brewton (Mrs. Harvey)

HOT HONEY PUNCH

¾ cup honey
1½ cups water
¼ teaspoon salt
6 whole cloves
1-2 sticks cinnamon
2 cups strong tea

1 20-ounce can pineapple juice
Juice of 2 lemons
12 maraschino cherries with
syrup
1 orange, seeded and thinly
sliced

Combine honey, water and spices. Simmer 5 minutes; strain. Add tea and juices; bring to a boil. Add cherries and orange slices. Makes 10 cups.

Martha Ann Horn (Mrs. Joe)

PERCOLATOR PUNCH

2 32-ounce bottles cranberry
juice cocktail
1 46-ounce can pineapple juice
1 cup firmly packed brown sugar

4 teaspoons whole cloves
12 (3-inch) sticks cinnamon
Rind of ¼ orange, cut into strips

In a 30-cup coffee pot place juices and brown sugar. In basket put spices and orange rind. Perk as for coffee. Makes 12-18 cups.

Lenda McCain (Mrs. Marvin)

WASSAIL BOWL

2 quarts apple cider
2 (3-inch) sticks cinnamon
½ teaspoon nutmeg
½ cup honey or light corn syrup

⅓ cup lemon juice
2 teaspoons grated lemon rind
2 20-ounce cans pineapple juice
2 cups vodka

Heat cider and cinnamon in large saucepan; bring to a boil. Simmer covered 5 minutes. Add remaining ingredients except vodka and simmer uncovered 5 minutes longer. Pour into punch bowl (placing silver ladle in bowl first to diffuse heat). Float spiced oranges on top. Add vodka just before serving.

Spiced Oranges

Oranges   Whole cloves

Decorate oranges with whole cloves ½-inch apart. Place in a pan with a little water. Bake at 325°F. for 30 minutes. Oranges will float.

Margaret Downer (Mrs. K. C.)

CLARENCE MOODY'S CHRISTMAS PUNCH

3 pieces fresh ginger
1 (3-inch) stick cinnamon
8 whole cloves
3-4 cardamon seeds
6 lemons, peeled and thinly
   sliced

6 small oranges, peeled and
   thinly sliced
1 gallon apple cider
1 quart canned pineapple juice
½ teaspoon salt
Rum

Place the spices in a bag of fine cheesecloth. Mix the lemon and orange slices with the juices in a large pot. Add the bag of spices and bring to a boil over very low heat. Simmer, stirring occasionally, for about 15 minutes. Add salt and stir vigorously. Just prior to serving add rum as desired.

June Greenwell (Mrs. Mark)
Mt. Dora, Florida

CHAMPAGNE PUNCH

1 46-ounce can pineapple juice
1 6-ounce can orange juice
concentrate, thawed

1 bottle sauterne
2 bottles champagne, chilled

In a large container mix first 3 ingredients and chill. At the table add chilled champagne.

Carolyn Finlayson (Mrs. Jimmy)

CREOLE CHAMPAGNE PUNCH

1 pound superfine sugar
1 cup strained lemon juice
1 cup strained orange juice
½ cup Curacao or other orange
flavored liqueur
1 quart champagne, chilled
1 quart dry white wine, chilled

1½ quarts (6 cups) club soda,
chilled
Ice mold or block of ice
Pineapple wedges and crushed
pineapple
2 cups fresh strawberries

Combine the sugar, juices and orange flavored liqueur in the punch bowl and stir to dissolve the sugar completely. Stir in the champagne, wine and club soda. Carefully place the ice in the bowl, then stir the pineapple (wedges and crushed) and strawberries into the punch. Makes about 5 quarts.

Fotula Slaughter (Mrs. Jim)

PLANTER'S PUNCH

1 12-ounce can frozen orange
juice concentrate
1¼ cups lemon juice
¾ cup pineapple juice

5 cups water
½ cup light rum
1 cup dark rum

Combine all ingredients except rum in a large container. Refrigerate until well-chilled. Serve over an ice ring in a punch bowl with the rum. Serves 12.

Martha Ann Horn (Mrs. Joe)

COFFEE PUNCH

2 quarts double strength coffee
1 cup sugar

2 quarts ice cubes and water
½ gallon chocolate ice cream

Make fresh coffee, add sugar and dissolve. Add ice cubes and water (to make 2 quarts). Just before serving, stir in ice cream until it melts. Serves 48.

Florence Stewart

LEMON VODKA

1 quart vodka
2 tablespoons superfine sugar
10 whole black peppercorns

Rind of 1 lemon, cut into long
strips ¼-inch wide

Pour off a shot glass of vodka to make room in bottle for other ingredients. Add sugar, peppercorns and lemon peel to bottle of vodka. Replace top and invert bottle several times to dissolve sugar. Refrigerate 7-10 days before serving. Keeps for months. Serve chilled or over ice. May be served with a meal in place of wine.

Georgia Dake (Mrs. James L.)

ORANGE BLUSH

2 6-ounce cans frozen orange
  juice concentrate, thawed
2 cups cranberry juice

½ cup sugar
4 cups sparkling water
  (club soda)

Combine undiluted orange juice, cranberry juice and sugar; chill thoroughly. Just before serving stir in sparkling water and pour over crushed ice in old-fashioned glasses. Serves 12.

Helen Kruse (Mrs. Foster)

ANDROS ISLAND GOOMBAY SMASH

3 ounces orange juice
3 ounces pineapple juice
3-4 ounces white rum
2 ounces coconut rum

1 ounce Nassau Royal Liqueur
Ice cubes
Club soda

Blend in blender with 4 ice cubes adding a splash of club soda. Serve over ice in tall glass with straw. Serves 4.

Judy Davidson (Mrs. John)

DERBY DAY JULEPS

1 cup sugar
2 cups water

2 quarts bourbon
Fresh mint

In a saucepan bring sugar and water to a boil over low heat, stirring to dissolve sugar. As soon as sugar is completely dissolved, remove from heat and cool thoroughly. Pour mixture into glass pitcher and add bourbon and half the mint leaves stirring well. Cover and refrigerate several hours. Remove and discard mint leaves from mixture. Fill silver julep cups or stemmed glasses with shaved ice; add bourbon mixture. Garnish each drink with fresh sprig of mint and serve with straw. Serves 20-30.

Judy Davidson (Mrs. John)

HOTEL NEGRESCO CHAMPAGNE COCKTAIL

2 tablespoons crème de Framboise
1 tablespoon Kirsch

Chilled champagne

Combine liqueurs in a chilled 8-ounce champagne glass and fill with chilled champagne. Makes 1 drink.

Note: This is from the barman at the Hotel Negresco in Nice, France. It is a "must" for anyone visiting Nice.

Caroline Ireland (Mrs. Charles W.)

STRAWBERRY DAIQUIRI

1 6-ounce can limeade
concentrate, thawed
2 teaspoons powdered sugar
½ cup rum
¼ cup Triple Sec

1 pound frozen sweetened
strawberries
½-¾ cup frozen non-dairy
whipped topping, thawed
Ice

In blender container combine lime concentrate, powdered sugar, rum and Triple Sec. Add half the strawberries; blend well. Repeat procedure with remaining strawberries. Add ice cubes 1 cup at a time to the blender mixture and crush. Continue adding ice cubes until desired consistency is reached. Add whipped topping to blender and blend well. Pour into glasses and top with additional whipped topping.

Stan Lane
Tucson, Arizona

BOARS HEAD COFFEE

1¼ ounces Amaretto
Freshly brewed coffee
Whipped cream

Kahlua
Maraschino cherry for garnish

Pour Amaretto into coffee cup; fill with coffee. Top generously with whipped cream; pour splash of Kahlua over and top with cherry.

The Boars Head Restaurant (Barry Ross)

SYLLABUB

2 cups white wine
1½ cups sugar, divided
⅓ cup lemon juice and rind
3 cups milk

2 cups light cream
4 egg whites
Nutmeg

Combine wine, 1 cup sugar, lemon juice and rind in a bowl, stirring until sugar dissolves. Add milk and cream; beat until frothy. In another bowl beat egg whites until stiff with remaining ½ cup sugar. Beat until peaks form. Pour wine mixture into punch bowl, top with spoonfuls of beaten egg white and grated nutmeg. Syllabub is a good substitute for eggnog.

Jenny Doster (Mrs. Hank)

BETH'S HOT BUTTERED RUM MIX

2 cups butter or margarine
2 cups sugar
2¼ cups firmly packed brown
  sugar
2 eggs, beaten

1 quart vanilla ice cream
2½ teaspoons cinnamon
2½ teaspoons nutmeg
Rum or bourbon

Cream together butter and sugars, add remaining ingredients and store in freezer until ready to use. To serve combine 1-1½ ounces rum or bourbon and 2 tablespoons mix in a mug. Add hot water as desired and stir.

Janie Jinks (Mrs. Russell)

ALMOND BUTTER BEVERAGE MIX

4 cups firmly packed brown sugar
1 cup butter or margarine,
  softened
⅔ cup Amaretto *or* ½ cup water
  plus 2 teaspoons almond
  extract

½ cup non-dairy coffee creamer
1 teaspoon ground cinnamon
1 teaspoon ground allspice

Beat together brown sugar, butter, Amaretto, creamer and spices until well blended. Place in decorative covered container for gift giving. Chill. Makes 5 cups.

Note: Gift instructions—Store in refrigerator up to 1 month. To serve spoon 1 tablespoon chilled mix into a mug; add 6 ounces hot coffee, hot wine, hot cocoa or hot milk. Serve immediately.

Nancy Wyatt (Mrs. Terrence)

SMOOTHIE (KIDS TREAT)

1 cup ice
½ cup apple juice
½ banana

1 tablespoon honey
3-4 strawberries

Combine all ingredients and mix until smooth in electric blender.

Note: May use 2 kinds of juice and any combination of fruit.

Gwyn Hill (Mrs. Alvin)

LEMONADE

8-10 lemons
1½ cups sugar

1½ cups very hot water
1 tablespoon grated lemon rind

Squeeze lemons to make 1½ cups juice. In 1-quart pitcher dissolve sugar in hot water. Add lemon rind and juice; refrigerate. To serve mix ¼ cup syrup to ¾ cup water.

Katharine Fuller (Mrs. Walter)

FRENCH MINT TEA

13 tea bags
¼ cup lightly packed fresh mint
  leaves
1 quart water
Juice of 2 freshly squeezed
  lemons

1 6-ounce can frozen orange
  juice concentrate
1 cup sugar
Fresh mint sprigs for garnish

Combine tea, mint leaves and water in large saucepan. Cover and bring to a boil. Immediately remove from heat; let steep 30 minutes. Add lemon juice, orange juice concentrate, sugar and additional water to make 2 quarts liquid. Strain and chill; serve over ice and garnish with mint leaves.

Dottie Hamlin (Mrs. Ronnie)

SANDRA CAMERON'S SUMMER TEA

4 (family-size) tea bags
1½-2 quarts water
2 cups sugar

½ cup lemon juice
1 6-ounce can pineapple juice

In 2-2½ quart saucepan place tea bags with water and heat. When water begins to bubble, pour liquid into a gallon container with sugar. Stir, then add lemon juice. Pour cold water over the tea bags which are still in the saucepan. Add to tea, then add pineapple juice. Stir and store in refrigerator.

Cathy Wilson (Mrs. Frank)
Atlanta, Georgia

FISHEL TEA

7 heaping teaspoons loose tea
1 quart boiling water
2 cups sugar

1 cup orange juice
1 cup lemon juice

Steep tea in boiling water for 10-15 minutes. Strain into 1-gallon container. Add remaining ingredients; stir. Fill container with cold water and mix. Refrigerate overnight for best flavor. Mix well before serving as it tends to settle slightly.

Louise Fishel (Mrs. John)

SOUTHERN SUN TEA

8 tea bags
1 quart cold water
¼ cup sugar

1 tablespoon lemon juice
Fresh mint sprigs

Combine tea bags and water in a clear glass jar or pitcher. Cover with lid or plastic wrap. Place in sun 7-10 hours until tea is desired strength. Remove tea bags; stir in sugar and lemon juice. Pour into glasses over ice and garnish with mint sprigs.

Marion Collins (Mrs. Charles)

SOUPS
& BREADS

Common Tern—Common terns are frequently seen diving for small fish in Gulf waters. They nest each summer on the secluded white-sand beaches of Bay County.

SOUPS

OYSTER SOUP

½ cup butter
¼ cup chopped onion
¼ cup chopped celery
4 tablespoons all-purpose
   flour
¼ cup chopped carrots

1 bay leaf
Garlic salt (optional)
Salt and pepper to taste
1 pint oysters
3 cups milk

Melt butter in saucepan and sauté onion and celery until tender. Blend in flour and cook 5 minutes over low heat, stirring constantly. Add remaining ingredients and simmer until oysters are heated through. Remove bay leaf. Serves 4.

Marie Bazemore (Mrs. Eugene J.)

LOBSTER BISQUE

¼ cup vegetable oil
1 large carrot, chopped
½ medium onion, sliced
2 ripe tomatoes, coarsely
   chopped
1 bay leaf
1 small stalk fresh thyme or
   dash of dried thyme
Meat of a 2 pound Maine
   lobster, cooked

¼ cup dry white wine
3 cups fish stock
¾ cup rice
Salt to taste
1 teaspoon white pepper
½ cup heavy cream
Dash of Tabasco

Heat oil in a large heavy saucepan; add vegetables and herbs. Add wine and simmer 5 minutes. Add fish stock, rice, salt and pepper; cook, covered, over low heat for 45 minutes. Remove bay leaf, strain or blend in food processor. Put the bisque over heat again, add cream and stir; cook 5 minutes more. Correct seasoning with Tabasco and salt if necessary. Add lobster meat and thin with small amount of milk if desired.

Robin Ross (Mrs. Barry W.)

MANGROVE BISQUE

1 pound bay scallops in juice
1 tablespoon Madeira wine
2¾ cups chicken broth
½ cup chopped carrot
¼ cup chopped onion
½ bay leaf
⅛ teaspoon marjoram
¼ cup dry white wine

3 tablespoons butter
   (no substitute)
3 tablespoons all-purpose flour
2 cups milk
1 teaspoon tomato paste
¼ cup heavy cream
Salt
White pepper

Parboil scallops for 1 minute in half their own juice. Remove to bowl with juice and finely chop scallops. Sprinkle with Madeira and set aside. Into saucepan add remaining half of scallop juice, chicken broth, vegetables, herbs and wine. Bring to a boil, cover and simmer for 30 minutes. Allow to stand several hours or overnight. Line a colander with cheesecloth, place it over a bowl and strain mixture through it. Melt butter in a large saucepan. Stir in flour until smooth then add broth, milk and tomato paste. Simmer about 15 minutes, stirring until smooth and thick. Add scallops with Madeira and the heavy cream. Season to taste with salt and white pepper. Serve with crusty black bread and green salad. Serves 4.

Nina Godwin (Mrs. Mark T.)

SHE CRAB SOUP

1 cup butter or margarine
1 cup all-purpose flour
1 quart milk
2 chicken bouillon cubes

2 cups light cream
1 pound crabmeat
White wine to taste

Melt butter in large saucepan. Add flour to make a paste; slowly add milk and bouillon. Heat, stirring constantly, until mixture is thick. Add cream and crabmeat. (For a thinner consistency add a small amount of milk.) Stir in wine to taste; correct seasoning with salt and pepper if desired.

Ruby Kiviecenski
Saint Andrews Bay Yacht Club

CRABMEAT AND MUSHROOM BISQUE

6 tablespoons butter or
  margarine, divided
4 teaspoons finely chopped
  onion
4 tablespoons finely chopped
  green pepper
1 scallion with top, coarsley
  chopped
2 tablespoons chopped parsley
1 cup sliced fresh mushrooms

2 tablespoons all-purpose flour
1½ cups milk
1 teaspoon salt
⅛ teaspoon pepper
¼ teaspoon ground mace
Dash of Tabasco
1 cup light cream
3 7½-ounce cans crabmeat
3 tablespoons dry sherry
  (optional)

In medium skillet heat 4 tablespoons butter, add vegetables and sauté until soft but not brown; set aside. In a large saucepan heat remaining butter, remove from heat. Stir in flour, gradually add milk; cook, stirring constantly, until smooth and thick. Stir in salt, pepper, mace and Tabasco. Add sautéed vegetables and cream. Bring to a boil, stirring constantly. Reduce heat, add crabmeat and simmer, uncovered, for 5 minutes. Just before serving, stir in sherry if desired.

Note: Sherry may be omitted from recipe but served at the table for those who like it.

Chris Dunlap

SEAFOOD GUMBO

1 46-ounce can tomato juice
2 10¾-ounce cans cream
  of mushroom soup
1 10-ounce package frozen okra
1 teaspoon salt
½ teaspoon garlic powder
½ teaspoon coarse pepper
¼ teaspoon oregano

2 tablespoons dried onions
1 teaspoon Tabasco
¼ cup Worcestershire sauce
1 pound shrimp
1 pound fish fillets, cut into
  chunks
½-1 pound scallops
¾ cup cooked rice (optional)

Combine all ingredients except seafood and rice. Cook over low heat until okra is half done. Add fish fillets. When okra is done, add shrimp and scallops. Cook 8 minutes; add rice just before serving if desired. Serve very hot with crackers. Serves 16.

Ann Kinnard (Mrs. Lee)

ARTICHOKE AND OYSTER SOUP

6 fresh artichokes
2 pints raw oysters and liquor
1 quart chicken stock
¾ teaspoon garlic powder
2 tablespoons paprika
1 teaspoon thyme
Dash-½ teaspoon cayenne pepper
1 teaspoon salt
¼ teaspoon white pepper
2 ribs celery with tops,
    chopped

4 sprigs parsley, chopped
¼ teaspoon Tabasco
⅓ cup cornstarch
½ cup water
2 tablespoons lemon juice
1 cup heavy cream
3-4 cups French breadcrumbs
½ cup butter or margarine

Wash artichokes; trim stem down level. Stand artichokes in about 3 inches of water in a large pot. Bring to a boil over medium heat and boil gently for about 45 minutes; drain. When cool, peel outside tougher leaves and scrape tender inner portion of each leaf into a bowl. Reserve middle, more tender leaves for dunking. Trim tender base of innermost leaves into bowl. Carefully scrape fuzzy top off of each choke and discard. Chop each choke into small pieces; set aside. Drain oysters into a bowl. Add enough water over oysters to make 3 cups liquid (including liquor). Chop drained oysters into small pieces; set aside. In a large pot put chicken stock, scrapings of artichoke leaves, oyster liquor, seasonings, celery, parsley and Tabasco, simmer 10 minutes. Pour mixture into food processor and blend until completely liquefied. Return to large pot over medium heat. Stir the cornstarch into the ½ cup water until well blended. Add to liquid and whisk lightly until thick. Add lemon juice, chopped artichokes and oysters; reduce to simmer. Sauté breadcrumbs in melted butter until crisp. Add cream and crumbs to large pot. (Use more or less crumbs to achieve desired thickness.) Simmer until oysters reach desired degree of doneness.

Salie Cotton (Mrs. B. Philip)

CRAB GUMBO

1 onion, finely chopped
3 tablespoons bacon fat
1 garlic clove, finely chopped
3 tablespoons all-purpose flour
2 1-pound cans tomatoes
Salt
Pepper
Celery salt

Worcestershire sauce
3 tablespoons catsup
1 10-ounce package frozen baby
    okra, sliced or equal amount
    fresh okra
1 pound crabmeat
50 shrimp, shelled and deveined

Brown onion in bacon fat. Add garlic and flour and brown well, stirring constantly to prevent burning. Add tomatoes, salt, pepper, celery salt and Worcestershire to taste, and catsup. Simmer 1½-2 hours. Add okra, crabmeat and shrimp; cook 30 minutes more. Serve over rice. Serves 6-8.

Jean Pitts (Mrs. Reynolds E.)

SHRIMP AND OKRA GUMBO

1 pound fresh okra
2 tablespoons olive oil
¼ cup butter or margarine
2 cups diced onion
2 green peppers, seeded and cut
    in ½-inch squares
2 garlic cloves, minced
¼ cup all-purpose flour
1 28-ounce can tomatoes
2 6-ounce cans tomato paste
2 10¾-ounce cans chicken
    broth

2 cups water
2 bay leaves
¼ teaspoon leaf thyme, crumbled
¼ teaspoon Tabasco
½ teaspoon Worcestershire sauce
2 teaspoons salt
2 pounds fresh shrimp, shelled
    and deveined or 1 10-ounce
    package frozen shelled and
    deveined shrimp
Hot cooked rice

Wash and dry okra; cut in ⅛-inch thick slices. Heat olive oil and butter in kettle or heavy saucepan over medium heat. Sauté okra, onion, green peppers and garlic 3-4 minutes, stirring frequently. Sprinkle with flour and stir until flour becomes golden brown. Add tomatoes, broth, water, bay leaves, thyme, Tabasco, Worcestershire and salt. Cover and bring to a boil; simmer 45 minutes. Add shrimp; cook 5 minutes longer. Correct seasoning to taste. Put a heaping spoonful of rice into each soup bowl. Ladle gumbo over rice. Serves 8.

Marie Bazemore (Mrs. Eugene J.)

CHILLED SHRIMP-CUCUMBER BISQUE

1 medium leek or 8 large green
  onions
3 tablespoons butter or
  margarine
3 medium cucumbers, 2 peeled
  and sliced, 1 grated
2 bay leaves
1½ tablespoons all-purpose
  flour

3 cups chicken broth
1 teaspoon salt
1 cup heavy cream
1½ tablespoons lemon juice
2 tablespoons finely chopped
  parsley
⅔ cup finely chopped cooked
  shrimp
Sour cream

Slice white portion of leek, reserve green top for another use. Melt butter in Dutch oven, add leek, 2 sliced cucumbers and bay leaves. Cover and cook over low heat about 20 minutes or until tender; remove bay leaves. Stir flour into cucumber mixture, cook 1 minute, stirring constantly. Gradually add broth, cook over medium heat, stirring constantly until thickened. Stir in salt. Pour soup mixture into container of electric blender; process 30 seconds. Chill soup at least 4 hours. Just before serving, stir in remaining cucumber (grated), cream, lemon juice, parsley and shrimp. Top with a dollop of sour cream. Serves 6.

Marie Bazemore (Mrs. Eugene J.)

GAZPACHO I

1 10½-ounce can condensed
   tomato soup
1 can cold water
3 tablespoons olive oil
2 tablespoons wine vinegar
1 teaspoon garlic salt
⅛ teaspoon cayenne pepper

1 avocado, sliced
1 medium ripe tomato, peeled
   and diced
12 ripe olives, sliced
½ cup thinly sliced cucumber
2 tablespoons thinly sliced
   green onion

Mix the first 6 ingredients together until blended. Add vegetables. Chill until flavors are blended and soup is well chilled. Serves 4-6.

Barbara Palmer (Mrs. Don)

GAZPACHO II

1 10½-ounce can condensed beef
   broth
2½ cups tomato juice
3 tablespoons lemon juice
2 chopped onions
1 garlic clove, sliced
   lengthwise

¼ teaspoon Tabasco
½ teaspoon salt
Dash of freshly ground pepper
Chopped green peppers
Chopped cucumbers
Chopped tomatoes

In a jar mix first 8 ingredients. Spear garlic on toothpicks. Cover and shake well; chill 4 hours. Remove garlic and place jar in freezer for about 1 hour but do not freeze. Divide chopped vegetables in soup bowls and pour mixture over the vegetables. Makes 4 large, 8 small servings.

Jean Ann Fleege (Mrs. Robert L.)
Pensacola, Florida

FRESH STRAWBERRY SOUP

2 pints strawberries, hulled
and halved
1 tablespoon cornstarch
1 cup orange juice

1 cup red wine
½ cup sugar
Sour cream
Strawberries for garnish

Pureé strawberries in food processor. In a saucepan blend cornstarch with ¼ cup orange juice, then add remaining orange juice, wine and sugar; bring to a boil. Remove from heat, add strawberries and chill. Serve cold with a large dollop of sour cream and garnish with a strawberry. Great for a brunch. Serves 6.

Marsha Lewis (Mrs. E. Clay, III)

COLD CUCUMBER SOUP

2 cups diced cucumber, peeled
and seeded
1 cup chicken stock
¼ cup celery leaves
¼ cup chives
¼ cup parsley

2 tablespoons butter
2 tablespoons all-purpose flour
1 cup light cream
Salt and pepper to taste
Fresh dill or lemon rind for
garnish

Into a blender container add cucumber, stock, celery, chives and parsley; blend until smooth. Make a roux with butter and flour and add contents of the blender to the roux. Cook for 5 minutes, remove from heat and add cream. Season with salt and pepper to taste. Chill; garnish with dill or lemon rind before serving. Serves 4.

Jean Ann Fleege (Mrs. Robert L.)
Pensacola, Florida

CHEESE SOUP

1 quart water
4 chicken bouillon cubes
1 large onion, chopped
1 cup chopped celery
1 green pepper, chopped
  (optional)
2½ cups diced potatoes

1 20-ounce package frozen
  California blend vegetables
2 10¾-ounce cans cream
  of chicken soup
1 pound pasteurized process
  cheese spread, cubed

Combine first 6 ingredients in a 4-quart saucepan. Cover and simmer 10 minutes, uncover and continue to simmer 20 minutes. Add frozen vegetables and soup, simmer until vegetables are tender and soup is heated. Add cheese, stirring occasionally, until cheese is melted. This is a very "hearty" soup. Serve with crusty bread and lettuce salad with tart dressing. Works in microwave also. Serves 8 or more.

Thelma Bozarth (Mrs. Charles)
Tuscola, Illinois

STEAK SOUP

2 pounds round steak, coarsely
  ground
1 cup butter or margarine,
  divided
1 medium onion, chopped
2 large carrots, chopped
3 ribs celery, chopped

1 cup all-purpose flour
1 28-ounce can tomatoes,
  chopped
1 tablespoon Worcestershire sauce
3 quarts beef stock
Salt and pepper to taste
1½ cups light cream

Brown round steak in ½ cup butter. Place meat in stock pot. Sauté onion, carrots and celery in remaining ½ cup butter. Combine in the pot with meat and stir in flour. Add remaining ingredients except cream. Simmer at least 1 hour, stirring occasionally. Just before serving, stir in cream. A tasty soup that freezes well.

Ruth Lark (Mrs. William E.)

CHEESY-BROCCOLI SOUP

2 cups chicken broth
2 cups (½-inch) egg noodles,
   uncooked
1 10-ounce package frozen
   chopped broccoli
1 large onion, chopped

2 tablespoons butter
2 garlic cloves
2½ cups milk
1 8-ounce package pasteurized
   process cheese spread, cubed

In a large saucepan bring chicken broth to a slow boil. Add noodles and cook 4 minutes. Add the broccoli. After it thaws, allow to return to a boil and continue boiling 3 minutes. Sauté onion in butter and add to the soup. Squeeze juice of garlic cloves into the soup mixture; return to a boil and cook 3 minutes. Add milk; when warm add cheese and stir until cheese is melted. Serves 6.

Millie Gwinn (Mrs. Paul J. Jr.)
Camden, Arkansas

CREAMY BROCCOLI SOUP

1 10¾-ounce can cream of
   potato soup, undiluted
1 10¾-ounce can cream of
   celery soup, undiluted
1¼ cups milk
1 teaspoon Dijon mustard

½ teaspoon dried whole thyme
¼ teaspoon dry mustard
¼ teaspoon dried whole basil
   (optional)
1 10-ounce package frozen
   chopped broccoli

In a 2-quart saucepan heat soups. Gradually add milk, stirring until smooth. Add remaining ingredients; cook over low heat for 40 minutes, stirring occasionally. Makes about 5 cups.

Marion Collins (Mrs. Charles)

CREAM OF BROCCOLI SOUP

3 tablespoons butter or
  margarine
½ cup white wine
⅓ cup diced leek
⅓ cup diced onion
⅓ cup diced celery

1 cup diced broccoli
3 tablespoons all-purpose flour
3 cups chicken stock
Salt and pepper
Thyme
1 cup light cream

Melt butter in heavy saucepan over low heat. Add wine and sauté vegetables 5 minutes. Blend in flour and gradually add chicken stock, stirring constantly to avoid lumps. Bring to a boil; season with salt, pepper and thyme. Simmer until vegetables are tender; add cream and serve.

Yui Fernandez (Mrs. Robert)

CHICKEN-VEGETABLE SOUP

2 chicken breasts, skinned and
  halved
1 cup long-grain natural brown
  rice
12 cups water
10 green onions with tops,
  chopped
¾-1 pound fresh mushrooms,
  sliced

1 large carrot, sliced
4-5 tablespoons fresh parsley,
  chopped
1 10-ounce package frozen
  chopped broccoli, thawed
1 heaping tablespoon Cavender's®
  Seasoning
Juice of 1 lemon (optional)
1 teaspoon sea salt

In large saucepan cook chicken and rice in water for about 40 minutes. Remove chicken and chop into bite-size pieces. Add chicken and remaining ingredients and cook 20 minutes or until vegetables are tender and rice has "opened". Serve in warmed soup bowls with a dollop of sour cream and crumbled dried parsley for garnish. Serves 8.

Holly Suber (Mrs. Stephen M. Jr.)

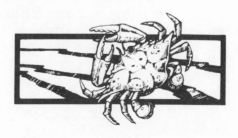

GREEK STYLE CHICKEN SOUP

1 4-pound chicken	1 carrot
2 lemons, divided	1 onion
8 cups hot water	1 rib celery
1 tablespoon salt	½ cup rice or pasta, uncooked
Few peppercorns	3 egg yolks

Rub chicken with 1 lemon and place in pot. Add water, salt and pepper. Slowly cook over low heat about 20 minutes; add carrot, onion and celery and continue cooking 30 minutes more. Remove fat during cooking process. Remove chicken and reserve for another use. Pour broth through strainer. Return broth to heat, adding rice, and boil 20 minutes. Remove from heat and allow to cool a few minutes. Beat egg yolks and juice of remaining lemon; slowly add to broth over low heat.

Calliope Bryant (Mrs. Rowlett)

CHICKEN AND SAUSAGE GUMBO

1 3-pound fryer, boned, skinned and cut into pieces or 3 whole chicken breasts	1 large onion, chopped
	1 small green pepper, chopped
	1 small red pepper, chopped
All-purpose flour	1 rib celery, trimmed and chopped
1 pound smoked sausage, cut into ½-inch slices (Andouille,® if possible)	1 bunch green onions, sliced
	¼ cup all-purpose flour
½ cup bacon drippings	1 quart chicken broth
2 garlic cloves, crushed	½ teaspoon salt
3-4 dried cayenne peppers, crushed	½ teaspoon pepper
	¾ pound fresh okra, chopped

Dust the chicken with flour and brown with the sausage in hot bacon drippings in a Dutch oven. Remove from pot, drain well; reserve drippings. Add garlic and cayenne peppers to reserved drippings. Sauté with vegetables until tender; drain well and set aside, reserving 2 tablespoons drippings. Stir in ¼ cup flour to reserved drippings and cook over medium heat, stirring constantly, until roux becomes orange-brown, about 10-15 minutes. Gradually add broth to roux, stirring until smooth. Add salt, pepper, chicken, sausage and reserved vegetables; cover and simmer 1-2 hours, stirring occasionally. Add okra for last 30 minutes of cooking time. Serve over rice.

John Robertson
Chicago, Illinois

BRUNSWICK STEW

1 chicken fryer, boiled and
  boned
2 pounds ground beef chuck,
  browned and drained
1 pound sausage, browned and
  drained
1 18-ounce bottle regular
  barbecue sauce
1 8-ounce bottle catsup
1 cup water

2 teaspoons Tabasco
7 potatoes, diced
3-4 carrots, diced
2 16-ounce cans tomatoes
1 16-ounce can corn with
  liquid, undrained
2 cups mixed vegetables
3 onions, chopped
Salt and pepper to taste

In a large kettle or Dutch oven mix all ingredients and cook over medium low heat until potatoes and carrots are done. Best if made the day before serving. Makes 4-6 quarts.

Donna Ashcraft (Mrs. Gary)
Tallahassee, Florida

JAMBALAYA

1½ cups diced cooked ham
1 cup chopped onion
¾ cup sliced celery
1 medium green pepper, cut into
  thin strips
1 garlic clove, minced
2 tablespoons vegetable oil
1 14½-ounce can chicken broth
1 15-ounce can tomato sauce

¾ cup water
1 cup chopped, cooked chicken
¾ cup uncooked rice
2 tablespoons minced parsley
1 bay leaf
¼ teaspoon leaf thyme
¼ teaspoon Worcestershire sauce
⅛ teaspoon red pepper

Sauté ham, onion, celery, green pepper and garlic in oil in large deep skillet until onion is soft. Add remaining ingredients. Bring to a boil, cover and simmer 40 minutes, stirring once or twice. Serves 4-6.

Note: Very thick. You may want to use less rice.

Karen Hosea (Mrs. Richard E.)

HODGE PODGE SOUP

6 cups water
¾ pound meaty ham hock
1 pound stew beef
4 medium potatoes, diced
2 carrots, diced
3-4 ribs celery, diced
1 medium onion, diced

1-2 garlic cloves, minced
2 1-pound cans garbanzo beans
½ pound Polish sausage, diced
Salt and pepper to taste
Dash of chili powder
Dash of dry mustard

In a large kettle or heavy saucepan combine water, ham hock and stew beef. Cook 1½ hours then add remaining ingredients. Cook 30 minutes over medium heat; lower heat and simmer 30-45 minutes longer. Garnish with crumbled bacon if desired.

Kathleen Vance (Mrs. Charles)

PURÉED MEXICAN BLACK BEAN SOUP

1 pound (2¼ cups) dried black
   beans
2½ quarts water
1 pound ham or ham hock
2 ribs celery, chopped
2 garlic cloves, minced
2 large onions, chopped
Salt to taste
½ teaspoon pepper

¼ teaspoon ground allspice
1 tablespoon beef stock or 3
   beef bouillon cubes
1 8-ounce can tomato sauce
½ cup dry red wine or 3
   tablespoons lemon juice
1 lemon, thinly sliced
2 cups sour cream

Combine beans and water in large kettle. Bring to a boil, boil 2 minutes. Cover; set aside for 1 hour. Add ham, celery, garlic, onions, salt, pepper, allspice and beef bouillon. Cover and simmer for 2-3 hours or until beans are soft. Remove ham and set aside. Stir in tomato sauce and wine. Whirl part of soup at a time through blender or food mill. Dice ham and add to soup. Correct seasoning with salt. Reheat soup and serve with lemon slices on top. Pass sour cream to spoon onto each serving. Serves 8-10.

Freddie Benton (Mrs. John)

BLACK BEAN SOUP

1 pound black beans or black
  turtle beans
Water
6 tablespoons olive oil,
  divided
1 medium ripe tomato
1 bay leaf
1½ medium onions, divided
1½ medium green peppers, divided

2 garlic cloves, divided
1 teaspoon crushed oregano
¼ teaspoon cumin
2 tablespoons wine vinegar
¾ tablespoon salt
½ teaspoon Tabasco
2 tablespoons dry sherry or
  cooking sherry

Wash beans and discard imperfect ones. Place in a 3-4 quart soup kettle with water to cover 2 inches above beans. Soak beans overnight. Next day, with the same soaking water, (if necessary add more water so that beans are still covered with 2 inches of water), add 2 tablespoons olive oil, 1 whole tomato, bay leaf, ½ onion, ½ green pepper and 1 crushed garlic clove. Bring to a boil over high heat. Cover and cook over moderate heat until beans are tender, about 1 hour. (Stir only with a wooden spoon.) Remove bay leaf and what is left of the tomato, onion, green pepper and garlic. In a skillet heat remaining olive oil and sauté remaining onion (chopped) and remaining green pepper (chopped) until transparent. Add remaining garlic clove (minced), crushed oregano (place oregano between palms of hands and crush to bring out true flavor of the herb), cumin, wine vinegar and salt. Stir to mix well and cook 2 minutes longer then add to beans. Stir in Tabasco, cover and cook for at least ½ hour. If soup is too thick, add a little more water. Correct seasoning and add sherry. Serve hot with cooked rice. Make approximately 2 quarts.

Dottie San Juan (Mrs Edward F.)

MINESTRONE WITH PESTO SAUCE

1 cup dried white navy beans
Water
2 10¾-ounce cans chicken
   broth
2½ teaspoons salt, divided
1 small head cabbage (about
   1½ pounds), shredded
4 carrots, sliced diagonally
   ¼-inch thick
2 medium potatoes, pared and
   cut into ½-inch cubes
1 14½-ounce can Italian style
   tomatoes

2 medium onions, thinly sliced
¼ cup olive or vegetable oil
1 rib celery, sliced diagonally
   ⅛-inch thick
2 zucchini, sliced in ½-inch
   thick rounds
1 large fresh tomato, peeled
   and cut into ½-inch cubes
1 garlic clove, crushed
¼ teaspoon pepper
¼ cup chopped parsley
1 cup broken spaghetti

The day before soak beans in water to cover and refrigerate overnight. Next day drain beans, add chicken broth and water, if necessary, to make 1 quart. Pour into 8-quart kettle and add 2 more quarts water, 2 teaspoons salt and beans. Bring to a boil, reduce heat and simmer, covered, for 1 hour. Add cabbage, carrots and potatoes to soup with canned tomatoes. Cover and cook ½ hour longer. In medium skillet heat oil and sauté onions about 5 minutes. Remove from heat and add celery, zucchini, fresh tomato, garlic, remaining ½ teaspoon salt and pepper. Cook slowly, uncovered, for 20 minutes. Add to bean mixture with parsley and spaghetti; cook slowly for 30 minutes. Serve with dollop of Pesto Sauce on top.

Pesto Sauce

¼ cup butter or margarine,
   softened
¼ cup grated Parmesan cheese
½ cup finely chopped parsley
1 garlic clove, pressed

1 teaspoon basil
½ teaspoon marjoram
¼ cup olive or vegetable oil
¼ cup chopped walnuts

Blend butter with Parmesan, parsley, garlic, basil and marjoram. Gradually add oil, beating constantly. Add nuts.

Jean Cardinale (Mrs. Richard)

BREADS

YORKSHIRE PUDDING

4 eggs
2 cups milk
2 cups all-purpose flour

1 teaspoon salt
½ teaspoon pepper
½ cup beef drippings

Beat the eggs with a wire whisk until very light; add remaining ingredients, except beef drippings and beat well. Put the drippings in a baking pan and place in the oven at 450°F. until it is very hot. Then add the batter. Bake 10 minutes at 450°F. reduce heat to 375°F. for 15 minutes. Pudding should be wonderfully light and crispy.

Robin Ross (Mrs. Barry)
Boars Head Restaurant

BLUE RIBBON BUTTERHORNS

3½ cups all-purpose flour,
   divided
1 package dry yeast
1¼ cups milk
¼ cup sugar

¼ cup shortening
1 teaspoon salt
1 egg
Butter or margarine

Mix 2 cups flour with the yeast; set aside. Heat and stir milk, sugar, shortening and salt until warm. Add to flour mixture; add the egg. Beat on low speed of mixer for ½ minute, then on high speed for 3 minutes. Stir in as much of the remaining flour as you can mix in with a spoon. Knead in enough of the remaining flour to make a moderately stiff dough. Knead until smooth about 6-8 minutes. Shape into a ball, place in a greased bowl and turn. Cover and let rise until doubled in bulk about 45-60 minutes. Punch down; divide into 3 equal parts. Cover; let rest 10 minutes. On lightly floured surface roll each ball to a 12-inch circle. Brush with melted butter. Cut each circle into 12 wedges. Begin rolling each wedge at the wide end and roll toward point, placing point down. Place rolls 2-3 inches apart on lightly greased baking sheets. Let rise and brush tops with melted butter just before baking. Let rise about 30-45 minutes and bake at 400°F. for 10-12 minutes or until brown, being careful not to burn.

Jamia Moncada

HUBERT'S FAVORITE ROLLS

2 cups water, divided
½ cup butter or margarine
½ cup shortening
¾ cup sugar
1½ teaspoons salt

2 packages dry yeast
2 eggs, slightly beaten
6 cups all-purpose flour
Melted butter or margarine

Bring 1 cup water to a boil; remove from heat. Add butter and shortening and stir until melted. Add sugar and salt; cool to lukewarm. In a large bowl place remaining 1 cup water at 105-115°F.; sprinkle in yeast and stir until dissolved. Add butter-sugar mixture and eggs. Add flour and mix thoroughly (dough will be soft). Cover and refrigerate overnight. About 2-2½ hours before serving, turn out onto a floured surface; roll to desired thickness. Cut in rounds, brush with melted butter and fold in half, pressing together. Brush tops with butter. Place on greased cookie sheet, cover and let rise 1½-2 hours. Bake at 400°F. for 12-15 minutes.

Karen Green (Mrs. Hubert)

BROWN ROLLS

1 cup shortening
¼ cup sugar
1 cup bran cereal
1 teaspoon salt
1 cup boiling water

2 packages dry yeast
1 cup lukewarm water
2 eggs
6 or more cups all-purpose flour
Softened butter or margarine

Put shortening, sugar, bran and salt in mixing bowl. Pour boiling water over. In a separate bowl soak yeast in lukewarm water. When bran mixture is cool, add eggs, yeast mixture and flour to make a soft dough. Roll out dough, cut into 2-inch circles, spread with softened butter and fold over. Place on greased baking sheets and bake at 375°F. for 20-25 minutes. Dough may be kept in refrigerator for a week or longer.

Ruthie Hunter (Mrs. Charles)

REFRIGERATOR ROLLS

1 package dry yeast
½ cup warm water
½ cup butter or margarine, softened
½ cup shortening, softened or vegetable oil
¾ cup sugar

1 cup unseasoned hot mashed potatoes
1 cup cold water
1½ teaspoons salt
About 6-6½ cups sifted all-purpose flour

In a large bowl sprinkle yeast into warm water; stir until dissolved. Stir in butter, shortening, sugar, potatoes. Add cold water, salt and enough flour to make a stiff dough. Place dough in a large greased bowl. Turn dough to grease all sides, cover tightly with foil and a clean towel and refrigerate. To use dough: cut off only as much as you need. Shape as desired, cover with towel and let rise in warm place until doubled. Bake at 425°F. for 20-25 minutes. Dough will keep 3-4 days in refrigerator. Makes 3 dozen.

Marion McNair (Mrs. Morris)

GRANDMOTHER HOLTMAN'S KUCHEN

1 medium potato, peeled and boiled
5 melted tablespoons butter or margarine, divided
¾ cup potato water (reserved from boiling potato)
1 cup sugar, divided

½ cup shortening
1½ teaspoons salt
1 egg
1 cup lukewarm water
1 package dry yeast
6½ cups all-purpose flour
1 teaspoon cinnamon

In blender combine potato, 1 tablespoon butter and ¾ cup potato water; blend until smooth; set aside. In large bowl cream ½ cup sugar, shortening and salt; add egg, beat. Add potato mixture; beat well. Mix lukewarm water with yeast, then mix into batter. Add flour, mixing until dough is stiff but not dry. Let mixture rise until doubled in bulk, punch down and let rise again (overnight in refrigerator if desired). Punch down and put dough into 2 buttered 13x9x2-inch pans. Brush with remaining melted butter; sprinkle with remaining sugar and cinnamon mixture. Let rise until doubled again. Bake at 350°F. for 20-25 minutes (does not brown). Slice in thin pieces and serve warm with butter. This freezes well.

Lillian Cooper (Mrs. Michael)

EASY CINNAMON ROLLS

2 cups self-rising flour
¼ cup shortening
⅔ cup milk

Melted butter or margarine
Cinnamon-sugar (Mixed to taste)

Make dough of flour, shortening and milk; knead for 2 minutes. Roll out into a rectangle and brush with melted butter. Sprinkle generously with cinnamon-sugar; roll up jelly-roll style. Slice and pat slightly into greased 9-inch round pan; brush again with melted butter. Bake at 425°F. for 10-15 minutes. Frost with a powdered sugar glaze.

Glaze

Confectioners sugar
Almond Flavoring

Sprinkle with nuts

Ann Bane (Mrs. Curtis)

CRESCENT DANISH ROLLS

2 10-ounce cans refrigerated
    crescent rolls

Preserves, to taste

Unroll crescents forming an 8x10-inch rectangle. Smooth out perforations. Spread filling on rectangle; roll lengthwise jellyroll fashion. Cut into slices 1-inch thick. Place on an ungreased baking sheet; flatten slightly. Top with preserves of your choice. Bake at 350°F. for 15 to 20 minutes. Drizzle glaze over warm rolls and serve. Quick, easy and delicious! Yield: 10 rolls.

Filling

1 8-ounce package cream cheese,
    softened

1 teaspoon lemon juice
½ cup sugar

Combine ingredients in order listed and mix until reaches spreading consistency and ingredients are well blended.

Glaze

½ cup confectioners sugar
1 teaspoon vanilla

2 to 3 teaspoons milk

Combine ingredients and mix until well blended.

Wilma Jasper (Mrs. Norman)

ORANGE ROLLS I

1 package dry yeast
¼ cup very warm water
1 cup sugar, divided
1 teaspoon salt
2 eggs
½ cup sour cream

½ cup butter or margarine,
  divided
3½ cups all-purpose flour,
  divided
2 tablespoons grated orange rind

Dissolve yeast in very warm water in large mixing bowl. Beat in ¼ cup sugar, salt, eggs, sour cream and 6 tablespoons melted butter with electric mixer. Gradually add 2¾ cups flour. Beat until smooth. Knead remaining flour into dough. Let rise in bowl in warm place until doubled in bulk, about 2 hours. Knead dough on well-floured surface about 15 times. Roll ½ of the dough to a 12-inch circle. Combine remaining ¾ cup sugar and orange rind. Brush dough with 1 tablespoon melted butter and sprinkle with half the orange-sugar mixture. Cut into 12 wedges. Roll up, starting with the wide end. Repeat with remaining dough. Place point side down in 3 rows in a greased 13x9-inch pan. Bake at 350°F. for 20 minutes. While still warm, spread with glaze.

Glaze

¾ cup sugar
½ cup sour cream

2 tablespoons orange juice
½ cup butter or margarine

Combine all ingredients and spread on warm rolls.

Ann Bane (Mrs. Curtis)

ORANGE ROLLS II

1 cup sugar
3¾ cups butter or margarine,
  divided
4 eggs
⅛ teaspoon salt

1 package dry yeast
3½ cups milk
½ teaspoon orange extract
½ teaspoon lemon extract
6½ cups all-purpose flour

In a large bowl blend sugar and ¾ cup butter. Beat eggs well and add to butter-sugar mixture. Dissolve salt and yeast in milk and add to mixture; add flavorings. Blend flour and knead lightly. Add more flour if necessary. Chill dough in refrigerator at least 1 hour. Roll out and spread with 1 cup butter. Fold over and chill again. Repeat twice—rolling out, spreading with butter and chilling each time. Roll out ⅛-inch thick and spread with filling, reserving some to frost rolls after they bake. Roll dough spread with filling into a long roll about ½-inch in diameter. Cut off 1-inch pieces and place in greased muffin pans. Place in warm place for 30 minutes. Bake at 375°F. for 15-20 minutes until light brown. Frost tops with remaining filling while rolls are still warm.

Filling

3 cups powdered sugar
½ cup butter or margarine

Juice and grated rind of 2
  oranges

Blend all ingredients together well.

Marjorie Shoemaker (Mrs. John H.)

MOMMA'S CORN LIGHT BREAD

3 cups plain white corn meal
  (not stone ground)
1 cup sugar
1 cup all-purpose flour
1 teaspoon salt

1 teaspoon baking powder
1 teaspoon soda
About ½ cup shortening
3 cups buttermilk

Sift dry ingredients together. Cut in shortening; stir in buttermilk. Grease bottom of an iron skillet and sprinkle with sugar. Pour in batter. Sprinkle with sugar; bake at 325°F. for 1 hour. May be baked in a regular skillet, Bundt pan or 2 loaf pans.

Note: In Tennessee this bread is traditionally served with barbecue.

Jane Keller (Mrs. Joe)

CORN BREAD

¼ cup shortening or vegetable
   oil
¼ cup sugar
1 egg, beaten
1¼ cups self-rising corn meal

¾ cup self-rising flour
¼ teaspoon soda
1 cup sour milk or 1 cup milk
   soured with either 1 tablespoon
   vinegar or lemon juice

Mix shortening, sugar and egg. Add remainder of ingredients alternately, mixing well. Bake in a well-greased pan at 375°F. for 20-25 minutes. Serves 8-10.

Genelle Wynn (Mrs. William W.)

THE FISH HOUSE "SAND DOLLARS"

1 cup water ground, fine corn
   meal
½ teaspoon salt

1½ cups hot water
4 teaspoons used vegetable oil

Combine corn meal and salt, add hot water and stir; it should be very thin. Add oil (that has been previously used, like what you've fried French fries in). Dip out a little batter on a hot grill that has been oiled or an old black skillet. Let it bubble some and brown on the underneath side; turn to brown on other side. Drain on paper towels.

The Fish House Restaurant
Mexico Beach, Florida

SOUR CREAM CORN BREAD

½ cup butter or margarine
1 cup cream style corn
1 cup sour cream

1 cup self-rising corn meal
2 eggs, beaten
½ medium onion, chopped

Preheat to 350°F. Melt butter in an 8-inch iron skillet. Mix other ingredients until blended. Pour melted butter into batter and mix well. Pour batter into the hot, buttered skillet. Bake at 350°F. for 35-40 minutes.

Ruthie Hunter (Mrs. Charles)

BUTTERMILK CORN STICKS

1⅓ cups corn meal
⅓ cup all-purpose flour
1 teaspoon baking powder
½ teaspoon soda
½ teaspoon salt

1 tablespoon sugar
1 cup buttermilk
1 egg, beaten
2 tablespoons melted shortening

Combine first 6 ingredients; stir in buttermilk and egg just until ingredients are moistened. Stir in shortening. Place 2 well-greased cast-iron corn stick pans in a 400°F. oven for 3 minutes or until hot. Remove pans from oven; spoon batter into pans filling ⅔ full. Bake at 400°F. for 12-15 minutes or until lightly browned. Makes 15 corn sticks.

Betty Gilbert (Mrs. J. J.)
Chipley, Florida

HUSH PUPPIES

1 cup chopped onions
2 cups sifted corn meal
1 cup all-purpose flour
1 teaspoon salt
¾ teaspoon pepper

2 heaping teaspoons baking
  powder
1 12-ounce can beer or more
  as needed

Mix and drop by spoonfuls into hot grease; cook until golden.

James I. Lark, Sr.

JOE SWANN'S HUSH PUPPIES

10 pounds water ground, coarse
  corn meal
1 cup all-purpose flour
1 cup salt
¼ cup baking powder

¼ cup soda
14 eggs
1 quart chopped onions
6-8 quarts buttermilk

Mix all ingredients together well. Let set for few minutes before spooning into hot grease. Serves 75-90.

Note: Cooking for a crowd.

Ann Bane (Mrs. Curtis)

SQUASH PUPPIES

5 medium yellow squash
Water
1 egg, beaten
½ cup buttermilk

1 medium onion, chopped
¾ cup self-rising corn meal
¼ cup all-purpose flour

Trim ends off squash; slice and place in a Dutch oven with water to cover. Cook over medium heat for 20 minutes or until tender. Drain well, mash and drain again. Combine squash with remaining ingredients. Drop mixture by scant tablespoonfuls into hot oil (350°F.). Fry 5 minutes or until golden brown. Makes about 2½ dozen.

Louverne Barron (Mrs. Dempsey)

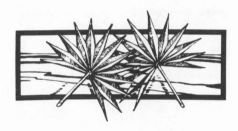

SESAME WAFER THINS

1¾ cups wheat flour
½ cup corn meal
2 tablespoons sugar
½ teaspoon salt
½ teaspoon baking soda

½ cup water
2 tablespoons vinegar
¼ cup butter, melted
Sesame seeds
Melted butter

Combine dry ingredients in a food processor. Process for 5 seconds to mix. In a measuring cup, combine water, vinegar and melted butter. Pour liquid into dry ingredients in processor with processor running. Process for 2 minutes or until a ball forms. Divide the dough into 30 balls. Roll each into a paper thin, 4½-inch, circle between 2 sheets of waxed paper. Lift top sheet of waxed paper and sprinkle with seeds and brush with melted butter. Replace paper and roll again. Peel off paper and gently transfer to an ungreased baking sheet. Bake at 375°F. for 8 to 10 minutes. Yield: 2½ dozen wafer thins.

Annette Rider (Mrs. James)

CHERYL WALKER'S LEMON MUFFINS

1 cup butter
1 cup sugar
4 eggs, separated
½ cup lemon juice

2 cups all-purpose flour
2 teaspoons baking powder
1 teaspoon salt
2 teaspoons grated lemon rind

Cream butter and sugar; add well-beaten egg yolks and beat until light. Add lemon juice alternately with flour which has been sifted with baking powder and salt. Mix thoroughly after each addition; do not overmix. Fold in stiffly beaten egg whites and grated lemon rind. Fill buttered muffin pans ¾ full and bake at 375°F. for about 20 minutes. These freeze well. Makes 24 muffins.

Bettina Mead Youd (Mrs. Richard)

PUMPKIN MUFFINS

½ cup butter or margarine
1¼ cups sugar
1¼ cups mashed pumpkin
2 eggs
1½ cups all-purpose flour
1 teaspoon baking powder
1 teaspoon cinnamon

¼ teaspoon nutmeg
¼ teaspoon salt
1 cup milk
½ cup chopped pecans or walnuts
½ cup raisins
Cinnamon-sugar

All ingredients should be at room temperature. Cream butter, sugar and pumpkin until smooth. Add eggs; blend well. Sift flour, baking powder and spices; add alternately with milk to egg batter. Do not overmix. Fold in nuts and raisins. Sprinkle a little cinnamon-sugar on top before baking. Bake in greased muffin tins at 375°F. for approximately 25 minutes or until done. Muffins may be frozen and reheated. Makes 2 dozen.

Variation: substitute 1¼ cups mashed sweet potato for pumpkin if desired.

The Greenbrier
White Sulphur Springs, West Virginia

APPLE MUFFINS

1½ cups firmly packed brown
   sugar
⅔ cup vegetable oil
1 egg
1 cup sour milk or buttermilk
1 teaspoon soda
1 teaspoon salt

1 teaspoon vanilla extract
2½ cups all-purpose flour
1½ cups diced apples
½ cup chopped pecans
⅓ cup sugar
1 teaspoon melted butter or
   margarine

Combine brown sugar, oil and egg in a mixing bowl. In a separate bowl combine sour milk, soda, salt and vanilla. Add milk mixture to sugar mixture alternately with flour, mixing well after each addition. Fold in apples and pecans. Pour into paper-lined muffin cups and sprinkle with mixture of sugar and melted butter. Bake at 325°F. for 30 minutes or until cake tester comes out clean. Makes about 15 muffins.

Frances Sulzychi (Mrs. Stanley)
Debbie Stout (Mrs. Gary)

BRAN MUFFINS

1 cup bran cereal
2 cups All Bran cereal
1 cup boiling water
2 eggs, beaten
½ cup shortening
1¼ cups sugar

2 cups buttermilk
2½ cups flour
2½ teaspoons soda
½ teaspoon salt
¾ cup raisins, optional

Combine first 3 ingredients and set aside. Combine eggs, shortening sugar and buttermilk. Mix until well blended; add to bran mixture. Sift together remaining ingredients except raisins. Add to buttermilk mixture. Stir in raisins. Place in jars with tight fitting lid and refrigerate. Use as needed. This mixture will keep up to seven weeks. Whole wheat flour may be used for added fiber or taste. Yield: 50 muffins.

Patty Segler (Mrs. Jack)

BRAN ORANGE MUFFINS

1 egg
1 cup orange juice
3 tablespoons vegetable oil
2 teaspoons grated orange rind
1½ cups bran cereal

1 cup unsifted all-purpose flour
2½ teaspoons baking powder
½ teaspoon salt
⅓ cup sugar
½ cup chopped toasted almonds

Preheat to 400°F. Beat together egg, orange juice, oil and orange rind. Stir in bran; let stand 5 minutes. On a sheet of aluminum foil combine flour, baking powder, salt, sugar and almonds. Add flour mixture to bran mixture; stir just until combined—do not overmix. Fill greased or paper-lined muffin tins until full. Bake at 400°F. 12-15 minutes or until done. Serve warm. Makes 12 large, 24-32 small muffins.

Edith Bozarth (Mrs. W. A.)

WHOLE WHEAT MUFFINS

1 cup all-purpose flour
2 teaspoons baking powder
1 teaspoon salt (optional)
1 cup whole wheat flour
¼ cup molasses

1 egg, beaten or egg substitute
1 cup skim milk
¼ cup corn oil margarine or
    safflower oil

Sift flour, baking powder and salt into a medium bowl; stir in the whole wheat flour and make a well in the center of the ingredients. Combine the molasses, egg, milk and margarine and add to the flour mixture, stirring lightly just until liquid is absorbed. Fill oiled muffin tins ⅔ full and bake at 400°F. for 20 minutes. Makes 1 dozen.

Dot Ennis (Mrs. Buford)

RAISIN BRAN MUFFINS

1 10-ounce package bran cereal
    with raisins
1½ cups sugar
2½ cups all-purpose flour
1 teaspoon salt

2½ teaspoons soda
2 eggs
½ cup butter or margarine, melted
2 cups buttermilk

Mix dry ingredients together; add eggs, butter and buttermilk. Stir with spoon until moistened. Fill greased muffin tins ½ full. Bake at 400°F. 15 minutes.

Susan Hughes
Gwyn Hill (Mrs. Alvin)

BRANANA MUFFINS

1 cup bran cereal
¾ cup skim milk
¼ cup mashed bananas
1 egg or egg substitute
¼ cup corn oil margarine,
    softened

1 cup all-purpose flour
2½ teaspoons baking powder
½ teaspoon salt (optional)
¼ cup sugar

Combine bran cereal, milk and mashed bananas; add egg and margarine. Beat well. Sift together flour, baking powder, salt and sugar. Add to bananas and cereal mixture; mix lightly until ingredients are moistened. Fill oiled muffin tins ⅔ full and bake at 400°F. for 25-30 minutes.

Variation: add ½ cup chopped dates and ½ teaspoon cinnamon.

Ruth Booker (Mrs. Nolen)

HOMEMADE BISCUITS

2 cups sifted self-rising flour
⅓ cup shortening

2 tablespoons buttermilk powder
¾ cup (approximately) cold milk

Preheat oven to 450°F. With pastry blender cut flour and shortening together until it resembles coarse meal. Mix in buttermilk powder; stir in cold milk and work with hands to form a soft dough. Turn out onto a floured surface, roll with a floured rolling pin to ½-inch thickness. Cut. Place in a greased pan. Bake at 450°F. for about 12 minutes.

Variations

Cheese Biscuits-add ¾ cup shredded sharp cheese
Sausage Biscuits-add ½ pound cooked sausage, well-drained
Onion Biscuits-add ½ cup sautéed chopped onions, drained
Parsley Biscuits-add 3 tablespoons finely chopped fresh parsley

Mary Lane Smallwood (Mrs. Henry)

DILL COTTAGE CHEESE BREAD

2 packages dry yeast
¾ cup warm water
2 teaspoons plus 2 tablespoons
  sugar, divided
2 eggs, at room temperature
2 cups creamy cottage cheese,
  at room temperature

2 tablespoons dill weed
2 tablespoons dehydrated onion
2 teaspoons salt
2 teaspoons baking powder
6½ cups bread flour

In a bowl mix yeast in warm water with 2 teaspoons sugar; proof (mixture should foam, if it doesn't then yeast is no good). Mix remaining ingredients except flour into yeast mixture. Add 4½ cups bread flour; mix well then add, ½ cup at a time, up to 2 cups more flour. Mix well. Let rise until doubled in bulk, punch down, let rest 5 minutes. Divide into 3 greased loaf pans. Allow bread to rise again; bake at 350°F. for 30-35 minutes. Cool. Bread may be frozen up to 4 months.

Debbie Stout (Mrs. Gary)

SALT FREE YEAST BREAD
A food processor recipe.

¾ cup water
3 tablespoons butter or margarine
1 egg, well beaten

2 envelopes dry yeast
3 cups white bread flour

Combine water and butter. Heat until very warm (120°F. to 130°F.) Grease a large mixing bowl and set aside. In food processor bowl with knife blade attached, process yeast and 1½ cups flour a few seconds to mix. With processor running, pour butter mixture and egg through the feed tube in a steady stream; process 10 to 15 seconds or until just mixed. Turn off food processor. Add remaining flour and process for 60 to 90 seconds or until dough is well mixed. Remove dough carefully, shape into a smooth ball and place in the greased bowl. Turn once to grease the top, cover and let rise in a warm place free from drafts for 1 hour or until doubled in bulk. Punch down, shape into a loaf and place in a greased 9x5x3-inch loaf pan. Cover and let rise 45 minutes or until doubled in bulk. Bake at 375°F. for 35 to 40 minutes or until loaf sounds hollow when tapped. Remove from oven and brush with butter. Cool on rack. Yield: 1 loaf.

Doris Fox Bailey

HEARTY WHEAT LOAF

2 tablespoons molasses
2 tablespoons honey
⅛ teaspoon cinnamon
2 tablespoons vegetable oil
1 teaspoon salt

1 cup hot water
1 cup cold water
1 package dry yeast
3 cups wheat flour
2 cups all-purpose flour

Place molasses, honey, cinnamon, oil, salt and hot water in a bowl. Stir to melt honey and molasses. Add cold water and yeast and stir. Add wheat flour then all-purpose flour; mix well. Knead, adding extra flour if sticky. Let rise in greased bowl until doubled in bulk, about 1½ hours. Punch down and place dough in an oiled loaf pan; let rise about 1 hour. Bake at 350°F. for 45 minutes.

Jean Pitts (Mrs. Reynolds E.)

PEPPER BREAD

2 packages dry yeast
2 cups water, divided
3 tablespoons plus a pinch of
 sugar, divided
1 teaspoon salt
2 tablespoons bacon fat
2 eggs, divided
1 teaspoon pepper

1 teaspoon oregano
½ cup crumbled bacon
½ cup grated Parmesan cheese
5 cups all-purpose flour
1 teaspoon milk
Pepper
Parmesan cheese

Dissolve yeast in ½ cup warm water, add pinch of sugar; proof 10 minutes. Combine remaining hot water, salt, remaining sugar and bacon fat in mixing bowl. Cool and add yeast. Beat in 1 egg, pepper, oregano, bacon and cheese. Add flour and mix until smooth. No kneading! Cover bowl and let rise until doubled in bulk. Punch down and divide dough in half. Place in 2 greased loaf pans, cover and let rise about 30 minutes. Bake at 400°F. for 10 minutes; reduce heat to 325°F. and bake for 20 minutes. After 15 minutes, brush loaves with remaining egg beaten with 1 teaspoon milk. Sprinkle with pepper and Parmesan cheese; return to oven for the last 5 minutes.

Hannelore Holland (Mrs. William)

VIDALIA ONION BREAD

1 large Vidalia onion, thinly
  sliced
6 tablespoons butter or
  margarine, divided
4 eggs, divided

1½ cups sour cream
1 teaspoon caraway seeds
½ teaspoon salt
½ cup milk
1¾ cups biscuit baking mix

Sauté onion in ¼ cup butter for 10 minutes or until golden brown; set aside. Slightly beat 3 eggs; add onion, sour cream, caraway seeds and salt. Stir well and set aside. Combine remaining 2 tablespoons butter, remaining egg and milk and stir just until moistened (dough will be slightly lumpy). Spread dough in a greased 12x8x2-inch pan. Spread onion mixture over dough. Bake at 375°F. for 30 minutes or until top is set. Serves 10-12.

Marion Collins (Mrs. Charles)

CRANBERRY NUT BREAD

½ cup butter or margarine, at
  room temperature
1 cup sugar
2 eggs
2 cups all-purpose flour
½ teaspoon salt
1 teaspoon baking powder

1 teaspoon soda
1 8-ounce carton sour cream
1 teaspoon almond extract
½ cup crushed nuts
1 16-ounce can whole cranberry
  sauce

Blend butter and sugar together in a mixing bowl. Add unbeaten eggs, 1 at a time, on medium speed of mixer. Reduce speed, add sifted dry ingredients alternating with sour cream. Add flavoring and nuts. Pour half of batter into a greased and floured 10-inch tube pan. Spread cranberry sauce over batter; add remaining batter. Bake at 350°F. for 50 minutes or until bread tests done. Cool in pan 5 minutes then remove to cool completely. Add glaze.

Glaze

¼ cup powdered sugar
1 tablespoon warm water

½ teaspoon almond extract

Mix well and drizzle over cranberry bread.

Karon Wakstein (Mrs. Gary)

BLUEBERRY GINGERBREAD

½ cup oil
1 cup sugar
½ teaspoon salt
3 tablespoons molasses
1 egg
2 cups flour

½ teaspoon ginger
1 teaspoon cinnamon
½ teaspoon nutmeg
1 teaspoon soda
1 cup fresh or frozen blueberries
1 cup buttermilk

Combine first 4 ingredients in order listed. Mix with electric mixer until well blended. Add egg. Beat another 30 seconds with mixer; set aside. Combine flour, ginger, cinnamon, nutmeg and soda. Dredge blueberries in 2 tablespoons of flour mixture; set aside. Add remaining flour mixture alternately with buttermilk, beating well after each addition. Stir in blueberries. Pour into 2, 9x5x3-inch, loaf pans or a 13x9x2-inch baking pan which have been greased and floured. Sprinkle top with brown sugar. Bake at 350°F. for 35 to 40 minutes. Yield: 2 loaves or a 13x9x2-inch pan gingerbread.

Brenda Veal (Mrs. James)

BLU'BANA BREAD

1 cup butter or margarine
2 cups sugar
4 eggs
2 teaspoons vanilla extract
5 medium bananas, mashed
4 cups all-purpose flour, divided

3 teaspoons allspice
2 teaspoons soda
1 teaspoon baking powder
½ teaspoon salt
2 cups blueberries, fresh or frozen

Preheat oven 325°F. Cream together butter and sugar; beat in eggs. Add vanilla; fold in mashed bananas. Fold in 2 cups flour. Measure 2 additional cups flour, reserving 2 tablespoons to coat blueberries. Place remaining flour in a sifter with allspice, soda, baking powder and salt. Sift and fold into creamed mixture. Sprinkle the reserved 2 tablespoons flour onto the blueberries, coat well then fold into the batter. Divide the batter into 2 greased and floured loaf pans. Bake at 325°F. for about 50 minutes. Test with toothpick for doneness.

Dr. Milton Acton

COCO-NUTTY BANANA BREAD

½ cup butter or margarine
1 cup sugar
2 eggs
2 cups mashed ripe bananas
2 cups all-purpose flour

1 teaspoon baking powder
1 teaspoon salt
½ cup toasted coconut
½ cup toasted pecans
½ cup walnuts (optional)

Cream butter and sugar; add eggs, 1 at a time, beating well after each. Stir in bananas. Combine dry ingredients and add to creamed mixture, stirring only until moistened. Add toasted coconut, pecans and walnuts if desired. Pour into greased and floured 9x5x3-inch loaf pan and bake at 350°F. for 50-60 minutes. Cool for 10 minutes before removing from pan.

Sherry Knight

CARROT WALNUT BREAD

1 cup vegetable oil
¼ cup sugar
2 eggs
1 teaspoon vanilla extract
1½ cups sifted all-purpose flour

½ teaspoon salt
1½ teaspoons soda
1½ teaspoons cinnamon
1½ cups grated carrots
1½ cups ground walnuts

Combine oil, sugar, eggs and vanilla in large bowl. Sift flour, salt, soda and cinnamon; add to sugar mixture. Stir in carrots and walnuts mix just until blended. Bake in a greased and lightly floured loaf pan at 350°F. for 1 hour. Cool in pan for 10 minutes, turn out on wire rack and cool completely. Top with Lemon Glaze.

Lemon Glaze

½ cup powdered sugar
1 teaspoon grated lemon rind

1 tablespoon lemon juice

Combine sugar, lemon rind and juice in a small bowl. Stir until smooth; drizzle over top and sides of bread.

Marion McNair (Mrs. Morris)

LEMON BREAD

½ cup butter or margarine
1 cup sugar
2 eggs, slightly beaten
1¼ cups all-purpose flour
1 teaspoon baking powder

¼ teaspoon salt
½ cup milk
½ cup chopped walnuts
Grated rind of 1 lemon

Cream together butter and sugar. Add eggs. Sift together flour, baking powder and salt. Stir into creamed mixture alternately with milk; add walnuts and lemon rind. Bake in greased and floured loaf pan at 350°F. for 1 hour. Remove from oven; pierce top of bread with fork. Pour topping over bread. Let cool, remove from pan and refrigerate until served.

Topping

¼ cup sugar

Juice of 1 lemon

Mix together in a saucepan and heat until slightly warm.

Pam Smoak (Mrs. Richard)

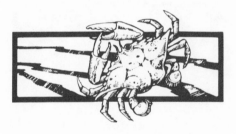

MOMA'S APRICOT BREAD

3 cups all-purpose flour
4 teaspoons baking powder
1 teaspoon salt
⅓ to ½ cup sugar
¼ cup butter or margarine

1 cup finely diced apricots
2 eggs, beaten
1 cup milk
1 teaspoon grated lemon rind
½ cup broken pecans

Sift together flour, baking powder, salt and sugar. Cut in butter until fine. Add apricots, eggs, milk and lemon rind; mix just until blended. Add to dry ingredients; stir, then add pecans. Pour into buttered loaf pan and bake at 350°F. for 1 hour.

Rosilin Mead
Louisa M. Salinas (Mrs. Bob)
Bettina M. Youd (Mrs. Richard)

SHARON'S NUTRITIOUS BANANA BREAD

3 bananas
¼ cup sour cream
½ cup butter or margarine
½ cup sugar
2 eggs
1 cup all-purpose flour

¼ cup whole-wheat flour
1 tablespoon baking powder
¼ teaspoon soda
1 cup wheat germ
1 teaspoon vanilla extract
2 cups pecan pieces

Cream together bananas, sour cream, butter and sugar. Add eggs and beat well. Add remaining ingredients to creamed mixture; pour into 2 greased and floured 9x5-inch loaf pans and bake at 350°F. for 30 minutes or until firm.

Sharon Mathews (Mrs. Marion)

ZUCCHINI BREAD

3 eggs
2 cups sugar
1 tablespoon cinnamon
1 teaspoon salt
1 cup vegetable oil or ½ cup
    butter or margarine and ½ cup
    shortening

1½ teaspoons soda
1 teaspoon baking powder
3 cups all-purpose flour
2 cups ground or grated peeled
    zucchini
1 cup chopped nuts
1 teaspoon vanilla extract

In a large bowl beat eggs. Combine sugar, cinnamon and salt and add to eggs; mix well. Add oil. Combine dry ingredients and add to mixture. Fold in zucchini, nuts and vanilla. Divide batter into 2 (9x5x3-inch) loaf pans. Bake at 325°F. for 1 hour. This freezes well.

Bertie Broaddus (Mrs. James)

BLUEBERRY COFFEE CAKE

2 cups all-purpose flour
2 teaspoons baking powder
¾ cup sugar
¼ cup butter or margarine

½ cup milk
1 egg
1 teaspoon vanilla extract
2 cups blueberries

Combine dry ingredients in large bowl. Cut in butter until crumbly. Make a well in center and add milk, egg and vanilla, stirring just until moistened. Fold in berries; pour into greased and floured 9-inch square pan. Sprinkle with topping. Bake at 350°F. for 30-35 minutes.

Topping

½ cup sugar
⅓ cup all-purpose flour
½ teaspoon cinnamon

¼ cup butter or margarine,
   softened

Mix all ingredients with fork until crumbly. Sprinkle over batter.

Lillian Dusseault

JEWISH COFFEE CAKE

Cake

1 cup butter or margarine
2 cups sugar
3 eggs
2¼ cups all-purpose flour
3½ teaspoons baking powder
1 teaspoon salt

1 13-ounce can evaporated
   milk
1 teaspoon vanilla extract
1 teaspoon almond extract
Chopped pecans

Cream butter and sugar; add eggs and mix well. Sift dry ingredients together. Add alternately with milk to creamed mixture; add flavorings. Pour half of batter into 13x9-inch pan, top with half of filling. Repeat, then cover top with chopped pecans. Bake at 350°F. for 45 minutes. Cool and slice.

Filling

¾ cup sugar
¼ cup cinnamon

¾ cup chopped pecans

Mix all together well; alternate with layers of cake batter.

Carolyn Fleming (Mrs. Robert)

CINNAMON-NUT COFFEE CAKE

3½ cups all-purpose flour,
 divided
1 package dry yeast
1 cup milk
¼ cup butter or margarine,
 divided

¾ cup sugar, divided
1 teaspoon salt
1 egg
1 teaspoon cinnamon
1 cup chopped pecans or toasted
 almonds

Combine 2 cups flour and yeast; set aside. Heat together milk, ½ cup butter, ¼ cup sugar and salt until warm; stir well. Add to flour; add egg. Beat at low speed of mixer for 30 seconds, scraping sides of bowl constantly. Beat 3 minutes at high speed. By hand stir in enough of remaining flour to make a stiff dough. Place dough in a greased bowl, turning once to grease surface. Cover, let rise until doubled in bulk, about 1½ hours. Turn out onto lightly floured surface. Divide dough in half. Roll each half of dough into a 12-inch square; brush each half with 2 tablespoons melted butter, sprinkle with ¼ cup sugar and ½ teaspoon cinnamon. Top with ½ cup pecans or almonds. Without stretching dough, fold one side over to within ½-inch of opposite side. Press edges together. Place on greased baking sheet, cover and let rise in warm place until almost doubled in bulk. Bake at 375°F. for 12-15 minutes; cool and frost.

Frosting

2 cups sifted powdered sugar
3 tablespoons hot water

¼ cup butter or margarine,
 softened

Blend ingredients to spreading consistency.

Jean Pitts (Mrs. Reynolds E.)

SHARON'S MUFFIN DONUTS

2 cups sugar, divided
3 cups all-purpose flour
1 tablespoon baking powder
1 teaspoon salt
½ teaspoon nutmeg
⅔ cup shortening

2 eggs
1 cup milk
¾ cup butter or margarine,
 melted
2 teaspoons cinnamon

Sift together 1 cup sugar, flour, baking powder, salt and nutmeg. Cut in shortening; add eggs and milk. Bake at 350°F. for 20 minutes in miniature muffin tins filled ¾ full. While warm, dip in melted butter and roll in mixture of remaining sugar and cinnamon. Makes about 50.

Jane Keller (Mrs. Joe)

SWEDISH TEA LOG

Dough

1 package dry yeast
¼ cup warm water
2¼ cups sifted all-purpose
   flour
2 tablespoons sugar
1 teaspoon salt

½ cup butter
¼ cup evaporated milk
1 egg, unbeaten
¼ cup currants or chopped
   raisins

Soften yeast in warm water; set aside. Sift together flour, sugar and salt in a mixing bowl. Cut in butter until particles are fine. Add milk, egg, currants and softened yeast; mix well. Cover and chill 2 hours or overnight. Divide dough into thirds. Roll out ⅓ on floured surface to a 12x6-inch rectangle. Spread with ⅓ of filling. Roll up starting with 12-inch side; seal. Place in crescent shape on foil-lined cookie sheet. Make cuts along outside edge 1-inch apart to within ½-inch of center. Turn cut pieces on sides; repeat with remaining dough. Let rise in warm place (85-90°F.) until light, about 45 minutes. Bake at 350°F. for 20-25 minutes until golden brown. Frost while warm.

Filling

¼ cup butter or margarine
½ cup firmly packed brown sugar

½ cup chopped pecans

In a mixing bowl cream butter; add brown sugar and cream well. Stir in chopped pecans.

Vanilla Glaze

2 tablespoons butter
1 cup sifted powdered sugar

½ teaspoon vanilla extract
1-2 tablespoons evaporated milk

In a saucepan brown butter; add sugar and vanilla. Stir in milk until of spreading consistency.

Dot Thomas (Mrs. Treaver)

WORLD'S EASIEST SOUFFLE

Butter
Grated Parmesan cheese
4 eggs
4 ounces sharp Cheddar cheese,
    cubed
3-ounce package cream cheese,
    cubed

⅓ cup milk, light cream or half
    and half
¼ cup grated Parmesan cheese
½ teaspoon onion salt
½ teaspoon dry mustard

Butter the bottom and sides of a 1 quart souffle dish or casserole; dust with Parmesan cheese; set aside. Combine remaining ingredients in order listed in a blender container. Cover and blend at medium speed for 30 seconds or until mixture is smooth. Blend on high for an additional 10 to 30 seconds. Pour mixture into pan and bake at 350°F. for 25 to 30 minutes or until puffly and delicately browned. Serve immediately. Serves 4.

Gail M. Fay

BREAKFAST CASSEROLE

16 slices bread
2 pounds sausage, browned
1 pound Cheddar cheese,
    shredded
1 8-ounce can mushrooms

6 eggs, well beaten
1 teaspoon salt
1 teaspoon dry mustard
4 cups milk

Layer first 4 ingredients except ½ cup cheese in a buttered 12x9x2-inch baking dish in the order listed. Mix remaining ingredients and pour over layers. Sprinkle with reserved Cheddar cheese. Cover and refrigerate overnight. Bake at 350°F. for 45 minutes.

Lenda McCain (Mrs. Marvin)

CONNIE'S BREAKFAST CASSEROLE

½ cup finely chopped onion
¼ cup chopped bell pepper
2 tablespoons butter
2 cups finely chopped cooked ham
3 eggs, slightly beaten

1 cup shredded Cheddar cheese
⅔ cup fine cracker crumbs (saltines)
1½ cups milk
Dash of pepper

Sauté onion and pepper in butter until translucent. Add remaining ingredients and mix until well blended. Pour into a 12x8x2-inch baking dish. Bake at 350°F. for 45 to 50 minutes. Serves 6.

Connie Morris (Mrs. Charles)
Ellicott City, Maryland

BLUEBERRY PANCAKES WITH SAUCE

1½ cups sifted all-purpose flour
2½ teaspoons baking powder
3 tablespooons sugar
¾ teaspoon salt
2 eggs, separated

1 cup milk
3 tablespoons melted butter or
   margarine
1 cup fresh blueberries

Sift dry ingredients. Beat egg yolks, combine with milk and butter; add to dry ingredients and mix until smooth. Stir in berries. Fold in stiffly beaten egg whites. Bake on hot greased griddle. Serve with Blueberry Sauce (recipe below). Makes 12 pancakes.

Blueberry Sauce

8 teaspoons cornstarch
2 cups water
2 cups fresh blueberries

1 cup sugar
2 tablespoons butter or margarine
2 teaspoons lemon juice

In a small saucepan mix cornstarch with water until smooth. Add blueberries and sugar and cook over low heat until thick and clear, stirring constantly. Blend in butter and lemon juice. May be served hot or cold. Makes 3 cups.

Mary Sue Southerland (Mrs. Steve)

ORANGE PECAN WAFFLES

4 eggs, separated
1 cup orange juice
1 cup milk
4 tablespoons grated orange
  rind
3 cups cake flour

4 tablespoons sugar
5 teaspoons baking powder
1 teaspoon salt
1 cup chopped pecans
¾ cup butter or margarine,
  melted and cooled

In a mixing bowl beat egg yolks until thick and lemon-colored. Add orange juice and milk and orange rind. Sift together flour, sugar, baking powder and salt; beat into yolk mixture until well blended. Stir in nuts and butter. Beat egg whites until stiff and fold into batter. Cook in waffle iron until brown and crisp. Serves 6.

Martha Middlemas (Mrs. Warren)

EVERYDAY PANCAKES

1 cup all-purpose flour
1 egg
1 cup milk

¼ teaspoon salt
1 tablespoon sugar
1 tablespoon baking powder

Mix all ingredients and bake on hot griddle. Makes about 10 pancakes. Doubles easily.

Nell Ennis (Mrs. Powell)

ROBERT'S FRENCH TOAST

1 loaf French bread
2 cups milk
4 eggs
½-1 teaspoon artificial
  sweetener

4 teaspoons orange flavored
  instant breakfast drink mix
  or ½ cup orange juice

Slice about 10-12 slices (¾-1 inch thick) from loaf. Mix remaining ingredients and pour over bread. Soak bread for 30 minutes, turn and cover. Leave another 30 minutes or overnight. Grease griddle and cook at 325°F. until brown on both sides, about 5 minutes. Serve with whipped topping and fresh strawberries. Serves 4.

Robert Cogburn

SALADS
& SALAD DRESSINGS

Day Lily—Blooming in late spring in a multitude of hues, the day lily graces many Bay County gardens.

SALADS

CRAB DELIGHT

1 10¾-ounce can cream of
  mushroom soup
1 envelope unflavored gelatin
1 tablespoon cold water
1 8-ounce package cream cheese,
  softened

¼ cup mayonnaise
1 tablespoon horseradish
Juice of 1 lemon
1 cup finely chopped celery
1 cup finely chopped onion
1 7-ounce can crabmeat, drained

In a saucepan heat soup; soften gelatin in water and add to soup. Cream the cheese into this mixture and set aside to cool. Add remaining ingredients. Pour into a 4-cup mold and refrigerate. Unmold and serve with crackers as a spread or slice and serve on a lettuce leaf as a salad. Serves 6.

Joni Wilcox
Anne Gagnet (Mrs. Sandy)
Pensacola, Florida

CRAB LOUIS SALAD

1½ pounds fresh crabmeat,
  flaked
1 cup mayonnaise
¼ cup Tarragon French Dressing
  (recipe below)

¼ cup chili sauce
2 tablespoons chopped chives
1 teaspoon horseradish
1 teaspoon Worcestershire sauce
Salt and pepper to taste

Flake crabmeat and arrange on bed of lettuce. Combine remaining ingredients and serve as dressing over crabmeat. Serves 6.

Tarragon French Dressing
6 tablespoons olive oil
2 tablespoons tarragon vinegar
1 teaspoon salt

1 teaspoon chopped fresh
  tarragon leaves

Blend all together well.

Caroline Ireland (Mrs. Charles)

PANHANDLE SALAD NIÇOISE

1 pound cooked crabmeat
½ pound cooked shrimp, shelled
½ pound cooked scamp or snapper,
  bones removed
1 3-ounce bottle capers,
  drained
2 red onions, thinly sliced and
  separated into rings
1 pound fresh mushrooms, halved
1 8½-ounce can artichoke hearts,
  drained and halved
1 7-ounce can hearts of Palms,
  drained and halved

3 shallots, finely chopped
2 tablespoons chopped fresh
  parsley
1 cup pitted ripe olives,
  sliced in half
1 7-ounce package blue cheese
  salad dressing mix
1 7-ounce package cheese
  Italian salad dressing mix
Vinegar

In a deep bowl assemble seafood, capers, onions, mushrooms, artichoke hearts, hearts of Palms, shallots, parsley, and olives. Prepare salad dressings according to package directions, using vinegar instead of water. Pour dressings over mixture and cover; refrigerate overnight. Stir carefully. Serve over leaf lettuce with steamed asparagus, French bread and wine (Pouilly-Blanc-Fume or other summer wine). Serves 6.

Nina Godwin (Mrs. Mark T.)

PARTY SHRIMP SALAD

1 hard-cooked egg, peeled
  and sliced
2 green onions, chopped
4 garlic cloves, crushed
¼ cup cooked, drained spinach
2 cups mayonnaise

1 tablespoon Worcestershire sauce
1 tablespoon mustard with
  horseradish
1 tablespoon lemon juice
2 pounds headless shrimp,
  boiled and peeled

In blender combine all ingredients except shrimp and puree until smooth; chill. Mound shrimp on lettuce-lined plate and drizzle sauce on top. Good as an appetizer or as a salad. Serves 6.

Amy Armstrong (Mrs. Larry)

SHRIMP SALAD

1 pound headless shrimp, boiled
   and peeled
½ cup mayonnaise
½ cup chopped celery
¼ cup chopped green onions

1 tablespoon chopped capers
2 hard-cooked eggs, peeled and
   chopped
Salt and pepper to taste

Mix all ingredients well; season to taste with salt and pepper. Chill and serve on a bed of lettuce or on an avocado half. Serves 4.

Jane Allen (Mrs. Newton)

TUNA MOUSSE

3 envelopes unflavored gelatin
¾ cup cold water
2 cups mayonnaise
3 7-ounce cans water packed
   tuna
1½ cups chopped celery

8 teaspoons sliced pimento-
   stuffed olives
1½ teaspoon salt
3 tablespoons lemon juice
3 tablespoons capers

Soften gelatin in cold water and place bowl of gelatin over hot water, stirring until dissolved. Cool and add mayonnaise and other ingredients. Refrigerate until congealed; serve with Cucumber Sauce. Serves 6.

Cucumber Sauce

1 unpared cucumber, grated
1 tablespoon grated onion
¼ cup mayonnaise
2 tablespoons vinegar

1 tablespoon chopped parsley
½ cup sour cream
Salt and pepper to taste

Combine all ingredients; blend until smooth.

Barbara Clemons (Mrs. Girard)

BAKED ORIENTAL CHICKEN SALAD

1 6-ounce package long-grain
  and wild rice
1 large onion, finely chopped
1 large fryer, boiled and de-
  boned and stock reserved
1 16-ounce can French style
  green beans

1 2-ounce jar pimento, drained
  and chopped
1 10¾-ounce can cream
  of mushroom soup, undiluted
¾ cup mayonnaise
1 can water chestnuts,
  sliced and drained

Cook rice according to package directions, adding the onion and using reserved chicken stock instead of water. When rice is done, mix all the remaining ingredients with the rice and put in a 13x9x2-inch pan. Bake at 350°F. for 30 minutes. Serves 6.

Carol Crisp (Mrs. Donald)

CHICKEN CRANBERRY MOLD

2 tablespoons unflavored
  gelatin, divided
1 cup cold water, divided
1 10¾-ounce can cream
  of chicken soup
¼ cup mayonnaise
1 tablespoon lemon juice
1 cup cooked, cubed chicken

¼ cup chopped celery
2 tablespoons chopped toasted
  almonds
1 tablespoon minced onions
1 16-ounce can whole cranberry
  sauce
1 11-ounce can mandarin
  oranges, drained

Soften 1 tablespoon gelatin in ½ cup cold water. Stir over hot water in top of double boiler until gelatin is dissolved. Blend soup, mayonnaise and lemon juice and stir into gelatin. Chill until mixture begins to thicken. Fold in chicken, celery, almonds and onions. Pour into a 1½-2 quart mold. Refrigerate until firm. Soften remaining tablespoon gelatin in remaining water as above. Crush the cranberry sauce and stir in softened gelatin. Fold in oranges and pour cranberry mixture over chicken layer in mold. Chill until set. Serves 8-10.

Betty Fensom (Mrs. Paul)
Port St. Joe, Florida

CHICKEN WITH TARRAGON
MAYONNAISE AND RICE SALAD

3 whole chicken breasts,
   skinned and boned
3 cups boiling water
2 carrots, diced
2 ribs celery, diced
1 small onion, sliced
Salt and freshly ground pepper
1 bay leaf
Tarragon Mayonnaise
   (recipe below)

3 cups cooked rice
½ cup diced fresh carrots,
   blanched
½ cup frozen green peas, thawed
1 cucumber, peeled, seeded and
   diced
3 large ripe tomatoes, scalded,
   peeled, seeded and shredded
French Vinaigrette Dressing
   (recipe below)

Combine first 7 ingredients in saucepan; cook until chicken is tender. Cool and cut chicken into bite-sized pieces. Moisten chicken with Tarragon Mayonnaise and chill. For rice salad, combine rice, carrots, peas, cucumber and tomatoes in a large bowl. Toss with French Vinaigrette Dressing. Serve at room temperature with chilled chicken and remaining Tarragon Mayonnaise. Serves 4-6.

Tarragon Mayonnaise

1½ cups mayonnaise
1 .21-ounce envelope brown
   bouillon powder

Freshly grated pepper
½ cup sour cream
½ teaspoon dried tarragon

Combine all ingredients well.

French Vinaigrette Dressing

1½ tablespoons red wine
   vinegar
½ teaspoon dry mustard
Salt and pepper to taste

1 small garlic clove, crushed
3-4 tablespoons olive oil
1 teaspoon sugar

Combine all ingredients in a covered container and shake well.

Gerry Sale (Mrs. Tom)

CHICKEN SALAD

½ cup salad dressing
½ cup sour cream
1 tablespoon lemon juice
Celery salt to taste
3 whole chicken breasts, skinned,
   boned, cooked and diced

1 cup sliced green seedless
   grapes
1 cup sliced macadamia nuts

Combine first 4 ingredients well then add chicken, grapes and nuts; chill well. Serve on bed of lettuce. Serves 8.

Rosemary Jenkins (Mrs. Eric)

CONGEALED CHICKEN SALAD

1 envelope unflavored gelatin
1 tablespoon cold water
1 cup boiling chicken stock
1 cup chopped, cooked chicken
1 cup chopped celery
1 2-ounce jar pimento,
   chopped

3 hard-cooked eggs, chopped
1 cup mayonnaise
Dash of thyme
Dash of basil
Dash of marjoram

Dissolve gelatin in cold water. Add boiling chicken stock; season with salt if necessary. Cool then add other ingredients. Pour into pan or molds and refrigerate. Serves 6.

Jean Pitts (Mrs. Reynolds E.)

CORNUCOPIA CHICKEN SALAD

1 cup finely diced chicken
   breast
½ cup finely diced celery

¼ cup diced toasted almonds
Mayonnaise to moisten
Salt to taste

Mix all ingredients well and serve chilled. 2 servings.

Lida Lewis (Mrs. James)

HOT CHICKEN SALAD

2 tablespoons butter or
 margarine
1 cup thinly sliced celery
½ cup chopped onion
½ cup mayonnaise
½ cup sour cream
1 tablespoon lemon juice
½ teaspoon salt

¼ teaspoon pepper
2 cups cooked chicken, cubed
½ cup slivered almonds, toasted
1 4-ounce can sliced mushrooms, drained
½ cup shredded Cheddar cheese
½ cup crushed potato chips

In a large skillet melt butter over medium heat. Add celery and onion. Cook about 4 minutes or until clear. Remove from heat; stir in mayonnaise, sour cream, lemon juice, salt and pepper until well blended. Add chicken, almonds, mushrooms and half the cheese. Toss to coat. Spoon into a 1½-quart casserole. Sprinkle with crushed potato chips and remaining cheese. Bake at 325°F. for 25-30 minutes or until heated through. May substitute turkey for chicken. Recipe is easily doubled. Serves 4.

Edith Bozarth (Mrs. W. A.)
Tuscola, Illinois

Jenny Doster (Mrs. Henry)

CHICKEN PASTA SALAD

1 8-ounce package corkscrew
 macaroni
½ cup mayonnaise
½ cup Italian salad dressing
3 tablspoons lemon juice
1 tablespoon prepared mustard
1 teaspoon pepper

½ teaspoon salt
3 cups cooked, cubed chicken
1 medium onion, chopped
1 cup diced cucumber
1 cup chopped celery
¾ cup sliced ripe olives

Cook macaroni according to package directions; drain and cool. Combine mayonnaise, salad dressing, lemon juice, mustard, pepper and salt and stir until blended. Add to macaroni and stir well. Stir in chicken, onion, cucumber, celery and olives; chill at least 2 hours. Serves 8.

Verna Burke (Mrs. Les)

OVERNIGHT LAYERED CHICKEN SALAD

6 cups shredded iceberg lettuce
¼ pound bean sprouts
1 8-ounce can water chestnuts,
    drained and sliced
½ cup sliced green onions
1 medium cucumber, thinly sliced
4 cups cooked, cubed chicken
2 10-ounce packages frozen
    Chinese pea pods, thawed

2 cups mayonnaise
2 teaspoons curry powder
1 tablespoon sugar
½ teaspoon ground ginger
½ cup Spanish-style peanuts
1-1½ dozen cherry tomatoes,
    halved

In a 4-quart serving dish spread lettuce in an even layer. Top with bean sprouts, water chestnuts, green onions, cucumber and chicken. Pat pea pods dry and arrange on top. Stir together mayonnaise, curry powder, sugar and ginger. Spread evenly over pea pods. Cover dish and refrigerate as long as 24 hours. To serve, garnish with peanuts and tomatoes. Serves 10-12.

Lorraine Koenigs
Pella, Iowa

CURRIED CHICKEN SALAD

¾ cup mayonnaise
1 teaspoon curry powder
2 teaspoons soy sauce
2 teaspoons lemon juice
2 cups cooked, cubed chicken
¼ cup sliced water chestnuts

½ pound seedless green grapes,
    halved
½ cup chopped celery
½ cup toasted, slivered almonds
1 8-ounce can pineapple chunks,
    drained

Combine mayonnaise with curry powder, soy sauce and lemon juice. Stir in remaining ingredients; chill. Serves 4.

Kathleen Vance (Mrs. Charles)

CORNED BEEF SALAD

1 12-ounce can corned beef
1 small onion
1 slice of bread
2 envelopes unflavored gelatin
½ cup cold water
2 beef bouillon cubes

1 cup boiling water
1 cup finely chopped celery
4 hard-cooked eggs, chopped
Worcestershire sauce to taste
1 cup mayonnaise

Grind corned beef, onion and bread. Dissolve gelatin in cold water; dissolve bouillon cubes in hot water. Mix all ingredients, pour into a 6-cup ring mold and chill 6-8 hours, preferably overnight. Serves 10-12.

Note: This is also good spread on crackers or rye bread; use only ½ cup celery; serves 24 or more.

Madelyn Gore (Mrs. George)

MEXICAN SALAD

1 pound ground beef
½ cup catsup
1 teaspoon chili powder
1 teaspoon oregano
Salt and pepper to taste
1 head lettuce, torn
2 tomatoes, chopped

1 cup shredded Cheddar cheese
1 2.2-ounce can sliced ripe
  olives
1 10-ounce package corn chips
½ cup mayonnaise
¼ cup taco sauce

Brown meat in a skillet; drain. Add catsup, chili powder, oregano, salt and pepper; simmer for 3-5 minutes. In a large bowl place torn lettuce. Add tomatoes, cheese and olives; add meat mixture and corn chips. Toss with mayonnaise and taco sauce; serve immediately. Serves 6-8.

Penny Whittaker (Mrs. Dennis)
Cupertino, California

TACO SALAD

1 pound ground beef
1 medium head lettuce
1 medium onion, chopped
3 tomatoes, chopped
¼ pound shredded Cheddar
cheese
1 15-ounce can red kidney
beans, drained

1 8-ounce bottle spicy, sweet
French salad dressing
1 8-ounce bottle mild taco
sauce
1 8-ounce package tortilla
chips, crushed

Brown ground beef; drain well and keep warm. Tear lettuce into a large bowl; assemble all ingredients in order listed; toss. Serve immediately for best results. Serves 6-8.

Laura Presley (Mrs. Larry)

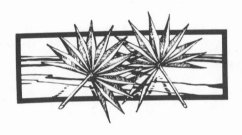

KEYSTONE PASTA SALAD

1 1-pound package sea-shell
macaroni, cooked and drained
¼ pound provolone cheese, diced
¼ pound hard salami, diced
3 tomatoes, chopped
3 green peppers, chopped
3 small onions, diced
3 ribs celery, diced

1 4-ounce can pitted ripe
olives
1 7-ounce jar green olives
1 tablespoon oregano
1 tablespoon salt
¾ cup vegetable oil
½ cup vinegar
1 teaspoon pepper

Mix all ingredients together well; marinate overnight. Serves 8.

Judy McGuire (Mrs. Walter E.)

SPINACH SALAD

1 package fresh spinach
2 hard-cooked eggs, peeled
 and chopped
4 green onions, chopped
1 cup sliced fresh mushrooms
6 slices bacon, cooked and
 crumbled
Grated Parmesan or Romano cheese
Croutons
½ cup vegetable oil

3 tablespoons wine vinegar
1 rounded tablespoon sour cream
½ teaspoon salt
½ teaspoon freshly ground
 pepper
1 tablespoon sugar
¼ teaspoon dry mustard
1 garlic clove, crushed or
 ⅛ teaspoon garlic powder
1 teaspoon dried parsley

Thoroughly wash spinach; remove stems and tear into bite-size pieces. Add eggs, onion, mushrooms and bacon. Sprinkle cheese and croutons on top. In blender combine remaining ingredients and blend well. Pour over spinach and toss lightly. Serves 6.

Nell Ennis (Mrs. Powell)

BEST EVER LAYERED SALAD

1 medium head lettuce, torn
1 bunch green onions, chopped
1 8-ounce can water chestnuts,
 sliced
½ cup chopped green pepper
2 ribs celery, sliced
1 10-ounce package frozen
 Chinese pea pods, thawed
 and crumbled
2 cups mayonnaise

2 teaspoons sugar
½ cup grated Parmesan cheese
1 teaspoon salt
¼ teaspoon garlic powder
¾ pound bacon, cooked and
 crumbled
3 hard-cooked eggs, peeled
 and sliced
2 tomatoes, sliced

Layer first 6 ingredients in order listed; spread mayonnaise on top to seal. Sprinkle sugar, cheese, salt, garlic powder, and bacon over all. Arrange eggs and tomatoes on top. Cover and chill 4 hours or up to 24 hours. Serves 10-12.

Ruth Lark (Mrs. William E.)

COLD ASPARAGUS SALAD

1½-2 pounds fresh young
   asparagus, ½-inch in diameter
   maximum

4 teaspoons soy sauce
1 teaspoon sugar
2 teaspoons sesame seed oil

Bend each asparagus stalk back until the tough root end snaps away; discard ends. Slice remaining stalks into 1½-inch lengths diagonally. There should be about 3 cups asparagus. Wash under cold water and parboil 1 minute; drain and rinse in cold water; pat dry. In glass bowl combine remaining ingredients, mixing until sugar is dissolved. Add asparagus and toss with wooden spoon. Chill no more than 2 hours. Serve on a bed of lettuce. Serves 4.

Connie Morris (Mrs. Charles)
Ellicott City, Maryland

PEA SALAD

½ cup sour cream
1 tablespoon mayonnaise
¼ teaspoon curry powder
1 tablespoon Worcestershire sauce

2 16-ounce cans small sweet
   peas, drained
⅔ cup dry roasted peanuts

Mix sour cream, mayonnaise, curry and Worcestershire; stir in peas and peanuts; chill. Serves 6-8.

Sue Shaw (Mrs. Sam)
Ozark, Alabama

CHILLED CAULIFLOWER SALAD

1 large head cauliflower, broken
   into flowerets
Salt and pepper
1 tablespoon Dijon mustard
1 cup mayonnaise

4 hard-cooked eggs, peeled and
   chopped
½ cup fresh parsley, finely
   chopped

Boil cauliflower for 20 minutes; rinse with cold water and chill. When chilled, arrange on serving dish; sprinkle with salt and pepper. Mix mustard and mayonnaise and spread over cauliflower. Stir eggs and parsley together and cover cauliflower; chill. Serves 6-8.

Dot Ennis (Mrs. Buford)

MANDARIN SALAD

Salad

¼ cup sliced almonds
1 tablespoon plus 1 teaspoon sugar
¼ head lettuce
¼ head romaine
1 cup chopped celery

2 green onions plus tops, thinly
  sliced
1 (11-ounce) can mandarin orange
  segments, drained

Cook almonds and sugar over a low heat, stirring constantly, until sugar is melted and almonds are coated. Cool and break apart. Store at room temperature until ready to serve. Tear lettuce and romaine into bite-sized pieces (about 4 cups). Place greens in plastic bag. Add celery and onion. Fasten bag, shake to mix ingredients. Refrigerate until 5 minutes before serving time. To serve; pour dressing into bag. Add mandarin orange segments and shake until greens and oranges are well coated with dressing. Add almonds and shake. Yield: 6 servings.

Note: To serve immediately do not refrigerate dressing or salad ingredients. Store salad no longer than 24 hours before adding dressing. Use only amount of dressing needed to coat greens.

Dressing

½ teaspoon salt
2 tablespoons sugar
¼ cup vegetable oil
Dash of red pepper sauce

Dash of pepper
2 tablespoons vinegar
1 tablespoon snipped parsley

Combine ingredients in jar with a tight-fitting lid. Shake well to thoroughly blend all ingredients. Refrigerate until ready to use.

Patricia Clayton Turner (Mrs. David J.)

SUMMER VEGETABLE SALAD

½ head cauliflower, cut into
  bite-size pieces
½ bunch broccoli, cut into bite-
  size pieces
2-3 ribs celery, cut into bite-
  size pieces
½ cup chopped onion

½ 16-ounce package frozen
  green peas
1 cup sour cream
½ .63-ounce package ranch style
  salad dressing mix
½ cup mayonnaise

Combine vegetables and mix with remaining ingredients; chill before serving. Serves 6.

Brenda Miller (Mrs. Darwin)

CAESAR SALAD

1 head Romaine lettuce
1 garlic clove, crushed
3 anchovies, crushed
¼ cup vegetable oil
2 tablespoons red wine vinegar
1 egg

½ teaspoon Worcestershire sauce
Juice of 1 lemon
½ teaspoon dry mustard
Freshly grated Parmesan cheese
Croutons (recipe below)
Salt and pepper

Rinse lettuce, drain and roll in paper towels. Refrigerate several hours. In a wooden salad bowl crush garlic and anchovies. Add oil, vinegar, egg, Worcestershire, lemon juice and dry mustard; mix thoroughly. Add torn lettuce. Toss with Parmesan and croutons; salt and pepper to taste. Serves 6.

Croutons

Bread cubes
Olive oil

Garlic powder

Brush bread cubes with olive oil and sprinkle with garlic powder. Bake at 350°F. for 3-5 minutes or until crisp.

Marie Bazemore (Mrs Eugene, Jr.)

ORIENTAL SLAW

¾ cup mayonnaise
2 tablespoons soy sauce
2 teaspoons sugar
1 teaspoon salt
1 head cabbage, shredded
½ cup chopped green onions

1 8-ounce can water chestnuts,
    drained and sliced
1 8-ounce can bamboo shoots,
    drained and diced
3 tablespoons chopped pimento

Mix first 4 ingredients. Add remaining ingredients and toss until mixture is well coated. Serves 8-10.

Jean Pitts (Mrs. Reynolds E.)

GARDEN SLAW

8 cups finely shredded cabbage
2 carrots, grated
1 green pepper, cut into thin strips
1 cup chopped onion
1 envelope unflavored gelatin
¼ cup cold water

⅔ cup sugar
⅔ cup vinegar
2 teaspoons celery seed
1½ teaspoons salt
¼ teaspoon pepper
⅔ cup vegetable oil

Mix cabbage, carrots, green pepper and onion; chill in refrigerator. Soften gelatin in cold water; set aside. In a saucepan mix sugar, vinegar, celery seed, salt and pepper and bring to a boil. Stir in softened gelatin. Cool until slightly thick then beat well. Gradually beat in oil. Pour dressing over vegetables; toss lightly to coat. May be served immediately or refrigerated. Stir just before serving to separate pieces. Serves 10-12.

Margaret Nordan (Mrs. John Robert)

TOMATO-GREEK SALAD

Served at Captain Anderson's Restaurant.

Tomato wedges
Cucumber slices
Feta cheese
Greek or Calamata olives

Salonica peppers
Purple onion rings
Avocado wedges

Arrange desired combination of ingredients on individual salad plates. Pour dressing over salads and serve immediately.

Dressing

¾ cup olive oil
¼ cup red wine vinegar
Salt to taste

Freshly ground pepper to taste
Oregano to taste
Garlic to taste

Combine olive oil and vinegar in a small mixing bowl. Add salt, pepper, oregano and garlic to taste. Whip mixture until ingredients are well blended. Serve over salad ingredients. Do not allow dressing mixture to separate. If separation occurs, rewhip before using. Yield: 4 to 6 servings.

Captain Anderson's Restaurant

TOMATO-FETA SALAD

2 garlic cloves
2 pints cherry tomatoes, halved
½ cup pitted ripe olives
1½ cups crumbled feta cheese
¾ cup olive oil

¾ cup wine vinegar
1 teaspoon oregano
1 teaspoon thyme
½ teaspoon basil
Salt and pepper to taste

Rub inside of a wooden salad bowl with garlic; discard. Combine tomatoes, olives and cheese in salad bowl. Combine remaining ingredients; mix well. Pour over tomato mixture, tossing gently. Refrigerate at least 4 hours. Serves 8.

Melissa Sale (Mrs. Douglas)

MARINATED VEGETABLES

1 package cherry tomatoes
1 bunch fresh broccoli, broken
   into flowerets
1 package fresh mushrooms
½ head cauliflower, broken into
   flowerets

2 15-ounce cans artichoke
   hearts, drained
1 16-ounce bottle Italian
   salad dressing

Mix all ingredients and chill for several hours. Serve with toothpicks as an appetizer or on a lettuce leaf as a salad. Serves 8-10.

Darlene Fensom (Mrs. Chesley)

ASPARAGUS AND ARTICHOKE VINAIGRETTE

2 1-pound cans white asparagus,
   drained
1 8½-ounce can artichoke
   hearts, drained and quartered
¼ cup wine vinegar
¾ cup olive oil
1 teaspoon salt
½ teaspoon pepper

2 tablespoons chopped green
   onions
1 tablespoon capers (optional)
1 tablespoon chives
¼ teaspoon thyme
¼ teaspoon basil
2 tablespoons stuffed green
   olives, thinly sliced

Combine asparagus and artichokes in a large bowl. Combine remaining ingredients, blending well. Pour over vegetables and marinate 24 hours. Will keep several days. Serves 6-8.

Gail Ennis (Mrs. Charles)
Ft. Walton Beach, Florida

CUCUMBER MOLD

1 3-ounce package lemon
   flavored gelatin
1 teaspoon salt
1 cup boiling water
1-2 tablespoons vinegar

1 teaspoon grated onion
1 cup sour cream
¼ cup mayonnaise
1 cup finely chopped cucumber,
   drained

Dissolve gelatin and salt in boiling water. Add vinegar and onion; refrigerate until syrupy, then beat in sour cream, mayonnaise and cucumber. Pour into mold and refrigerate until firm. Serves 6.

Betty Jean Mills

MARINATED CHERRY TOMATOES

⅔ cup vegetable oil
¼ cup vinegar
1 garlic clove, minced
¼ cup fresh snipped parsley
¼ cup sliced green onions and
   tops

1 teaspoon salt
¼ teaspoon pepper
½ teaspoon dried thyme
1 package cherry tomatoes,
   peeled

Combine all ingredients except tomatoes; mix well. Pour over tomatoes. Cover and chill well. Serve with additional parsley and onions as garnish if desired.

Note: To peel cherry tomatoes, submerge a few at a time in boiling water; leave about 5 seconds. Remove, dry and cool slightly. Skin will pull off easily with a knife. Serves 6-8.

Dottie Hamlin (Mrs. Ronald B.)

CREOLE SALAD

1 8-ounce package sea shell
   macaroni, cooked and drained
3 cups chopped fresh tomatoes
½ cup chopped pimento stuffed
   olives

1 cup shredded Cheddar cheese
¼ cup grated onion
1 cup mayonnaise
Garlic salt to taste
Pepper to taste

Mix all ingredients well and refrigerate at least 6 hours before serving. Serves 6.

Nancy Wyatt (Mrs. Terrance)

GREEN BEAN SALAD

1 20-ounce can cut green
   beans, drained
2 20-ounce cans French style
   green beans, drained
1 20-ounce can small green
   peas, drained
1 green pepper, seeded and
   finely diced

1 cup diced crisp celery
¼ cup diced white onion
¼ cup sliced pimento
½ cup sliced water chestnuts
½ cup cider vinegar
1¼ cups sugar
½ cup vegetable oil

Combine vegetables, pimento and water chestnuts. Mix vinegar, sugar and oil and pour over vegetables; toss lightly to coat. Refrigerate 24 hours before serving. Serves 8.

Salie Cotton (Mrs. B. Philip)
Mary Ola Miller (Mrs. C. Edward)

CONGEALED SPINACH SALAD

1 3-ounce package lemon
   flavored gelatin
1 cup boiling water
1½ tablespoons vinegar
¾ cup smooth cottage cheese,
   well-drained
1 medium mild onion, grated

⅓ cup chopped celery
Dash of salt
1 10-ounce package frozen
   chopped spinach, thawed,
   drained and squeezed
½ cup mayonnaise

Dissolve gelatin in boiling water. Chill until gelatin begins to thicken. Fold in vinegar, cottage cheese, onion, celery, salt and spinach; mix thoroughly. Fold in mayonnaise and mix well. Pour into pan, cover and chill overnight. May be doubled or tripled—foolproof! Serves 6-8.

Martha Bingham (Mrs. T. Y.)

CONGEALED VEGETABLE SALAD

1 6-ounce package lemon
   flavored gelatin
1 3-ounce package lemon
   flavored gelatin
3 cups boiling water
1½ tablespoons vinegar
2 medium tomatoes, peeled and
   chopped

3 green onions, thinly sliced
1 avocado, peeled and diced
¾ cup chopped celery
1 cup mayonnaise
¼ cup chopped green olives
Dash of hot pepper sauce

Dissolve gelatin in boiling water; chill until slightly thickened. Stir in vinegar, tomatoes, onions, avocado and celery; chill until set. Mix mayonnaise with chopped olives and dash of hot pepper sauce. To serve, cut salad into squares and place on lettuce leaf. Top with spoonful of mayonnaise mixture. Serves 8-10.

Joan Fleming

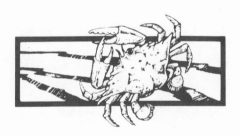

GREEN GODDESS MOLDS

1 3-ounce package lemon
   flavored gelatin
2 chicken bouillon cubes
1 cup boiling water
½ cup cold water
½ cup green goddess salad
   dressing

1 tablespoon lemon juice
1 14½-ounce can asparagus
   tips, drained
½ cup diced celery

Dissolve gelatin and bouillon cubes in boiling water. Add cold water, salad dressing and lemon juice. Beat with rotary beater until smooth. Chill until partially set. Fold in asparagus and celery. Turn into 6 (½-cup) molds; chill until firm. Serves 6.

Nancy Hull (Mrs. Deck)

SOUTHWESTERN NOODLE SALAD

1 pound small to medium shell
  macaroni, cooked al dente,
  thoroughly drained
⅔ cup cider vinegar
¼ cup vegetable oil
1 cup minced celery
½ cup chopped green pepper
6 green onions, minced
1 2-ounce jar pimento, drained
  and chopped
3 generous dashes Worcestershire
  sauce
3 dashes hot pepper sauce

1 tablespoon minced, roasted
  green chili pepper
1 teaspoon salt
½ teaspoon freshly ground pepper
1 15-ounce can black-eyed
  peas, drained
1 12-ounce can corn, drained
½ cup pitted ripe olives,
  drained and chopped
1 2-ounce jar pimento stuffed
  olives, drained and chopped
⅓ cup mayonnaise

Place macaroni in a large bowl; pour vinegar over and let stand while preparing other ingredients. Add all other ingredients to macaroni and mix well. Cover and refrigerate 2-3 days. Taste for seasoning before serving. Serves 8-10.

Betsy Gray Hannon
Tucson, Arizona

PASTA SALAD

¾ cup (6-ounces) pasta shells,
  spinach and plain
2-ounces fresh pea pods
2-ounces roasted cashews
1 14-ounce can artichoke
  hearts, drained
1 bunch green onions, chopped
1 package cherry tomatoes
3 cucumbers, sliced
¼ cup olive oil
½ cup vegetable oil
2 teaspoons Dijon mustard

Grated rind of 1 lemon
2 tablespoons tarragon vinegar
2 tablespoons wine vinegar
1 tablespoon fresh or dried
  dill
1 tablespoon fresh or dried
  oregano
1 tablespoon fresh or dried
  basil
2 garlic cloves, crushed
Salt and freshly ground pepper
  to taste

Cook pasta; drain and rinse with cold water. Combine pasta with pea pods, cashews, artichoke hearts and vegetables. Mix remaining ingredients well and pour over vegetables; toss to coat. Refrigerate overnight. Serves 8-10.

Jackie Sullivan (Mrs. Frank)

VERMICELLI SALAD

1 16-ounce package vermicelli, broken into 2-inch pieces
6 cups boiling salted water
¼ cup vegetable oil
3 tablespoons lemon juice
1 tablespoon MSG
1 cup chopped celery
½ cup chopped onion
1 cup chopped green pepper
1 2-ounce jar pimento, drained and chopped
1 4-ounce can pitted ripe olives, thinly sliced
¼ cup mayonnaise
Seasoned salt to taste

In a large saucepan cook vermicilli for 10 minutes in boiling salted water; drain well. Marinate overnight with oil, lemon juice and MSG. Next day add celery, onion, green pepper, pimento and olives; mix well with mayonnaise. Add seasoned salt. Keeps well in refrigerator. Serves about 20.

Elsie Nelson

TABOOLI

2 cups bulgur wheat
4½ cups cold water
1 large cucumber, peeled and finely chopped
4 large tomatoes, peeled and finely chopped
1¼ cups fresh minced parsley
¾ cup minced green onions
2 teaspoons salt
2 teaspoons freshly ground pepper
½ cup olive oil
½ cup fresh lemon juice
¼ teaspoon crushed garlic
A small handful or 1 cup pine nuts
2 ribs celery, finely chopped

Soak bulgur in cold water for at least 1 hour; drain well. Mix remaining ingredients together. Cover and refrigerate several hours. Great with heavy meats—lamb, pork, beef or goose. May serve inside pita bread as in the Middle East. Serves 6-8.

Nina Godwin (Mrs. Mark T.)

ARTICHOKE RICE SALAD

1 6-ounce package vermicelli
  fried rice mix with almonds
1 green pepper, seeded and
  chopped
2 green onions, chopped
1 4-ounce can pitted ripe
  olives, drained and sliced

1 6-ounce jar artichoke hearts,
  drained and sliced and juice
  reserved
1 cup mayonnaise
½ teaspoon curry powder

Prepare rice according to package directions; cool. Add chopped pepper, onions, olives and artichokes. Mix reserved artichoke juice with mayonnaise and curry powder. Mix and toss with rice mixture. Chill overnight. May add cubed chicken or shrimp. Serves 6.

Hope Tucker

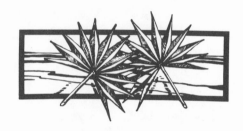

SOUR CREAM POTATO SALAD

4 hard-cooked eggs
⅔ cup mayonnaise
¾ cup sour cream
1½ teaspoons mustard with
  horseradish
½ pound bacon
⅓ cup chopped green onions

7 cup cooked, cubed, fresh
  white potatoes
⅓ cup Italian salad dressing
Salt to taste
Celery seed to taste
Parsley for garnish

Cut eggs in half and remove yolks. Mash yolks and blend in mayonnaise, sour cream and mustard. Cook bacon until crisp; drain and crumble. Chop egg whites and combine with bacon, onion, potatoes and salad dressing. Fold in mayonnaise mixture and season with salt and celery seed. Garnish with parsley sprigs. Serves 8-10.

Ann Bane (Mrs. Curtis)

SPANISH POTATO SALAD

6 potatoes, cooked, peeled and
cut into ½-inch slices
4 hard-cooked eggs, peeled
and quartered
1 pound fresh green beans,
cooked until tender
and drained

1 onion, sliced
Pimento stuffed olives
(optional)
6 tablespoons olive oil
2 tablespoons vinegar
Salt and pepper

Arrange potatoes, eggs, green beans and onion slices on serving platter. Garnish with stuffed olives if desired. Dress with oil, vinegar, salt and pepper to taste. Serve warm or at room temperature. Serves 6.

Yvi Fernandez (Mrs. Robert)

FLUFFY MIXED FRUIT SALAD

1 3-ounce package cream cheese,
softened
1 5-ounce jar neufchatel or
cream cheese spread with
pimento
1 20-ounce can sliced peaches,
drained and juice reserved

1 20-ounce can pineapple
chunks, drained
1 16-ounce can mandarin orange
sections, drained
1 cup miniature marshmallows
1 cup heavy cream, whipped

Beat together cream cheese and cheese spread. Cut up peaches, reserving ¼-cup of the peach syrup. Beat reserved peach syrup into the cheese mixture. Fold in fruits and marshmallows; fold in whipped cream. Chill 5-6 hours or overnight. Serves 10-12.

Note: More fruit may be added to this if you want to increase the number to serve, but it is not necessary to increase any of the other ingredients unless you would like more marshmallows.

Helen Kruse (Mrs. Foster)

MINTED MELON COCKTAIL

1 cup sugar
2 cups water
10 mint leaves
¼ cup lemon juice
2 cups cantaloupe balls

2 cups honeydew melon balls
2 cups strawberries or sliced
   peaches
Mint sprigs

Combine sugar, water and mint leaves in saucepan; stir well. Bring to a boil over medium heat and boil 2 minutes; discard mint leaves. Add lemon juice, stirring well. Chill thoroughly. Combine fruit in a dish. Pour syrup mixture over fruit; marinate several hours. Garnish with mint sprigs. Serves 8-10.

Jackie Sullivan (Mrs. Frank)

WALDORF SALAD

2 cups diced apples (half red
   delicious, half golden
   delicious)
3 tablespoon lemon juice
3 tablespoons sweet sherry
1 tablespoon honey

1 cup diced celery
1 cup chopped dates
½ cup chopped walnuts
½ teaspoon celery seed
½ cup sour cream
½ cup mayonnaise

Marinate apples in lemon juice, sherry and honey for 15 minutes. Mix all other ingredients and chill. Then mix all together; chill 3-4 hours before serving. Serves 8.

Joan Fleming

PINK FROZEN FRUIT SALAD

1 20-ounce can crushed pineapple, well-drained
1 21-ounce can cherry pie
   filling
1 14-ounce can sweetened
   condensed milk

1 8-ounce container frozen
   non-dairy whipped topping,
   thawed

Mix all ingredients. Pour into an 8-inch square pan and freeze. Cut into squares and serve on lettuce leaves. Serves 9.

Dot Ennis (Mrs. Buford)
Claudia Shumaker (Mrs. Robert)

CRANBERRY FLUFF

2 cups raw cranberries, ground
3 cups miniature marshmallows
¾ cup sugar
2 cups tart apples, unpared
and diced

½ cup seedless green grapes
½ cup chopped nuts
¼ teaspoon salt
1 cup heavy cream, whipped

Combine cranberries, marshmallows and sugar. Chill several hours or overnight. Add apples, grapes, nuts and salt; stir gently. Fold in whipped cream and serve. A different cranberry salad for the holidays. Serves 8-10.

Faye Carroll (Mrs. John)
Kissimmee, Florida

GRAPEFRUIT SURPRISE

6 grapefruit
2 3-ounce packages lemon
flavored gelatin
2 3-ounce packages cherry
flavored gelatin
6 cups liquid (reserved grapefruit juice and water)

2 20-ounce cans crushed pineapple, drained reserving
juice
1 14-ounce can mandarin oranges,
drained, reserving juice

Cut grapefruit in halves; remove pulp and juice, reserving juice. Mix gelatin according to package directions, using juice plus water for the needed liquid. Add the fruit; chill until partially set. Pour mixture into grapefruit shells; chill until firm. Serve on lettuce leaf garnished with lemon slice. Serves 12.

Note: Grapefruit may be cut into quarters after gelatin is set in order to serve more people. Cut a small slice on the bottom of grapefruit shells to insure its sitting properly on the plate.

Carol Carswell (Mrs. James)

FROZEN CRANBERRY SALAD

1 14-ounce can sweetened
condensed milk
¼ cup lemon juice
½ cup chopped nuts
1 20-ounce can crushed pineapple, drained

1 16-ounce can whole cranberry
sauce
1 8-ounce container frozen
non-dairy whipped topping,
thawed

Combine condensed milk and lemon juice; stir in nuts, pineapple and cranberry sauce. Fold in whipped topping. Freeze in an 8-inch square pan. Thaw slightly before cutting into squares to serve. Serves 9.

Penny Quantz

FROZEN ORANGE JUICE SALAD

½ cup sugar
2 cups water
3 tablespoons lemon juice
1 10-ounce jar maraschino
cherries, drained

1 6-ounce can frozen orange
juice concentrate, thawed
1 15½-ounce can unsweetened
crushed pineapple, undrained
3 bananas, thinly sliced

Dissolve sugar in water; add remaining ingredients; freeze. Take out of freezer about 15 minutes before serving. Spoon into serving bowls or cups. Serves 12.

Kathy Johnston (Mrs. Mark)

BUTTERMILK SALAD

1 15½-ounce can crushed pineapple with juice
1 6-ounce package strawberry,
peach or apricot flavored
gelatin

2 cups buttermilk
1 12-ounce container frozen
non-dairy whipped topping,
thawed
½ cup chopped nuts

Heat pineapple with juice; add gelatin and stir until dissolved. Cool then add buttermilk, whipped topping and nuts. Pour into a 13x9-inch pan. Chill until firm. Serves 12.

Susie Harvey (Mrs. Chester)
Linda Laurence (Mrs William)
Mrs. James R. Maxwell

APRICOT COOLER

2 3-ounce packages apricot
flavored gelatin
1½ cups boiling water
1 28-ounce can apricots,
quartered, drained and
juice reserved
1 11-ounce can mandarin oranges,
drained and juice reserved

1 quart vanilla ice cream,
softened
½ cup chopped pecans or walnuts
1 3-ounce package cream cheese,
softened
1 tablespoon mayonnaise
1 tablespoon fruit juice
Fine nut crumbs

Dissolve gelatin in boiling water; add 2 cups reserved fruit juice. Fold in ice cream. Add apricots, oranges and nuts. Pour into a 13x9-inch pan and chill until firm. Cream together cream cheese, mayonnaise and 1 tablespoon fruit juice until smooth. To serve cut salad into squares and top with 1 teaspoonful topping per serving. Sprinkle with fine nut crumbs. Serves 12.

Lillie Brewton (Mrs. Harvey)

SAWDUST SALAD

1 3-ounce package lemon
flavored gelatin
1 3-ounce package orange
flavored gelatin
3½ cups water
1 15½-ounce can crushed pineapple, drained and juice
reserved
2-3 bananas, sliced
½ cup pecans or walnuts,
chopped (optional)

2 eggs
1 cup pineapple juice
¾ cup sugar
2 teaspoons all-purpose flour
1 cup heavy cream, whipped
1 3-ounce package cream cheese,
softened
1½-2 cups shredded Cheddar
cheese

Combine gelatin with 2 cups boiling water and 1½ cups tap water; add bananas, pineapple and nuts if desired. Chill until set in refrigerator. Combine eggs, pineapple juice, sugar and flour in a saucepan and boil until thick; cool and spread over gelatin. Cream and beat together the whipped cream and cream cheese; spread over the custard mixture and sprinkle with shredded cheese. Serves 10-12.

Lillian Cooper (Mrs. Michael)
Dot Marshall (Mrs. J. W., Sr.)
Ernestine Williams (Mrs. Raymond)

PRETZEL SALAD

1 6-ounce package strawberry
gelatin
2 cups boiling water
2 10-ounce packages frozen
strawberries with juice,
thawed
2 cups coarsely crushed pretzels
¾ cup butter or margarine,
melted

3 tablespoons plus 1 cup sugar,
divided
1 8-ounce package cream cheese,
softened
1 8-ounce container frozen
non-dairy whipped topping,
thawed

Combine gelatin and boiling water, stirring until gelatin is dissolved. Stir in strawberries with juice. Chill until partially set. Combine crushed pretzels, melted butter and 3 tablespoons sugar. Pat into a 13x9x2-inch pan. Bake at 400°F. for 8 minutes; cool completely. Cream together cream cheese and remaining 1 cup sugar; fold in whipped topping. Spread cream cheese mixture over pretzel crust. Pour partially set gelatin mixture over all; chill several hours or overnight. Serves 12.

Julie Fulcher (Mrs. Jerry)
Sherry Knight

GREEN PARTY SALAD

¼ pound marshmallows
1 cup milk
1 3-ounce package lime flavored
gelatin
2 3-ounce packages cream cheese,
cubed

1 15½-ounce can crushed pineapple, drained
1 cup whipped cream
⅔ cup mayonnaise
1 cup finely chopped pecans

Melt marshmallows with milk in top of double boiler. Pour hot mixture over gelatin, stirring until gelatin is dissolved. Stir in cream cheese. When cheese is dissolved, add pineapple: cool. Blend in whipped cream, mayonnaise and nuts. Chill until firm. Cut into squares to serve on lettuce leaves. Serves 6-8.

Marion Collins (Mrs. Charles)

CONGEALED BLUEBERRY SALAD

2 3-ounce packages raspberry
flavored gelatin
2 cups boiling water
1 15-ounce can blueberries,
drained and juice reserved
1 8-ounce can crushed pineapple, drained and juice
reserved

Water (optional)
1 8-ounce package cream cheese,
softened
½ cup sugar
1 8-ounce carton sour cream
½ teaspoon vanilla extract
½ cup chopped pecans

Dissolve gelatin in boiling water. Combine juices of blueberries and pineapple adding water if necessary to make 1 cup liquid. Add liquid to gelatin mixture; stir in drained fruit. Pour into a 2-quart flat pan and chill until firm. Combine cream cheese, sugar, sour cream and vanilla; blend well. Spread over gelatin and sprinkle with pecans. Serves 10-12.

Kathy Barr (Mrs. Jimmy)
Mrs. Jim Brock
Birmingham, Alabama

CRANBERRY SALAD

1 envelope unflavored gelatin
4 tablespoons or more orange
juice, divided
1 8-ounce can crushed pineapple, drained and juice
reserved

1 3-ounce package raspberry or
strawberry flavored gelatin
1 3-ounce package cream cheese
1 cup whole cranberry sauce
½ cup chopped nuts
½ cup chopped celery

Soften unflavored gelatin in 2 tablespoons orange juice; set aside. Add orange juice to reserved pineapple juice to make 1½ cups liquid. Bring liquid to a boil. Stir in softened gelatin and raspberry gelatin, stirring to dissolve; cool. Blend cream cheese with 2 tablespoons orange juice to soften. Stir pineapple and cranberry sauce into cream cheese. Add cooled gelatin mixture. Stir in nuts and celery. Pour into 8 individual molds that have been rinsed with cold water. Chill until firm. Best when made the day before it is to be served. Serves 8.

Jean Lewis (Mrs. Albert)

ORANGE-CRANBERRY CONGEALED SALAD WITH COOKED PINEAPPLE DRESSING

2 3-ounce packages red
raspberry flavored gelatin
1 cup boiling water
1 6-ounce can frozen orange
juice concentrate, undiluted
1 14-ounce jar cranberry-orange
relish
1 8-ounce can crushed pineapple, drained and juice
reserved

½-1 cup chopped pecans
(optional)
2 tablespoons all-purpose flour
1 tablespoon butter or margarine
1 teaspoon vanilla extract or
rum extract
1 teaspoon cinnamon
1 tablespoon whole cloves

Dissolve gelatin in boiling water. Add undiluted orange juice and stir until melted. Add relish, drained pinapple and nuts if desired. Pour into mold; refrigerate until set. In small saucepan blend reserved pineapple juice and flour; cook over medium heat, stirring constantly, until thick. Remove from heat and add butter; cool slightly. Add flavoring, cinnamon and whole cloves. Serve dressing in separate dish for spooning over salad as desired. Serves 8.

Gretchen Vann (Mrs. Leroy)

LO-CAL CHERRY SALAD

1 17-ounce can dark, pitted
cherries, drained and juice
reserved
Water
1 6-ounce package cherry
flavored sugar free gelatin
1 8-ounce package cream cheese,
softened

1 envelope sugar equivalent
1 20-ounce can crushed pineapple with juice, undrained
1 cup chopped pecans
1 12-ounce can diet cola
carbonated beverage

Add water to cherry juice to make 1½ cups liquid. Heat liquid in a saucepan with gelatin, stirring until gelatin is dissolved. Blend in cream cheese. Add sugar equivalent, pineapple with juice, pecans, cola and cherries. Pour into pan; chill until firm. Serves 12-14.

Gail Ennis (Mrs. Charles)
Ft. Walton Beach, Florida

Ruthie Hunter (Mrs. Charles)

MOLDED AMBROSIA

1 cup graham cracker crumbs
¼ cup butter or margarine, melted
1 cup crushed pineapple, drained and juice reserved
1 3-ounce package orange flavored gelatin
⅓ cup sugar
1 cup hot water
1 cup sour cream
¼ teaspoon vanilla extract
1 cup diced oranges
½ cup coconut
1 cup chopped nuts

Combine crumbs and butter; reserve ⅓ cup for topping. Press crumb mixture into the bottom of an 8-inch square baking dish. Drain pineapple, reserving syrup. Dissolve gelatin and sugar in hot water; stir in reserved syrup. Chill until partially set. Add sour cream and vanilla. Whip until fluffy. Fold in pineapple, oranges, coconut and nuts. Pour over crumbs and sprinkle top with reserved crumbs. Chill until firm. Serves 6-8.

Anna Marie Baugh

AIOLI MAYONNAISE

2 egg yolks
1 tablespoon Dijon mustard
1 teaspoon hot Chinese mustard
6-8 garlic cloves, peeled and crushed
1 teaspoon salt
1½ cups peanut oil
½ teaspoon cold water
2 teaspoons wine vinegar or 2 teaspoons lemon juice

Place egg yolks, mustards, garlic and salt in small mixing bowl; mix at low speed. At medium speed, add peanut oil in a slow stream to the bowl. Caution: beat thoroughly after each small stream of oil is added. (Adding too much at once will curdle the mayonnaise. Once the mayonnaise is creamy, then you may add larger amounts of the oil.) Add salt to taste. Add the water, mixing on low speed; this will make it smooth. For a slightly sour taste add vinegar or lemon juice.

Note: This is a traditional French mayonnaise served in southern France. It is excellent with any type cold seafood or fresh vegetables.

Frances Carey (Mrs. Robert)

SALAD DRESSINGS

AUNT FAYE'S SALAD DRESSING

1 cup sugar
Dash of garlic salt
1 tablespoon dry mustard
1 tablespoon celery seed

1 cup corn oil
½ cup white vinegar
1 10¾-ounce can tomato soup
Dash of pepper

Combine all ingredients in a blender. Blend about 30 seconds. Place dressing in a saucepan and boil for 5 minutes; cool and refrigerate. Keeps about 2 weeks.

Judith Laird (Mrs. Richard)

BLUE CHEESE LEMON DRESSING

¼ pound blue cheese
¾ cup vegetable oil
1 teaspoon grated lemon rind
¼ cup lemon juice
1 cup sour cream

1 large or 2 small garlic
   cloves, minced
½ teaspoon MSG
1 teaspoon salt (optional)

Mash cheese with knife blade in food processor; blend in oil. Add grated lemon rind, juice, sour cream, garlic and MSG. Process until smooth. Taste and add salt if necessary (some blue cheese is saltier than others). Cover and chill for serveral hours. Bring to room temperature before serving. Will keep refrigerated for 2 weeks. A good topping for baked potatoes as well as salads.

Betty Smith (Mrs. Corbett E.)

DIET FRENCH DRESSING

1 cup water
½ teaspoon garlic salt
1 cup catsup
⅓ cup vinegar
1 tablespoon prepared mustard

½ teaspoon pepper
½ teaspoon paprika
2 drops hot pepper sauce
Artificial sweetener equivalent
   to 2 teaspoons sugar

Place all ingredients in blender and blend well; refrigerate. Makes 2¼ cups.

Madelyn Gore (Mrs. George)

CAESAR SALAD DRESSING

5 large garlic cloves
10-12 anchovy filets
5 eggs
2 tablespoons coarsely ground
   pepper

1½ cups olive oil
3 lemons
⅔ cup grated Parmesan cheese

Mash the garlic and anchovies with a fork until mixture is of a pulpy consistency; add remaining ingredients 1 at a time, blending well after each addition. Makes almost 1 quart.

Rowlett W. Bryant

POPPY SEED DRESSING

1½ cups sugar
2 teaspoons dry mustard
2 teaspoons salt
⅔ cup vinegar

3 tablespoons onion juice
2 cups vegetable oil
   (not olive oil)
3 tablespoons poppy seeds

Mix sugar, mustard, salt and vinegar. Add onion juice and stir in thoroughly. Add oil slowly, beating constantly and continue to beat until thick. Add poppy seeds and beat for 3 minutes. Store in refrigerator. Especially good on grapefruit. Makes 3½ cups.

Bettina Youd (Mrs. Richard)

OLD FASHIONED FRENCH DRESSING

1 cup sugar
½ teaspoon salt
½ teaspoon white pepper
1 teaspoon dry mustard
1 teaspoon celery seed
1 teaspoon paprika

Garlic powder to taste
2 cups vegetable oil
¾ cup vinegar
Juice of 2 lemons
2-4 tablespoons grated onion

Mix all dry ingredients; add remaining ingredients, cover and shake well.

Dorothy Logue Durham

HOT SPINACH SALAD DRESSING

3 tablespoons bacon fat
3 tablespoons lemon juice
3 tablespoons wine vinegar
1 tablespoon Worcestershire
  sauce

1 tablespoon Dijon mustard
1 tablespoon brown sugar
1 tablespoon sugar
Salt and pepper to taste

Thoroughly mix all ingredients. Just before serving heat dressing and pour over spinach.

Judy Davidson (Mrs. John)

DRESSING FOR FRUIT

1 cup sour cream
2 tablespoons powdered sugar
¼ cup chopped pecans

1 teaspoon vanilla extract
¼ teaspoon salt

Mix all ingredients; serve with fresh fruit.

Isabell Hall (Mrs. Kent)

APRICOT FRUIT SALAD DRESSING

½ cup mayonnaise
½ cup sour cream
⅓ cup apricot preserves

2 tablespoons lemon juice
Dash of salt

Mix all ingredients. Good on mixed fruit salads, peach salads, etc.

Isabell Hall (Mrs. Kent)

SPECIAL FRUIT SALAD DRESSING

¼ cup sugar
½ teaspoon salt
1½ tablespoons all-purpose flour

1 egg
2 tablespoons vinegar
¾ cup pineapple juice

Mix in order listed and stir well. Cook over low heat until thick, stirring constantly; chill. Serve on mixed fruit or use as a dip for fruit.

Katharine Fuller (Mrs. Walter)

Snapper and Grouper — Red snapper and Nassau grouper, some of our tastiest seafood, abound in the Gulf of Mexico.

SEAFOOD

SELECTION AND PREPARATION

May we suggest....

that fresh fish have clear, cloudless, bulging eyes, firm flesh and bright gills. All fresh fish should be purchased whole with heads to determine freshness.

that shrimp is fresh when there is no head discoloration and a strong "fishy" or iodine odor is not present.

that fresh seafood be frozen in water in small freezer bags or containers to maintain flavor and texture. All seafood should be thawed in the refrigerator whenever time allows.

that thawed scallops sit in salted ice water several hours before cooking to retain their fullness and flavor.

that shrimp boil in a large quantity of rapidly boiling water so that they are free-swimming. Add shrimp after water has boiled for at least a minute. Boil no longer than 1-2 minutes (depending upon size) and remove promptly. Do not overcook shrimp or any other seafood!

that fresh crabmeat be spread on a cookie sheet and placed in a 200° oven for 10 minutes so that all pieces of shell turn bright white. The crabmeat remains uncooked and all shell is easily seen and removed.

that fish fillets and pieces be measured at their thickest points and be broiled or baked 10 minutes per inch.

that all fried fish (snapper, grouper, flounder, scamp, mackerel) be cut into finger-sized pieces, no more than ¾ of an inch thick, salted and peppered to taste, coated in a mixture of ¾ fine cornmeal to ¼ flour and deep fried at 350° until fish flakes easily. Shrimp and soft-shell crabs may also be prepared in this manner. An outdoor fryer is ideal.

that lean fish such as swordfish, flounder, snapper, grouper and shellfish be basted during grilling with butter or a marinade to prevent drying. Fish with more oil content such as mackerel, mullet and pompano can be grilled without added oil.

that grilled seafood be cooked over flameless, gray coals 4 inches above the heat source. A hinged wire grill basket may be used. Seafood should be turned only once to prevent drying.

LIGHT CRAB QUICHE

1 4-ounce can sliced mushrooms, drained and liquid reserved
1 teaspoon butter or margarine
1 9-inch baked pastry shell
1½ cups lump crabmeat
1⅓ cups shredded Swiss cheese
¾ cup sour cream
¼ cup mayonnaise
½ teaspoon salt
1 teaspoon all-purpose flour
Light cream
3 eggs, slightly beaten

Sauté mushrooms in butter; scatter in pastry shell. Sprinkle the crab, then the cheese over mushrooms. Mix sour cream and mayonnaise, reserved mushroom liquid, salt and flour. Add enough light cream to make 2 cups liquid. Blend in eggs and pour all into pastry shell. Bake at 350°F. for 25 minutes until almost set in center.

Georgia Dake (Mrs. James L.)

CRAB SOUFFLÉ

¼ cup melted butter or margarine
11 slices white bread
1 pound crabmeat or 2 7½-ounce cans
1 cup shredded Cheddar cheese
1 tablespoon onion flakes
3 cups milk
4 eggs, beaten
1½ teaspoons salt
¼ teaspoon pepper
Paprika

Melt butter in a 13x9-inch baking dish. Cut crusts from bread. Place 6 slices in bottom of pan and cut 5 slices in half and place around edges of pan to form crust. Spread crabmeat over bread; sprinkle on cheese and onion flakes. Combine milk, eggs, salt, pepper and mix well. Pour over crab mixture; sprinkle with paprika. Bake at 375°F. for 45 minutes or until brown and knife inserted near center comes out clean.

Chris Corry (Mrs. James)

CRABMEAT QUICHE

1½ cups crabmeat, fresh or
    canned
1 tablespoon finely chopped
    celery
1 tablespoon chopped onion
1 tablespoon finely chopped
    parsley
2 tablespoons sherry
1 (9-inch) unbaked pastry shell
    or Pâté Brisee

5 eggs, divided
½ cup Swiss cheese
2 cups cream or 1 cup each milk
    and cream
½ teaspoon salt
¼ teaspoon white pepper
¼ teaspoon nutmeg

Pick over crabmeat to remove bits of shell and cartilage. Combine the crabmeat, celery, onion, parsley and sherry and refrigerate 1 hour. Line a pie plate with pastry and bake at 450°F. for 5 minutes, remove from oven and brush with 1 beaten egg. Bake 3 minutes longer and cool for 5 minutes. Sprinkle the crabmeat in the partially baked pastry shell and top with Swiss cheese. Combine the remaining eggs, cream, salt, pepper and nutmeg in food processor and pour over the mixture in the pastry shell. Bake at 450°F. for 10 minutes, reduce heat to 350°F. and bake 30-40 minutes or until a knife inserted 1-inch from pastry edge comes out clean. Let cool 10 minutes and serve as an hors d'oeuvre or main dish.

Dee Redding (Mrs. Ben)

CRABMEAT DRESSING

¼ cup butter
½ cup minced onion
½ cup minced celery
¼ cup minced green pepper
½ pound crabmeat
1 tablespoon lemon juice

1 cup fresh breadcrumbs
2 eggs, slightly beaten
1 tablespoon minced parsley
¼ teaspoon pepper
½ teaspoon paprika
1 teaspoon dry mustard

Melt butter in a skillet and sauté onion, celery and green pepper until wilted. Add crabmeat. Stir a few seconds; add lemon juice. Remove from heat, add breadcrumbs, beaten eggs and remaining ingredients. Leftovers may be put in ramekins, topped with cheese and baked. Makes 2 cups.

June Greenwell (Mrs. Mark)
Mt. Dora, Florida

MEETING STREET CRAB

¼ cup butter or margarine	1 teaspoon salt
¼ cup all-purpose flour	Pepper to taste
1 cup light cream	¼ cup sherry
1 cup shredded Cheddar cheese,	1 pound flaked crabmeat
divided	Paprika

In a saucepan make roux of butter and flour. Add cream, ½ cup cheese, salt, pepper and sherry. Cook over low heat, stirring constantly, until thick and smooth and cheese is melted. Remove from heat, add crabmeat and pour into 2-quart baking dish. Sprinkle with remaining cheese. Bake at 425°F. for 10-15 minutes until cheese melts. Sprinkle with paprika. Serves 4.

Penny Whittaker (Mrs. Dennis)
Cupertino, California

CRABMEAT ST. FRANCIS

1 pound lump crabmeat, picked	4 eggs, beaten
of shell	1 cup light cream
½ cup mayonnaise	2 cups shredded Swiss cheese,
1 cup minced celery	divided
2 tablespoons chopped pimento	1 10¾-ounce can cream of
8 slices white bread, cubed	mushroom soup

Mix crabmeat, mayonnaise, celery and pimento together. Place half the bread cubes in the bottom of a 1½-quart casserole. Cover with crab mixture and remainder of bread cubes. Combine eggs, cream and pour over casserole; sprinkle with half the Swiss cheese; Bake at 350°F. for 15 minutes. Spread the undiluted mushroom soup and remaining Swiss cheese over casserole; bake 45 minutes longer. Serves 6.

Note: This is a wonderful appetizer or luncheon entrée which may be made ahead and reheated in oven or microwave.

Betty Steinbrecher (Mrs. Raymond)

ARTICHOKES WITH CRAB OR SHRIMP

12 artichoke hearts, cooked
1 7½-ounce can crabmeat or
 ¾ pound cooked shrimp
1 cup canned mushrooms, drained
2 tablespoons butter or margarine
1¼ cups medium white sauce

1 tablespoon Worcestershire sauce
¼ cup dry sherry
Salt and pepper to taste
¼ cup grated Parmesan cheese
Paprika
Fresh parsley for garnish

Arrange artichokes in a buttered shallow baking dish; spread crab or shrimp over and around artichokes. Sauté mushrooms in butter; spread over the seafood. Combine white sauce, Worcestershire, sherry, salt and pepper; pour over all in casserole. Top with cheese and paprika. Bake at 375°F. for 20-30 minutes; garnish with parsley. Serves 4.

Darlene Fensom (Mrs. Chesley)

SOFT SHELL CRABS AMANDINE
(A very rich but delicious dish)

8 small soft shell crabs,
 cleaned
Salt and pepper
¾ cup all-purpose flour
½ cup vegetable oil

½ cup clarified butter
2 tablespoons butter
½ cup sliced almonds
¼ cup red wine vinegar
½ cup heavy cream

Season crabs with salt and pepper and dip in flour. Heat oil and clarified butter in a large skillet until very hot. Place crabs in skillet for about 3 minutes on each side. Remove from pan and arrange in rows on a serving platter; keep warm. Add butter to a skillet and heat until golden brown. Add almonds, toasting them quickly in the butter. Pour in vinegar and reduce until dry. Pour in cream and cook for 5 minutes, stirring until thick and smooth. Pour sauce over crabs. Serves 4.

Martha Middlemas (Mrs. Warren)

SHRIMP STUFFED PEPPERS
(A great stuffing for fish!)

4 green peppers
½ cup butter or margarine
1 onion, finely chopped
3-4 ribs celery, finely chopped
2 garlic cloves, crushed
1-1½ pounds shrimp, cleaned,
   peeled and deveined

2 tablespoons dried parsley
Tabasco to taste
Salt and pepper to taste
1 tablespoon catsup
½ cup grated Parmesan cheese,
   divided
¾ cup Italian breadcrumbs

Cut green peppers in half vertically, remove seeds and stems. Place in a pan of hot water and blanch; drain and set aside. In a large skillet melt butter. Add onion, celery, garlic and sauté until tender. Place shrimp in skillet and gently stir until shrimp are pink. Add parsley, Tabasco, salt, pepper, catsup and ¼ cup Parmesan. Gradually add breadcrumbs until moisture is reduced to form a moist stuffing. Stuff peppers and place in baking dish. Sprinkle remaining cheese on top of peppers and bake at 350°F. for 20-30 minutes.

Patti Jack (Mrs. E. Terry)

SHRIMP CASSEROLE I

3 pounds medium shrimp, cleaned
   and shelled
1 tablespoon lemon juice
3 tablespoons vegetable oil
¼ cup minced onion
¼ cup chopped green pepper
2 tablespoons butter or margarine
1 cup raw rice, cooked

1 10¾-ounce can tomato soup
1 cup heavy cream
¼ cup sherry
1 teaspoon salt
⅛ teaspoon pepper
⅛ teaspoon mace
Tabasco sauce to taste

Cook shrimp until pink and drain. Marinate shrimp in lemon juice and oil for 2-3 hours. Sauté onion and green pepper in butter for 5 minutes. Combine rice, onion, pepper, soup, shrimp, cream, sherry and seasonings. Bake in 2-quart casserole for 35 minutes at 350°F. Serves 6-8.

Mary Lou Alfred (Mrs. Harry)

SHRIMP CASSEROLE II

¾-1 pound fresh mushrooms
1 garlic clove, minced
½ cup chopped celery
1 cup chopped onion
1 cup chopped green pepper
¾ cup butter, divided

2 cups cooked shrimp
2 cups cooked rice
½ teaspoon chili powder
1 20-ounce can tomatoes, drained
¼ teaspoon salt

Cook mushrooms, garlic, celery, onion and green pepper in ¼ cup butter until tender. Combine with remaining ingredients except ½ cup butter and place in a greased casserole. Pour remaining melted butter over casserole and bake at 300°F. for 40-50 minutes. Serves 6.

Mrs. David Marshall (Renate)
Carol Crisp (Mrs. Donald)

SHRIMP CASSEROLE III

1 pound cooked shrimp
1 cup mayonnaise
1 2-ounce jar sliced pimento
1 garlic clove, minced or
⅛ teaspoon garlic powder
2 teaspoons Worcestershire sauce
3 hard-cooked eggs, diced

½ teaspoon salt
¼ teaspoon pepper
2 10¾-ounce cans cream of
mushroom soup
1 cup breadcrumbs
½ cup sliced almonds
3 tablespoons butter

Combine all ingredients except breadcrumbs, almonds and butter; mix well. Place in a large greased casserole and sprinkle with breadcrumbs. Top with almonds and dot with butter. Bake at 350°F. for 20 minutes. Serve over rice. Serves 8.

Sibyl Mizell (Mrs. Joe)

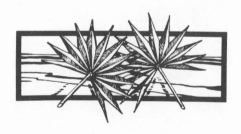

SHRIMP CASSEROLE IV

2 tablespoons butter
8 ounces fresh mushrooms,
  sliced
1 tablespoon all-purpose flour
1 10¾-ounce can cream of
  shrimp soup
1 8-ounce carton sour cream
2 tablespoons finely chopped
  parsley

1½ tablespoons chopped chives
2 tablespoons chopped green
  onions
Pinch of pepper
1½ pounds shrimp, shelled,
  deveined and cooked
Breadcrumbs

In a large skillet heat butter and sauté mushrooms. Stir in flour and soup until thick, stirring constantly. Add sour cream, parsley, chives, onions and pepper; add shrimp and stir. Place in casserole and bake at 350°F. for 20-25 minutes; top with breadcrumbs and bake 2 minutes longer.

Note: I prefer making my own breadcrumbs. Toast bread and pinch into small pieces. Put in a pan that has ½ cup melted margarine in it. Toss crumbs well and put in 325°F. oven for 20 minutes, stirring 3 times.

Gay Sudduth (Mrs. Rowe)

SHRIMP CASSEROLE V

2 ¾-pound packages frozen
  peeled shrimp
2 cups raw rice, cooked
2 10½-ounce cans Newburg sauce
1 10¾-ounce can cream of
  celery soup
1 4-ounce can sliced mushrooms
  with liquid

1½ teaspoons curry powder
¼ teaspoon celery salt
½ teaspoon Worcestershire sauce
2 cups shredded mild Cheddar
  cheese

Mix all ingredients together the day before, place in baking dish and refrigerate. Bake at 350°F. for 1¼ hours. Serves 10.

Nancy Hull (Mrs. Deck)

NEW ORLEANS SHRIMP

2 cups butter or margarine
¼ teaspoon pepper
6 shakes cayenne pepper
2 teaspoons fresh lemon juice
½ teaspoon liquid crab boil

1 teaspoon Worcestershire sauce
1½ teaspoons salt
3 dozen large shrimp, washed
  and unshelled

Melt butter in a 13x9x2-inch pan in oven at 350°F. Remove from oven and add all ingredients except shrimp; blend well. Add shrimp, return to oven and bring to a boil. Boil for 20 minutes. Taste for doneness; when 95% done, remove and let set. Serves 4.

Note: Serve in a bowl with French bread to dip in the sauce and with lots of napkins and a bib!

Kathryn Olivier (Mrs. Jules)

ELEANOR'S MELON AND PRAWNS A LA SYROSS

1 small onion, chopped
2 tablespoons vegetable oil
1 tablespoon all-purpose flour
1 tablespoon curry powder
½ cup chicken stock
Juice of 1 lemon
2 tablespoons chutney

2 teaspoons tomato paste
½ cup mayonnaise
½ cantaloupe or wedge of honeydew melon per person, chilled
2-2½ pounds shrimp, cleaned,
  deveined and cooked

Sauté the onion in oil for 3 minutes; add flour and curry and cook over low heat for 3 minutes. Add the stock, lemon juice, chutney and tomato paste. Simmer for 10 minutes. Cool the mixture and add the mayonnaise. Add the mixture to the shrimp until well-coated; reserve remaining mayonnaise for another use. Pile into chilled melon. Increase shrimp if used as a main course. This is enough mayonnaise for 4½ pounds shrimp. Serves 8 as appetizer.

Note: Eleanor was the Irish cook in a Greek villa and served this for starters, but it is a nice luncheon dish. The curried mayonnaise is also good with eggs or chicken.

Martha Middlemas (Mrs. Warren)

BARBECUED SHRIMP BROIL

1¼-1½ pounds shrimp, unshelled
3 ribs celery with leaves, very
  coarsley chopped
1 garlic clove, chopped
Juice of 2 lemons
½ cup butter, cubed

2 tablespoons cracked pepper
1 tablespoon Worcestershire sauce
1½ teaspoons salt
½ teaspoon hot sauce
Lemon wedges

Wash shrimp and place in very large shallow pan. Add celery and garlic; squeeze juice of lemons over top. Dot with butter and sprinkle with remaining ingredients except lemon wedges. Place shrimp under broiler until butter melts and shrimp start to turn pink, about 5 minutes, stirring several times. When all shrimp are slightly pink, reduce temperature to 350°F. and bake for 15-20 minutes longer.

Ella Russ (Mrs. Carl S.)

SHRIMP BAYOU

2 pounds cooked, peeled large
  shrimp, chilled
⅔ cup finely chopped celery
¼ cup thinly sliced green onions
⅔ cup finely chopped green
  pepper
2 tablespoons finely chopped
  chives

1 cup vegetable oil
½ cup chili sauce
3 tablespoons lemon juice
2 tablespoons horseradish
1 tablespoon prepared mustard
½ teaspoon paprika
½ teaspoon salt
1-2 dashes hot sauce

Put shrimp in a large bowl; add celery, onion, green pepper and chives. Combine remaining ingredients and pour over shrimp; mix gently. Cover and refrigerate 12 hours before serving, stirring 2-3 times. Serve as an appetizer or salad.

Katharine Fuller (Mrs. Walter)

BEER BATTER FRIED SHRIMP

Beer Batter

¾ cup all-purpose flour
½ cup flat beer, at room
   temperature
Salt to taste

1 teaspoon peanut, vegetable
   or corn oil
1 egg, separated

Place flour in a bowl and stir in the beer, salt and oil; stir to slightly blend. (There should be a few small lumps.) Cover bowl with plastic wrap and let stand in warm place about 3 hours. Stir in egg yolk. When ready to cook, beat the egg white until stiff and fold into batter. Makes enough for 1½ pounds shrimp.

Fried Shrimp

1½ pounds shrimp, shelled,
   deveined and tail segment
   intact
1½ tablespoons cornstarch
1 tablespoon dry sherry

2 tablespoons finely chopped
   parsley
Salt to taste
Peanut, vegetable or corn oil
   for deep-frying

Combine shrimp with cornstarch, sherry and parsley. Heat oil for deep-frying. Add a few shrimp at a time to the beer batter and drop, 1 at a time, into the hot oil. Cook, turning as necessary to brown evenly; drain. Sprinkle with salt.

Sue Brancato (Mrs. Joseph)
Thiells, New York

CURRIED SHRIMP

1 cup finely chopped onions
1 cup finely chopped celery
2 tablespoons butter
1 10¾-ounce can cream of
   mushroom soup

1 13-ounce can evaporated
   milk
Salt and pepper to taste
3-4 pounds cooked shrimp
Curry powder to taste

Sauté onions and celery in butter in a large skillet until well done. Add soup, milk, salt and pepper. Simmer and add cooked shrimp and curry. Be careful—not too much curry!

Emory Ray

SHRIMP AU GRATIN SUPREME

1 pound shrimp or ½ pound shrimp
    and ½ pound scallops
Water
4 tablespoons butter, divided
3 tablespoons chopped onions
1½ cups whole milk
¼ cup all-purpose flour

½ teaspoon salt
¼ teaspoon dry mustard
Dash of pepper
1 cup shredded pasteurized
    process cheese spread, divided
¼ cup dry breadcrumbs

Cut shrimp into small pieces and simmer lightly in water in saucepan until pink. Drain and set aside. While shrimp are cooling, put 3 tablespoons butter in a saucepan, add chopped onions and cook them until clear. Gradually add the milk and heat. Mix together flour, salt, dry mustard and pepper; slowly blend into the milk, stirring constantly until smooth. When the sauce has thickened, add ¾ cup cheese and cook and stir sauce until the cheese has melted. Add the shrimp and simmer for about 2 minutes. Pour shrimp and sauce into a large greased casserole dish or individual ramekins. Mix together the remaining ¼ cup cheese, breadcrumbs and remaining 1 tablespoon butter and sprinkle over the casserole. Bake at 400°F. for about 15 minutes. Serves 4.

Note: Recipe doubles easily.

Rowlett Bryant

SHRIMP SCAMPI

1½ pounds fresh shrimp, shelled
    and deveined
½ cup butter or margarine
1 tablespoon lemon juice
4 large garlic cloves, minced

1 teaspoon salt
½ teaspoon oregano leaves
⅛ teaspoon pepper
¼ cup chopped parsley
Lemon wedges

About 20 minutes before serving, preheat broiler. Place shrimp in single layer in bottom of broiler pan. In small saucepan heat butter, lemon juice, garlic, salt, oregano and pepper over low heat until butter is melted. Pour mixture over shrimp, turning shrimp to coat evenly. Broil 5-8 minutes until shrimp is pink. Spoon shrimp and mixture onto platter and sprinkle with parsley; garnish with lemon wedges. Serves 6.

Kathy Barr (Mrs. Jimmy)
Helen Ullman (Mrs. Albert)

SHRIMP ÉTOUFFÉE

½ cup butter
½ cup coarsely chopped onions
½ cup or more coarsely chopped celery
1 cup coarsely chopped green onion
1 cup coarsely chopped green pepper
2 cups sliced mushrooms
2 tablespoons finely chopped parsley
2 minced garlic cloves

½ cup water
1 tablespoon all-purpose flour
⅓ cup dry sherry
1½ pounds raw headless shrimp, shelled
Juice of ½ lemon
¼ teaspoon salt
¼ teaspoon white pepper
1 teaspoon tomato paste
2 teaspoons Worcestershire sauce
Few drops Tabasco

In a large skillet melt butter and quickly stir-fry all vegetables; cook over medium heat 5 minutes, stirring constantly. Gradually add water, flour, and sherry, stirring constantly. Stir in shrimp and remaining ingredients, cover and simmer 8-10 minutes, stirring occasionally. Serve over hot buttered rice. Serves 6.

Anda Gagnet (Mrs. Ted)

SHRIMP QUICHE

1 unbaked pastry shell
¼ cup sliced green onions
¾ cup chopped cooked shrimp
1 cup shredded Swiss cheese
1 cup mayonnaise

2 eggs
⅓ cup milk
¼ teaspoon salt
¼ teaspoon dried dill weed

Fill pastry shell with green onions, shrimp and cheese. Beat remaining ingredients until smooth and pour into pastry shell. Bake at 400°F. for 30 minutes or until set in center and browned. Cool slightly before serving. Serves 6-8.

Ann McElheney (Mrs. Lorie E.)

SHRIMP SPECIAL

2 7-ounce packages frozen
Chinese pea pods
Boiling water
3 chicken bouillon cubes
50 large shrimp (about 3 pounds),
peeled and deveined

⅔ cup chopped green onion
3 tablespoons soy sauce
½ teaspoon salt
¼ cup cornstarch
¼ cup cold water
4 medium tomatoes, cut into ⅛

Pour boiling water over frozen pea pods and break apart with a fork; drain. Dissolve bouillon cubes in 2½ cups boiling water; add shrimp, onion, soy sauce and salt. Bring to a boil and cook, uncovered, for 3 minutes, stirring constantly. Combine cornstarch and cold water and stir into cooked mixture, stirring constantly until it thickens and bubbles. Add tomatoes and pea pods and cook over low heat for a few minutes longer until mixture is heated through. Serves 10.

Patty Sikes (Mrs. Lamar)

BARBECUE SHRIMP I

1 cup butter or margarine
1 tablespoon Italian seasoning
¾ tablespoon pepper

1 garlic clove, crushed
2 pounds large shrimp, unshelled

Place butter in a roasting pan and melt, add seasoning and stir; add shrimp. Cover and bake at 350°F. for 20-30 minutes. Serve with French bread to dip into butter sauce.

Barbara Clemons (Mrs. Girard)

BARBECUE SHRIMP II

2 pounds headless shrimp,
unshelled
½ cup butter
2 tablespoons Worcestershire
sauce

½ cup cooking sherry
Dash of Tabasco sauce
Salt
Pepper

Place shrimp in a single layer in oblong baking dish. Slice butter into pats and place over shrimp. Pour Worcestershire and sherry over shrimp; sprinkle with Tabasco sauce, salt and pepper. Bake at 350°F. for 20 minutes.

Tina Kovaleski (Mrs. Charles)

SAUTÉED SHRIMP

2 pounds fresh raw shrimp,
   shelled
Garlic salt
Mr. Marinade® or
   (Dale's® steak sauce)

Butter or margarine
Green onions with tops (optional)

In a small bowl about 45 minutes prior to cooking, place shrimp that has been sprinkled with garlic salt and bottled marinade or steak sauce to cover. Let stand for 30-45 minutes. Sauté shrimp in a small amount of butter in a large skillet until pink. Remove from heat and let sit in skillet for about 5 minutes before serving over fried or wild rice. May sauté a little finely chopped green onion with shrimp if desired.

Carolyn Smoot (Mrs. Ray)

SHRIMP CREOLE

1 teaspoon bacon grease
2-2½ tablespoons butter or
   margarine
1 onion, chopped
1 garlic clove, chopped
½ large green pepper, chopped
½ cup chopped celery
½ cup chopped fresh parsley
1 1-pound can tomatoes
½ 6-ounce can tomato paste

½ 10-ounce bottle catsup
1 6-ounce can tomato juice
Sugar
Salt
Pepper
Worcestershire sauce
Hot sauce
Oregano
50 shrimp, shelled and deveined

In a large kettle or Dutch oven melt bacon grease and butter; brown vegetables. Add tomatoes, tomato paste, catsup and tomato juice. Add seasonings to taste. Cook over low heat 4-6 hours or longer; add shrimp the last hour.

Jean Pitts (Mrs. Ronnie)

LOUISE'S SHRIMP TEMPURA

Medium-large shrimp
Bacon slices, cut into thirds
Pancake mix

Beer
Vegetable oil

Wrap shrimp with bacon and secure with a toothpick. Make a batter of 1 part pancake mix and 1 part beer. Fry shrimp in hot oil until golden brown.

William E. Lark

CHINESE-STYLE SHRIMP IN PATTY SHELLS

1 13¾-ounce can chicken
   broth
2 tablespoons cornstarch
1½ tablespoons soy sauce
3 tablespoons peanut oil
1 teaspoon minced garlic
1½ cups Chinese pea pods, cut
   into 1-inch pieces
¼ cup sliced scallions or green
   onions

1 3-ounce can water chestnuts,
   sliced and drained
2 8-ounce packages frozen cooked
   shrimp, thawed and drained
1 package frozen patty shells,
   prepared according to
   package directions

Mix chicken broth, cornstarch and soy sauce; set aside. In a large skillet heat oil over high heat. Add garlic, peas and onions; stir-fry until almost tender crisp. Add water chestnuts and shrimp and stir in chicken broth mixture; cook, stirring constantly, until sauce thickens and comes just to a boil. Serve over baked patty shells. Serves 6.

June Greenwell (Mrs. Mark)
Mt. Dora, Florida

EASY SHRIMP CURRY

¼ cup chopped onion
1 teaspoon curry powder
1 tablespoon butter or margarine
1 10¾-ounce can cream of
   shrimp soup

1 cup sour cream
2 cups cooked shrimp

Sauté onion and curry powder in butter until onion is tender. Add soup; set pan over hot water and stir until smooth. Add sour cream and shrimp. Heat thoroughly; serve over hot rice. Serves 4-6.

Darlene Fensom (Mrs. Chesley)

SHRIMP JOSETTE

¼ cup olive oil
3 pounds large fresh headless
  shrimp, shelled and deveined
1 medium yellow onion, chopped
5 large garlic cloves, peeled
  and crushed
1 cup warmed cognac
2 cups warmed dry white wine
1 tablespoon all-purpose flour

1 6-ounce can tomato paste
¼ teaspoon dried thyme or
  1 fresh sprig
1 bay leaf
⅛ teaspoon red pepper
⅛ teaspoon cayenne pepper
Salt to taste
¼ cup chopped fresh parsley

In a large heavy skillet heat oil until moderately hot. Add shrimp and sauté until pink. Add onion and garlic; sauté until onion is opaque(do not let garlic brown). Add warmed cognac and wine. Flambé mixture until fire extinguishes. Mix flour and tomato paste well. Add to shrimp and mix thoroughly. Add seasonings and simmer, stirring occasionally, for 5-10 minutes over low heat. Remove bay leaf and thyme sprig. Serve on bed of rice with shrimp topped with chopped parsley. Serves 6-8.

Note: Other shellfish may be used: lobster is excellent.

Frances Carey (Mrs. Robert E.)

SHRIMP AND SAUSAGE JAMBALAYA

2 cups raw rice
1 green pepper, chopped
1 bunch green onions, chopped
1-2 pounds smoked sausage
1-2 pounds small to medium
  shrimp
1 10½-ounce can beef bouillon

1 10½-ounce can French onion
  soup
1 8-ounce can tomato sauce
Salt and pepper
1 tablespoon Tony Chacheres®
  creole seasoning
½ cup butter or margarine

In a 13x9x2-inch baking dish put rice, green pepper and onions. Slice sausage into small rounds and add along with shrimp. Add soups, tomato sauce, salt and pepper to taste, Sprinkle creole seasoning freely over the top. Stir to mix all ingredients. Place pats of butter on top; bake at 350°F. for 1-1¼ hours, stirring every 20 minutes. Serves 4-6.

Amy Mason (Mrs. Ed)

CHAR-GRILLED SHRIMP

5 pounds headless shrimp, 16 to 20
    count

Peel and devein shrimp; arrange on wooden or metal skewers. Immerse skewered shrimp into marinade. Refrigerate for 2 to 18 hours. Cook shrimp for 6 minutes over a medium-hot charcoal grill, turning after 3 minutes and basting with marinade while cooking. Yield: 25 to 30 servings as an appetizer; 8 to 10 servings as an entrée.

Marinade

¼ cup lemon juice   1 ounce seasoned salt
1½ cups vegetable oil   5 cups water

Combine ingredients. Mix until well blended.

Note: This simple and easy to prepare dish will double as an appetizer or entrée. If using smaller shrimp, shorten cooking time.

Boar's Head Restaurant

HOODED GRILL FISH

Ice cream salt   ½ cup butter
1 large snapper, grouper or   2 teaspoons paprika
    flounder (about 2-4 pounds)   Pepper to taste
½ cup lemon juice

Place heavy duty aluminum foil on heavy cookie sheet and cover with at least ¼-inch ice cream salt. Score fish in diamond shapes and place fish, belly side down, on salt. Place on grill 3-4 inches above medium hot charcoal and cook 15-20 minutes with hood down, basting frequently with mixture of remaining ingredients. Fish is done when it flakes easily and pulls away from center bone. Cooking time depends on size of fish and intensity of heat. Do not overcook.

George Gore

FRIED CATFISH

12 catfish fillets, halved
1 cup prepared mustard, divided
1¼ cups white cornmeal
½ teaspoon salt
½ teaspoon black pepper

1-1½ teaspoons red pepper
Vegetable oil
Parsley
Lemon wedges
Purple onion rings

Brush fillets lightly with half the mustard. Place cornmeal, salt and pepper in a plastic bag; drop in catfish one at a time and shake until completely coated. Brush fillets lightly with remaining mustard; return to bag and shake again. Fry fillets in deep hot oil (330°F.) until they float to the top and are golden brown; drain well. Transfer to serving platter; garnish with parsley, lemon wedges and onion rings. Serve hot. Serves 12.

Helen Arnold (Mrs. J. R.)

BAKED ELEGANCE OF FARM RAISED CATFISH

4 pan-dressed farm raised catfish
   (1-1½ pounds each), fresh
   or frozen

2 cups water
2 teaspoons seasoned salt
Sauce Jerrold (recipe below)

Thaw fish if frozen. Rinse, then pat dry inside and out with paper towels. Score fish on one side at 1-inch intervals making a diamond shaped pattern. Pour water in the bottom of a broiler pan; oil rack well. Sprinkle seasoned salt on both sides of fish. Place fish, scored side up, on broiler rack and bake at 350°F. for 20 minutes, basting with Sauce Jerrold. Continue to cook 20 minutes longer or until fish flakes easily when tested with a fork. Just before fish is done, baste again. Serve fish with remaining sauce, heated. Serves 4.

Sauce Jerrold

2 tablespoons mayonnaise
2 tablespoons prepared mustard
2 teaspoons onion juice
2 teaspoons garlic juice
2 teaspoons lemon juice

2 teaspoons cream style prepared
   horseradish
½ teaspoon hot pepper sauce
1 cup butter or margarine

In a small saucepan combine mayonnaise and mustard. Add onion juice, garlic juice, lemon juice, horseradish and hot pepper sauce. Blend into a smooth mixture. Place over low heat and add butter, a small amount at a time, stirring it into mayonnaise mixture as it melts. Makes approximately 1½ cups.

Helen Arnold (Mrs. J. R.)

BAKED FISH WITH SPINACH STUFFING

Spinach Stuffing

¼ cup butter
3 tablespoons finely chopped
shallots or scallions
½ cup finely chopped, cooked
fresh spinach, squeezed dry and
firmly packed or 1 10-ounce
package frozen chopped spinach,
thawed and squeezed
completely dry

2½ cups fresh breadcrumbs
(use 6 slices if homemade.)
2-4 tablespoons heavy cream
¼ teaspoon lemon juice
½ teaspoon salt
Freshly ground pepper

In a heavy 6-8 inch stainless-steel or enameled skillet melt butter over moderate heat and cook shallots for 2 minutes or until soft but not brown. Add the spinach and cook over high heat, stirring constantly, for 2-3 minutes to evaporate most of the moisture. Transfer to a large mixing bowl. Add breadcrumbs, cream, lemon juice, salt and pepper; gently toss them all together. Season with more lemon juice, salt or pepper if needed.

Fish

1 4-5 pound whole red snapper, cleaned and scaled with backbone removed but head and tail left on (or pollack, lake trout, cod, rockfish, whitefish, salmon or mackerel)
7 tablespoons butter, divided
Salt and pepper

1 cup dry white wine
Watercress sprigs, lemon wedges

Wash fish inside and out under running water; dry thoroughly with paper towels. Fill fish with the stuffing, close the opening with small skewers and criss-crossed kitchen string as you would lace a turkey. Brush 2 tablespoons melted butter on the bottom of a shallow baking and serving dish large enough to hold the fish. (If you prefer to serve the fish on a platter, line the dish with a long piece of foil oiled or buttered on both sides to make it easy to handle later.) Place the fish in the dish, brush top with another 2 tablespoons melted butter; salt and pepper it. Combine 2 tablespoons melted butter with wine and pour around the fish. Bring to a simmer on top of the stove then bake, uncovered, at 400°F., basting every 5-7 minutes with pan juices, for 40-50 minutes. If the wine evaporates, add up to ¾ cup more as needed. The fish should be just firm when pressed lightly with a finger. Remove the pan from oven and if the fish will be served from the baking dish, use a bulb baster to transfer the juices to a small saucepan. If the fish will be served from a platter, carefully lift the foil and fish from the baking dish, using the long ends of foil as handles. Gently slide the fish from the foil to the platter. Then pour the juices into a small saucepan. Boil the juices down over high heat until they are syrupy. Remove from heat, stir in remaining 1 tablespoon soft butter and pour sauce over the fish. Serves 6-8.

John Henry Sherman

POACHED FISH WITH MOUSSELINE SAUCE

Fish

6 large lettuce leaves
6 fish fillets
3 tablespoons butter

½ cup green onions, chopped
1 cup clam juice or fish stock

Blanch lettuce leaves in boiling water. Wrap each fillet in a lettuce leaf. Melt butter in a skillet and sprinkle shallots over butter. Place wrapped fillets over shallots, cover with clam juice; simmer for 20 minutes over low heat. Keep fish in refrigerator until ready to serve; reserve poaching liquid. Warm in oven when ready to serve.

Mousseline Sauce

3 egg yolks
½ cup heavy cream
¼ cup reserved poaching liquid
¾ cup butter, cut into
    10 pieces

Salt and pepper
Lemon juice

Beat egg yolks, cream and poaching liquid over low heat until slightly thick (will coat the wires of the whisk). Remove from heat and beat in butter, one piece at a time, beating until each is almost absorbed before adding another. The sauce will thicken like a hollandaise. Taste for seasoning and add drops of lemon juice. Sauce may be kept in refrigerator and reheated in double boiler. Pour over poached fish to serve.

Hannelore Holland (Mrs. William)

BAKED STUFFED FISH WITH SHRIMP SAUCE

6 small fish (red snapper or
any fish you prefer) or 1
(5-6 pound) large fish

Salt and pepper

If one large fish is used, use only half the stuffing recipe. Season fish with salt and pepper. Fill each fish with stuffing and close opening with toothpick.

Stuffing

1 large onion, chopped
⅓ cup vegetable oil
¼ cup chopped celery
1 green pepper, chopped
1 large garlic clove, chopped

½ cup green onion tops
2 tablespoons parsley flakes
½ cup breadcrumbs
½ cup tomato sauce
Salt and pepper to taste

In a saucepan combine onion, oil and celery and cook for 8 minutes; remove from heat. Add other ingredients. Stir together into a ball—it must not be too soft. If too soft, add more crumbs. If too dry, add a little water.

Shrimp Sauce

1 large onion, chopped
½ cup green onion tops, chopped
2 garlic cloves
¼ cup chopped celery
1 green pepper, chopped
⅔ cup vegetable oil
½ pound whole shrimp

1 28-ounce can whole tomatoes
with liquid
1 lemon, sliced
2 tablespoons parsley flakes
¼ teaspoon thyme
1 tablespoon all-purpose flour
Salt and pepper to taste

Place chopped onion, onion tops, garlic, celery and green pepper over fish. Pour oil over top then add shrimp, tomatoes, lemon slices, parsley and thyme. Mix flour with a little juice from tomatoes; pour over all. Add salt and pepper to taste (use no water). Place fish in baking dish and bake covered at 350°F. for 30 minutes. Uncover and bake 30 minutes longer. Serves 6.

Mrs. K. P. Allen, Sr.
Meridian, Mississippi

REX'S BAKED GROUPER

2 pounds fillet of grouper,
  skinned
½ teaspoon salt
¼ teaspoon pepper
Butter or margarine
3 tablespoons lemon juice

3 tablespoons chopped scallion
  tops
Dash of Tabasco
1½ cups sour cream
½ cup mayonnaise
Paprika

Wash fillets and pat dry. Rub salt and pepper on fish and arrange in buttered baking dish in a single layer. Mix remaining ingredients except paprika. Spread over fillets. Sprinkle with paprika and bake at 375°F. for 15 minutes. Place under broiler for a few minutes to brown. Serve immediately. Serves 4.

June Harrison (Mrs. Jerry)

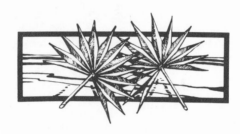

CRAB-STUFFED FLOUNDER

1 medium onion, chopped
2 tablespoons butter
½ cup breadcrumbs
Salt and pepper
1 teaspoon parsley
1 teaspoon chives
½ teaspoon celery salt
Juice of 1 lemon, divided

1 4-ounce can chopped mushrooms
1 8-ounce package frozen crabmeat
1½ pounds flounder or filet
  of sole
Paprika
Garlic powder
Sesame seed

In a large skillet sauté onions in butter. Add breadcrumbs, salt and pepper to taste, parsley, chives, celery salt, juice of half lemon, mushrooms and flaked crabmeat. Spread mixture on 1 length of fillet of flounder; fold in half and fasten with toothpicks. Sprinkle with juice of remaining half lemon. Dot with butter. Season with salt, pepper, parsley, paprika, garlic powder, breadcrumbs and sesame seed to taste. Bake at 350°F. for 25 minutes.

Susan Siragusa (Mrs. Robert)

GRILLED SWORDFISH

1 1-pound swordfish steak
Salt
1 lemon
Freshly ground pepper

¼ cup butter or margarine
¼ cup olive oil
1 tablespoon Worcestershire sauce
Paprika

Wash and dry the swordfish; rub with a little salt, lemon, pepper and paprika. Make a basting sauce of butter, oil and Worcestershire and spread a little on fish. Set aside until ready to grill. Grill seasoned swordfish for approximately 15 minutes, depending on thickness (do not overcook). Brush occasionally with basting sauce. Cut into serving pieces, squeeze a little fresh lemon over fish and top with serving sauce; garnish with lemon and parsley.

Serving Sauce

½ cup white vermouth
¾ cup clarified butter
¼ cup olive oil
Fresh parsley leaves, minced
Freshly ground pepper

Salt
Garlic powder
Fresh lemon juice
1-2 teaspoons cornstarch
¼-⅓ cup chicken broth

In a saucepan pour white vermouth; boil, reducing to 1-2 tablespoons. Add butter, olive oil, parsley, and seasonings to taste, being careful not to add too much. In a small bowl mix together cornstarch and chicken broth. Add this to the mixture in saucepan. Cook and stir until thickened. Add or delete seasonings as desired. Keep warm or reheat carefully when ready.

Valerie Bergeron
Germantown, Tennessee

FISH HASH

½ cup butter
1½ cups chopped onions
2 cups raw potatoes, peeled and
   finely chopped

2 cups cooked fish, broken into
   pieces (mackerel, grouper,
   snapper)
Salt and pepper to taste

Melt butter in a heavy skillet; add onions and potatoes. Cover and cook slowly over medium heat until mixture is very soft. Add fish, uncover, raise heat and stir. As hash begins to brown, turn it over to spread the crisp part throughout. Season to taste with salt and pepper. Cook until crisp on both sides. Serve with tomato relish or chili sauce and toasted muffins. Serves 2.

Dot Ennis (Mrs. Buford)

RED SNAPPER CASSEROLE

6 4-ounce snapper or grouper
  fillets
Salt and pepper
All-purpose flour
¼ cup butter

¾ cup mild green chili sauce
3 cups shredded Monterey Jack
  cheese
1½ cups shredded Cheddar cheese
2 tablespoons minced parsley

Season fillets with salt and pepper; coat with flour. Sauté fillets in melted butter 2 at a time, using more butter if needed. Transfer fillets to individual casseroles or large pieces of foil sprayed with non-stick coating. Divide sauce and cheeses among them. Bake at 350°F. for 12-15 minutes depending on thickness of fillets. Sprinkle with parsley. Serves 6.

Sue Harris (Mrs. Casper)

SAUTÉED RED SNAPPER

1 8-ounce fresh red snapper
  fillet
Milk
Seasoned all-purpose flour
  (seasoned with salt, pepper and
  garlic powder)

¼ cup clarified butter
2 tablespoons fresh lemon juice
6 tablespoons dry white wine
1 tablespoon capers, drained well

Cover fish with milk and let stand in refrigerator at least 4 hours. When ready to cook, remove fish from milk and dust lightly with seasoned flour. Heat butter in a 10-inch ovenproof skillet over medium high heat. Add fish and sauté until brown on both sides. Remove from skillet and keep warm. Reduce heat, add lemon juice and wine to pan juices. Simmer about 1 minute until well blended. Return fish to skillet and bake at 375°F. about 5 minutes or until fish flakes easily. Transfer to heated plate and sprinkle with capers. Serves 1.

Dot Ennis (Mrs. Buford)

POMPANO EN PAPILLOTE

6 pompano fillets
1 cup rosé wine
¼ cup butter
½ cup finely chopped mushrooms
1 tablespoon minced shallots

1 cup condensed bisque of tomato
  soup
1½ cups diced cooked lobster
  (canned if necessary)

Place fish in shallow pan. Add wine and butter, mushrooms and shallots. Cover and simmer over low heat for 15 minutes or until fish flakes. Drain and remove fish. Place each on a 12-inch square of foil. Boil liquid remaining in skillet until almost all absorbed. Stir in soup. Top fish with lobster. Put sauce over fish, seal tightly with foil. Bake at 400°F. for 15 minutes until package "puffs". May be made in advance. Serves 6. (Flounder fillets may be used in place of pompano.)

Richard Youd

SCAMP AMANDINE

4 (8-ounce) scamp fillets, ½ inch
  thick or less
3 tablespoons seasoning mixture
  (recipe below)
1½ cups all-purpose flour
5 tablespoons olive oil

¼ cup white wine
¼ cup Amaretto
3 tablespoons freshly squeezed lemon
  juice
¾ cup toasted slivered almonds

Sprinkle fillets with seasoning mixture on fleshy side. Dust with flour. Heat oil in skillet to 375°F. Add fish, seasoned side down. Sauté for 3 to 5 minutes or until browned. Turn and sauté an additional 2 minutes; remove from pan. Add wine, Amaretto and lemon juice to skillet. Cook for 2 minutes, stirring constantly. Add almonds to mixture. Stir until blended. Spoon over fish and serve immediately. Yield: 4 servings.

Seasoning Mixture

4 tablespoons instant beef bouillon
½ tablespoon black pepper

½ tablespoon each: oregano leaves,
  thyme leaves, sweet basil leaves,
  granulated garlic and rosemary
  leaves.

Combine ingredients. Mix until well blended. Store unused portion in an airtight container.

The Greenhouse Restaurant

GRILLED GROUPER OR SCAMP

1 large fillet of grouper or
  scamp, cut into 4-inch
  square pieces
½ cup low-calorie Italian salad
  dressing
½ cup white wine
1 teaspoon garlic powder

1 teaspoon Cavender's Greek
  Seasoning®
1 teaspoon Italian seasoning
2 tablespoons olive oil
Melted butter or margarine
1 large bunch green onions,
  chopped

Marinate grouper overnight in mixture of all ingredients except butter and green onions. Spray grill with non-stick coating. Place grouper directly on hot grill. Cook about 8-10 minutes on each side. Take up on warmed platter and pour melted butter and green onions over top; serve immediately.

Pat Syfrett (Mrs. Frank)

CURRY BROILED KING MACKEREL

2 mackeral fillets or
  4 mackeral steaks
⅓ cup steak sauce
¼ cup ketchup

¼ cup melted butter
1 tablespoon vinegar
1 teaspoon salt
½ teaspoon curry powder

Mix ingredients together, baste fish, then broil.

Maureen Hess (Mrs. Glenn)

WINE FISH

Butter or margarine
1 onion, sliced
¼-½ cup white wine

Small, fresh boneless fillets
  (snapper, grouper, bass or
  any white meat fish)

Melt butter, covering bottom of skillet. Over medium heat lightly brown onion slices in skillet. Remove onions from pan and brown fillets quickly on each side (not until done). Reduce heat to low, return onions to pan; add wine to cover. Cover and simmer about 10 minutes, being careful not to overcook.

Dr. Owen Reese, Jr.

MEDITERRANEAN-STYLE CHARCOAL BROILED POMPANO
...as served at Captain Anderson's Restaurant...

1½ pounds pompano per serving
Salt to taste

Pepper to taste
Olive oil

Salt and pepper belly of cleaned pompano. Oil fish until well covered. Place on charcoal grill making sure coals have burned down so they look gray and dusty. Cook for 5 to 6 minutes per side depending on size of fish. Do Not Overcook; turn fish only once per side. Pour marinade over fish after removing from grill. Yield: 1 serving.

Note: Snapper, grouper, scamp, swordfish and blue and yellow-fin tuna fillets can also be prepared in this manner.

Johnny and Jimmy Patronis

SUPER SEAFOOD CASSEROLE

3 tablespoons butter or margarine
2 cups chopped celery
1 cup chopped onions
1 cup green pepper chopped
2 cups sour cream
1 cup light cream
¼ cup chopped pimento
2 tablespoons lemon juice

1 teaspoon Worcestershire sauce
2 4-ounce cans sliced mushrooms, drained
2 cups cooked rice
1 pound cooked shrimp
½ pound cooked crabmeat
Breadcrumbs
Melted butter

In a large skillet melt butter and sauté celery, onions and green pepper. Add sour cream, light cream, pimento, lemon juice, Worcestershire, mushrooms, rice and seafood. Place in a 13x9x2-inch baking dish; top with breadcrumbs and melted butter. Bake at 350°F. for 25 minutes. Serves 6-8.

Pat Syfrett (Mrs. Frank)

SHRIMP AND CRAB AU GRATIN

¾ cup all-purpose flour
4 cups milk, divided
1 8-ounce jar pasteurized
processed (Cheese Whiz®) cheese
spread
¼ teaspoon pepper

¼ teaspoon Tabasco
1 pound shrimp, cooked
1 pound crabmeat, cooked
4 cups (1-pound) shredded Cheddar
cheese

Mix flour and a little milk to form a smooth paste. Pour remaining milk into a medium saucepan and heat over medium heat. Add cheese spread and stir until melted and milk is hot. Slowly stir in flour mixture and cook, stirring constantly, until mixture thickens. Add pepper, Tabasco, shrimp and crabmeat. Mixture should be a thick consistency. Pour into a large casserole dish and top with grated cheese. Bake 20-30 minutes at 350°F. Serves 6.

Ann Bane (Mrs. Curtis)

SEAFOOD CASSEROLE I

¾ cup butter
13 tablespoons all-purpose flour
3 cups light cream
1½ teaspoons salt
½ teaspoon red pepper
2 cups shredded sharp Cheddar
cheese
1 tablespoon onion juice
1⅓ cups sherry
2 pounds white lump crabmeat

2 pounds shrimp, cleaned and
shelled
1 pound raw scallops
2 8-ounce cans water chestnuts,
drained and sliced
2 14-ounce cans artichoke
hearts, halved
1 cup slivered almonds
Grated Parmesan cheese

Melt butter in a large skillet and add flour. Stir over medium heat for 3 minutes then add cream, salt and pepper. Stir constantly and continue cooking until thick. Add cheese and stir until cheese melts. Add onion juice and sherry and stir. Line 2 large buttered casseroles with crabmeat, shrimp, scallops, water chestnuts and artichoke hearts. Pour in cream sauce. Sprinkle with almonds and Parmesan cheese. Bake at 325°F. for 30 minutes. Serves 20-24. Doubles easily.

Marie Bazemore (Mrs. Eugene J.)

SEAFOOD CASSEROLE II

2 10¾-ounce cans cream
  of shrimp soup
½ cup mayonnaise
1 small onion, grated
¾ cup milk
Salt
White pepper
Seasoned salt
Ground nutmeg
Cayenne pepper
3 pounds shrimp, cleaned and
  cooked

1 7½-ounce can crabmeat,
  drained
1½ cups raw, long-grain rice,
  cooked until dry and fluffy
1½ cups diced celery
1 6-ounce can water chestnuts,
  drained and sliced
3 tablespooons fresh parsley,
  minced
Paprika
Slivered almonds

Blend soup into mayonnaise in a large bowl. Stir until smooth; add onion then milk. Season heavily with salt, white pepper, seasoned salt, nutmeg and cayenne pepper. Taste until seasoned to your liking. Combine mixture with seafood and rice. Add celery, water chestnuts and parsley. Stir until mixed. (Add a few tablespoons milk if mixture seems dry; it should be moist.) Turn into a large shallow, greased casserole. Sprinkle paprika over casserole and scatter slivered almonds generously over top. Bake, uncovered, at 350°F. for about 30 minutes or until hot and bubbly. Freezes well. Serves 10.

Mollie Austin
Pompano Beach, Florida

GULFCOAST COQUILLE

1 pound fresh scallops in juice
½ pound shrimp, shelled and cut
  in half if large
1 pint oysters in juice
3 tablespoons butter
¼ cup dry white wine
1 cup fresh mushrooms, finely
  chopped

1 teaspoon fresh lemon juice
¼ cup shallots, finely diced
Cayenne pepper to taste
6 dashes of Tabasco
Salt and pepper to taste
½ cup water (more if needed)
3 garlic cloves, chopped
½ cup grated Parmesan cheese

In long broiler pan combine all ingredients except cheese. Cover and refrigerate several hours. Remove from refrigerator and when it reaches room temperature, place under broiler for 5 minutes. Stir well and add liquid (water) if needed. Add cheese and place under broiler again until bubbling hot. Serve in bowls with crusty bread for dipping in juice. May be assembled the day before. Serves 6.

Nina Godwin (Mrs. Mark T.)

CORNUCOPIA SEAFOOD CRÊPES

6 tablespoons butter
⅓ cup all-purpose flour
1 teaspoon salt
1¼ cups homemade chicken broth
1 cup light cream

¼ cup dry sherry
3 cups cooked seafood (shrimp,
    scallops, crabmeat)
1 pound fresh mushrooms, sautéed
16 crêpes

Melt butter, stir in flour and salt. Add chicken broth and cream, whisking constantly until sauce is thick. Stir in sherry; add seafood and mushrooms. Place a
large spoonful in each crêpe and roll up. Place crêpes in a single layer, seam side
down, in a 13x9x2-inch baking dish. Bake at 350°F. for about 20 minutes.

Crêpes

4 eggs
¼ teaspoon salt
2 cups all-purpose flour

2¼ cups milk
¼ cup melted butter

Combine ingredients in blender jar; blend for about 1 minute. Scrape down sides
with rubber spatula and blend for 15 seconds more or until smooth. Refrigerate
batter for at least 1 hour. Cook on crêpe griddle or in crêpe pan or small skillet.
Makes about 32-36 crêpes.

Lida Lewis (Mrs. James)

OYSTER CAKES HOLLANDAISE

2 tablespoons finely chopped
    onion
4 tablespoons butter or
    margarine, divided
2 eggs, beaten
3 cups soft breadcrumbs
    (4 slices bread)
1 pint oysters, drained and
    finely chopped

½ cup finely chopped celery
¼ cup milk
2 tablespoons snipped parsley
1 tablespoon lemon juice
½ teaspoon salt
½ teaspoon paprika
¾ cup fine dry breadcrumbs
Hollandaise sauce

In saucepan cook onion in 2 tablespoons butter until tender but not brown.
Combine eggs, soft breadcrumbs, oysters, celery, milk, parsley, lemon juice, salt
and paprika with cooked onion. Chill 2 hours or until ready to serve. Shape into 8
(½-inch thick) patties. Coat with fine dry breadcrumbs. Melt remaining butter in
a skillet; brown cakes, reduce heat and cook slowly for 6-8 minutes. Pour
hollandaise over cakes. Serves 4.

Ann Aldrich Logue

OYSTERS ROCKEFELLER

Oysters   Ice cream salt

Remove oysters from shells; wash and drain them. Put back into the shells, set on a pan of hot ice cream salt and run under the broiler for 5 minutes. Cover with sauce and return to broiler until the sauce melts and browns.

Oyster Rockefeller Sauce

1 large bunch spring onions, chopped
1 large bunch parsley, chopped
½ cup butter
4 cans strained spinach or (4 bunches) fresh or frozen
1 tablespoon celery salt
¾ tablespoon anchovy paste

2 tablespoons Worcestershire sauce
2 tablespoons hot sauce
1 tablespoon fresh horseradish
2 teaspoons basil
1 teaspoon marjoram
2 tablespoons absinthe
1 tablespoon bitters

In a covered pot slowly cook onions, parsley and butter until soft, about 20 minutes. Run through blender or food processor and return to pot. Add spinach and celery salt, anchovy paste, Worcestershire, hot pepper sauce, horseradish, basil and marjoram. Bring to a boil then remove from heat and add absinthe and bitters. Serves 8.

Ann Aldrich Logue

OYSTER CASSEROLE

1 pint oysters, drained
1 cup chopped green onion tops
⅔ cup fresh snipped parsley
1 cup cracker crumbs
½ cup butter or margarine, melted

2 tablespoons Worcestershire sauce
1 teaspoon dry mustard
Juice of 1 lemon

Place oysters in the bottom of a 10x6x2-inch pan. Sprinkle with onion tops and parsley. Top with cracker crumbs. Mix butter, Worcestershire sauce, mustard and lemon juice and pour over all. Bake at 375°F. for 20 minutes. Serves 4-6.

Jane Allen (Mrs. Newton)

OYSTERS LAFITTE

7 tablespoons butter or margarine, divided
¼ cup chopped shallots or green onions
2 cups chopped mushrooms
¼ cup chopped parsley
1 cup chopped, cooked shrimp
2 garlic cloves, minced
½ cup dry white wine

2 dozen oysters on the half shell, drained and liquid reserved
½ teaspoon salt
Dash of cayenne pepper
1 cup heavy cream
2 tablespoons all-purpose flour
Rock salt
2 tablespoons breadcrumbs

Heat ¼ cup butter in skillet over medium heat. Add shallots, mushrooms, parsley, shrimp and garlic. Cook 1 minute. Add wine, oyster liquid, salt and cayenne. Bring to a boil; simmer 1 minute. Stir in cream. Blend 1 tablespoon melted butter with flour until smooth. Add to mushroom-shrimp mixture, stirring until sauce is thick. Correct seasoning to taste. Arrange oysters on a bed of rock salt in a ovenproof platter. Place about 2 tablespoons shrimp mixture over each oyster. Sprinkle with breadcrumbs. Dot with remaining butter; bake at 450°F. for 15-20 minutes. Serves 6-8.

Marie Bazemore (Mrs. Eugene J.)

BAYOU OYSTER BAKE

1 pint fresh oysters
3 slices bacon
1 cup chopped onion
½ cup butter or margarine
1 8-ounce package herb seasoned stuffing mix
1 1-pound can tomatoes
1 10¾-ounce can cream of mushroom soup

1 8-ounce carton sour cream
1 cup shredded sharp Cheddar cheese
½ cup chopped green pepper
½ cup chopped celery
1 teaspoon horseradish

Drain oysters; set aside. In a large skillet fry bacon until crisp; remove bacon to absorbent paper. Add onion and butter to bacon drippings and cook onion until tender but not brown. Stir in stuffing mix. In a 2-quart bowl combine oysters with remaining ingredients. Spread half the herb stuffing mixture evenly in a well-greased 3-quart baking dish. Add the oyster mixture. Top with remaining herb stuffing mixture. Bake at 350°F. for 45-50 minutes. Garnish with crumbled bacon. Serves 12-16.

Wanda Patterson, (Mrs. James R.)

SCALLOPS WITH PASTA

1 pound fresh pasta
3-4 garlic cloves
⅓ cup chopped parsley
3 cups scallops, cleaned and
   patted dry
All-purpose flour

¼ cup butter
¼ cup homemade breadcrumbs
Juice of 1 large lemon
Salt and pepper to taste
Olive oil

If making your own pasta, have it ready to cook; try to start the pasta and scallops cooking at about the same time. Mince the garlic and mix with parsley; set aside. Flour the scallops and sauté in butter in a large pan (they will brown better if not crowded). Add more butter if needed. When scallops are browned, remove them to a warm platter. Stir the garlic-parsley mixture with the breadcrumbs in the pan (adding more butter if necessary) until the crumbs have absorbed the butter. Add lemon juice, salt and pepper to taste. Remove from heat; drain pasta when done and toss with enough olive oil to coat. Top with scallops and then with crumb mixture. Serves 4-6.

Candis Harbison (Mrs. Joe)

SCALLOP DISH

1½ pounds fresh or frozen
   scallops
¾ cup dry white wine
1 tablespoon lemon juice
¾ teaspoon salt, divided
1 cup sliced fresh mushrooms
2 tablespoons thinly sliced
   green onions

1 garlic clove, minced
6 tablespoons butter or
   margarine, divided
⅓ cup all-purpose flour
⅓ teaspoon nutmeg
Dash of white pepper
1 cup milk
1 cup soft breadcrumbs

Thaw scallops, if frozen. In saucepan combine scallops, wine, lemon juice and ½ teaspoon salt. Bring to a boil; reduce heat, cover and simmer 2-4 minutes or until scallops are opaque in appearance. Drain, reserving 1 cup of the wine mixture (add water if necessary to make 1 cup liquid). Cook mushrooms, green onions and garlic in ¼ cup butter until tender, stirring occasionally. Blend in flour, nutmeg, white pepper and remaining ¼ teaspoon salt. Add milk and the reserved 1 cup wine mixture all at once. Cook and stir until thick and bubbly. Add scallops and heat through. Spoon mixture into 6 buttered baking shells. Toss breadcrumbs with the remaining 2 tablespoons butter; sprinkle over scallop mixture. Bake at 400°F. for 10-20 minutes or until nicely browned.

Ann Bane (Mrs. Curtis)

COQUILLES ST. JACQUES

2 pounds fresh scallops
Dry white wine
¼ teaspoon dried tarragon
¼ teaspoon chervil
¼ cup butter
4 shallots, minced

2 pounds mushrooms, sliced
¼ cup all-purpose flour
1 cup heavy cream
¼ cup brandy
2 cups shredded Gruyere or
    Swiss cheese, divided

Place scallops in a large heavy saucepan. Add wine, barely covering scallops. Add tarragon and chervil and simmer, uncovered, 3-4 minutes or until scallops are very white. Drain scallops, reserving ½ cup of the liquid. In another pan heat butter and sauté shallots and mushrooms until just cooked but not browned. Stir in flour. Gradually stir in heavy cream and reserved liquid. Stir over low heat until sauce bubbles and thickens. Stir in 1 cup cheese until melted. Season to taste with salt and pepper. Stir in drained scallops, then spoon into 8 small shallow ramekins. Sprinkle remaining cheese on top. Place under broiler until cheese is lightly browned. May be prepared early in the day and placed under broiler before serving. Serves 8.

Judy Davidson (Mrs. John)

SCALLOPS BELLE MEUNIERE

¼ cup chopped green onions
¼ cup sliced mushrooms
6 tablespoons butter
¼ cup white wine or vermouth

1 tablespoon brandy
Juice of 1 lemon
2 cups cleaned scallops
1 tablespoon chopped parsley

Sauté onions and mushrooms in butter until onions are tender. Add wine, brandy and lemon juice; simmer a few minutes to reduce the alcohol. Add scallops and cook over medium heat until scallops are no longer translucent. Be careful not to overcook or the scallops will dry out. Serve over rice or patty shells; sprinkle with parsley. Serves 4 as an appetizer; 2-3 as main dish.

Candis Harbison (Mrs. Joe)

COQUILLES SAUTÉES

1½ pounds Bay scallops
4 tablespoons olive oil or margarine
3 ounces white table wine

3 tablespoons seasoning mixture (see recipe below)
2 cups whipping cream

Drain scallops and pat dry. Heat oil in skillet over a medium-high to high heat until 375°F. Add scallops and sauté for 2½ minutes, stirring constantly. Remove scallops and set aside. Reserve all pan juices and add wine and seasoning mixture. Continue to cook over a medium-high heat for 3 minutes or until mixture is reduced in volume. Reduce heat and add cream. Simmer for 10 minutes or until sauce thickens, stirring constantly. Return scallops to sauce and cook for an additional 5 to 8 minutes or until thoroughly heated. Serve over rice or noodles. Yield: 4 servings.

Seasoning Mixture

4 tablespoons instant beef bouillon
½ tablespoon black pepper

½ tablespoon each: oregano leaves, thyme leaves, sweet basil leaves, granulated garlic and rosemary leaves

Combine all seasonings. Mix until well blended. Store unused portion in an airtight container.

The Greenhouse Restaurant

TUNA-CHEESE CROISSANTS

1 6½-ounce can tuna
1 cup shredded Cheddar cheese
3 hard-cooked eggs, chopped
2 tablespoons minced onion
3 tablespoons chopped olives
    (about 10)

2 tablespoons pickle relish
½ cup mayonnaise
Croissants

Mix ingredients for filling together; slice croissants horizontally. Spread mixture on bottom half of bun. Replace top and wrap in foil. Bake at 350°F. for 20 minutes. Makes 6.

Louise Reese (Mrs. William)
Greenville, South Carolina

TUNA AND ASPARAGUS CASSEROLE

1 8-ounce package macaroni
  twists or elbow macaroni
3 tablespoons butter or
  margarine
3 tablespoons all-purpose flour
1 teaspoon salt

2 cups milk
1 cup shredded sharp Cheddar
  cheese
1 9¼-ounce can tuna
1 15-ounce can asparagus
  spears

Cook macaroni according to package directions; drain. While macaroni is cooking, make sauce as follows: melt butter in saucepan and blend in flour and salt. Gradually add milk and stir until smooth and slightly thick. Remove from heat and add cheese. Stir until cheese melts. Place macaroni in greased 2-quart glass baking dish. Pour half the cheese sauce over macaroni; spread tuna over macaroni and then arrange asparagus spears over tuna. Pour remaining cheese sauce over top. Bake at 350°F. for 30 minutes. Serves 10-12.

Wanda Patterson (Mrs. James R.)

CURRIED SALMON CROQUETTES

¼ cup butter
¼ cup all-purpose flour
½ teaspoon salt
⅛ teaspoon pepper
¾ cup milk
1 cup quick-cooking oats

1 16-ounce can red salmon,
  drained
1 egg, beaten
1½ cups dry breadcrumbs
Vegetable oil for deep frying

Melt butter in saucepan. Stir in flour, salt and pepper. Slowly add milk, stirring constantly. Cook over medium heat until mixture has thickened. Remove from heat and stir in oats and salmon. Cool thoroughly. Shape into 8 croquettes. Roll each in flour, then dip in egg and finally into breadcrumbs. Heat oil to 375°F. Fry the croquettes until they are golden brown, about 2-3 minutes. Turn to brown both sides. Drain on paper towels to remove excess oil.

Sauce

1 10¾-ounce can cream of
  mushroom soup
1 cup light cream

1 tablespoon lemon juice
½ teaspoon curry powder

Combine all ingredients; bring to a boil. Remove from heat and serve over the hot croquettes.

Ann Bane (Mrs. Curtis)

LINGUINE WITH ANCHOVY SAUCE
(A good main course starter!)

1 pound linguine
1 cup butter
½ cup vegetable oil
1 2-ounce can anchovy fillets,
cut in pieces

1 bunch fresh broccoli, cut,
cleaned and cooked
½ cup chopped pecans or walnuts
Freshly ground pepper to taste

Cook linguine according to package directions; drain and set aside. Meanwhile melt butter in oil and add anchovy pieces. Sauté anchovies until they melt. In a large serving bowl arrange pasta and cooked broccoli. Pour anchovy sauce over all, add nuts and pepper, toss well and serve. Serves 4.

Susan Siragusa (Mrs. Robert)

CLAMS OREGANATO

Scant ¼ cup olive oil, divided
1 10-ounce can choppped clams,
drained and liquid reserved
½ cup seasoned breadcrumbs

¼ teaspoon oregano
2 garlic cloves, chopped
3 ounces mozzarella cheese,
diced

Mix 2 tablespoons oil with all other ingredients, adding 3 tablespoons of reserved clam liquid. Mix well and spoon into shell-shaped ramekins. Sprinkle with additional breadcrumbs and drizzle with remaining 2 tablespoons oil and clam liquid on top. Bake at 350°F. for 10 minutes. Place under broiler for 5 minutes or until golden brown. Serves 6.

Susan Siragusa (Mrs. Robert)

REMOULADE SAUCE

⅓ cup fresh chopped parsley
or a 2 tablespoons dried parsley
3 green onions, chopped
2 cup mayonnaise
¼ cup sugar
¼ cup vegetable oil

Juice of ½ lemon
1 tablespoon capers
1 tablespoon grated onion
1 tablespoon creole mustard
¼ teaspoon salt

Combine all ingredients in blender at medium to high speed until smooth.

Edna Pope (Mrs. Merritt)

BASTING SAUCE FOR KING MACKEREL

½ cup catsup
¼ cup oil
3 tablespoons lemon juice
2 tablespoons liquid smoke
2 tablespoons vinegar
1 teaspoon Worchestershire
1 teaspoon salt

½ teaspoon dry mustard
½ teaspoon grated onion
¼ teaspoon paprika
1 clove garlic, minced
 (or garlic powder)
3 drops hot pepper sauce

Combine all; baste fish with mixture either on the grill or in the oven.

Renate Marshall (Mrs. David)
Dothan, Alabama

COCKTAIL SAUCE

1 20-ounce bottle catsup
½ cup cider vinegar
1 cup sugar

1 1-ounce box Coleman's® dry
 mustard

Mix all ingredients and refrigerate. Keeps well in refrigerator.

Dot Ennis (Mrs. Buford)

HOMEMADE TARTAR SAUCE

1 cup good quality mayonnaise
1 medium onion, chopped

Juice of 1 lemon
½ cup chopped dill pickle relish

Mix together all ingredients and chill. Serve with all types of seafood.

Boar's Head Restaurant

POULTRY
& GAME

Brown Pelican—Having once almost disappeared from Gulf shores, brown pelicans are again skimming over St. Andrews Bay and perching on the pilings of our marinas.

POULTRY & GAME

STIR-FRIED CHICKEN BREASTS WITH HOISIN SAUCE

2¾-pound each whole chicken
breasts, diced in ½-inch cubes
1 tablespoon cornstarch
1 tablespoon Chinese rice wine
or pale dry sherry
1 tablespoon soy sauce
¼ cup vegetable oil, divided
1 medium green pepper, seeded
and diced in ½-inch squares
6 water chestnuts, diced in
¼-inch cubes

¼ pound fresh mushrooms, diced
in ¼-inch cubes
½ teaspoon salt
2 tablespoons hoisin sauce
(available in specialty section
of grocery store or Oriental
food store)
¼ cup roasted cashews or almonds

Sprinkle chicken cubes with cornstarch, toss to coat; pour in wine and soy sauce, toss. Set a wok or 10-inch skillet over high heat for 30 seconds. Pour in 1 tablespoon oil, swirl in pan and heat for 30 seconds (lower heat if oil smokes). Immediately add peppers, water chestnuts, mushrooms and salt and stir-fry briskly for 2-3 minutes. Scoop out vegetables with slotted spoon and set aside. Pour remaining 3 tablespoons oil into pan, heat almost to smoking and drop in marinated chicken. Stir-fry over high heat for 2-3 minutes until chicken turns white and firm. Add hoisin sauce, stir well with chicken. Add the reserved vegetables and cook 1 minute longer. Drop in cashews or almonds and stir to heat through. Transfer all to a heated platter. Serves 4 as main course; 6-8 as side dish.

Susan Siragusa (Mrs. Robert)

CHICKEN AND SPINACH NOODLE CASSEROLE

3 whole chicken breasts, split
Salted water
2 8-ounce packages spinach
noodles
1 cup chopped green pepper
1 cup chopped onion
1 cup chopped celery
½ cup melted butter or margarine,
divided
1 8-ounce package processed
cheese, cubed

1 10¾-ounce can cream of
mushroom soup
1 3-ounce jar pimento-stuffed
olives, sliced (or more to
taste)
1 4½-ounce jar sliced mushrooms, drained
1 cup crushed bite-size Cheddar
cheese crackers (optional)

Cook chicken in salted water for 25-30 minutes or until tender; drain, reserving stock. Bone chicken and cut meat into bite-size pieces; set aside. Cook noodles in stock until tender; drain and set aside. Sauté green pepper, onion and celery in ¼ cup butter until tender; add cheese. Cook stirring constantly, until cheese melts. Stir in soup, olives and mushrooms; cook until bubbly. Add chicken and noodles, mixing well. Spoon into greased 13x9x2-inch baking dish. Combine crumbs and butter over top. Bake at 325°F. for 40 minutes. Serves 8-10.

Gail Ennis (Mrs. Charles)

MANICOTTI CRÊPES

2 chicken breasts
1 cup ricotta cheese
½ cup mozzarella cheese
¼ cup Parmesan cheese
1 egg
Chopped parsley or parsley flakes

Salt and pepper
Chopped green onions
Slivered almonds (optional)
12 crepes
1 15-ounce can tomato sauce

Cook chicken or use leftover chicken, chop in food processor and mix with cheeses, egg, parsley, salt and pepper to taste, onions and almonds. Fill crêpes and layer in casserole dish. Top with tomato sauce and additional cheese. Bake at 350°F. for 10 minutes. May be frozen.

Jean Greene

CHICKEN BAKED IN WHITE WINE

Marinade

¾ cup white wine
¼ cup vegetable oil
1 large garlic clove, finely
　minced
1 large onion, finely minced
⅛ teaspoon cayenne pepper

Freshly ground pepper to taste
1 teaspoon poultry seasoning
1 tablespoon fresh or dried
　parsley, finely minced
1 teaspoon salt (optional)

Combine ingredients and allow to stand 6-8 hours.

1 chicken fryer, halved or
　cut into pieces or
　4 chicken breasts

Arrange chicken, skin side down, in casserole or baking pan. Pour marinade over chicken, cover and refrigerate until cooking time. Remove from refrigerator, uncover, turn chicken (skin side up) and bake at 350°F. for 1-1½ hours until brown and tender. Baste occasionally; serve with pan drippings. Serve with your favorite style of rice. Serves 4-6.

Shirley Penewitt (Mrs. Paul)

CHICKEN À LA BASQUE

2 tablespoons butter
2 tablespoons olive oil
2 cups sliced mushrooms
4 large whole chicken breasts
　or 1 chicken fryer

4 teaspoons garlic salt
2 teaspoons oregano
1 teaspoon paprika
½ cup sliced green onions
1 cup white wine

Melt butter in large skillet, add oil and sauté mushrooms until golden; remove and reserve. Brown chicken on both sides. Sprinkle with garlic salt, oregano, paprika and onions. Top with mushrooms and add wine. Cover and simmer 45 minutes until chicken is tender and flavors are blended. Serves 4 generously.

Kathleen Vance (Mrs. Charles)

CHICKEN BREASTS WITH WALNUT SAUCE

2 chicken breasts per person
¼ cup or more all-purpose flour
Salt and pepper
2 tablespoons butter or margarine
1 tablespoon vegetable oil
3 fresh scallions, chopped

1 tablespoon chopped parsley
1 cup chopped mushrooms
1 cup water
1 ounce brandy (optional)
1 cup plain yogurt or sour cream
½ cup ground walnuts

Flour chicken lightly and sprinkle with salt and pepper. Heat fats in a large skillet and add chicken. Brown 5 minutes on each side. Add scallions, parsley, mushrooms and water. Bring to a boil, cover and reduce heat. Cook over low heat for 25 minutes or until tender. Remove chicken from pan. Mix in brandy, yogurt or sour cream and walnuts, adding a little more water if a thinner sauce is desired. Pour over breasts and serve on a bed of rice pilaf.

Fotula Slaughter (Mrs. Jim)

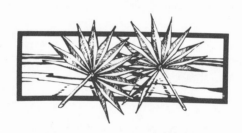

CHICKEN CASHEW CASSEROLE

2 cups diced celery
½ cup chopped onion
¼ cup butter or margarine,
   melted
1 cup chicken broth (no fat)
2 10¾-ounce cans cream
   of mushroom soup

12 drops hot sauce (Tabasco)
4-5 cups cooked, diced chicken
   (2 fryers)
1 cup cashew nuts
2 5-ounce cans fried Chinese
   noodles

Sauté celery and onion in butter. Add broth, soup, hot sauce and chicken; stir. Cover and simmer 5 minutes over medium low heat. Place in buttered 13x9-inch dish. Bake at 350°F. 25-30 minutes. Add cashews and noodles over top about halfway through cooking time. Serves 4-6.

Ernestine Williams (Mrs. Raymond)

CHICKEN À L'ABRICOT

2 3-pound chickens or 6 chicken
  breasts
Salt and pepper
Zest of 1 orange removed and
  minced
1 18-ounce jar apricot preserves
1 garlic clove, split

½ cup orange juice
¼ cup water
3 tablespoons cognac
2 tablespoons red wine vinegar
1 teaspoon salt
2 medium oranges, thinly sliced
  for garnish

Season birds with salt and pepper; roast at 325°F. for 1¼-1½ hours. In a bowl blend remaining ingredients; pour over chicken and refrigerate overnight. Bring to room temperature; brush birds with glaze and bake at 350°F. for 30 minutes. Serves 6-8.

Larry Williams
Dothan, Alabama

CHICKEN LICKEN

¼ cup butter or margarine
1 3-pound chicken, cut into
  pieces or 4 large chicken
  breasts
1 large onion, chopped
1 garlic clove, minced
¾ teaspoon salt
1½ teaspoons paprika

1 teaspoon ground ginger
¼ teaspoon chili powder
1 12-ounce can tomatoes,
  broken up
1 6-ounce can mushroom sauce
2 tablespoons cornstarch
1 cup evaporated milk

Melt butter in large skillet and brown chicken pieces well. Remove chicken from pan. Brown onion and garlic, add seasonings, tomatoes and mushroom sauce. Add chicken; simmer, covered, 40 minutes or until chicken is tender. Remove chicken from pan. Blend cornstarch with milk to smooth paste; stir into sauce. Mix well, add chicken and simmer gently 5 minutes. Serve over hot cooked noodles. Serves 4-8.

Lillian Cooper (Mrs. Michael)

CHICKEN JUBILEE

Chicken pieces for 8 servings
Salt and pepper
½ cup butter or margarine
Minced garlic or garlic salt
½ cup raisins
1 cup water

1 tablespoon instant onion
1 12-ounce bottle chili sauce
½ cup firmly packed brown sugar
1 tablespoon Worcestershire sauce
1 cup sherry
1 16½-ounce can pitted cherries

Place chicken pieces on broiler pan. Season lightly with salt and pepper. Brush chicken with melted butter flavored with garlic. Broil chicken until golden brown on both sides. Remove chicken to shallow baking pan. Mix all remaining ingredients except sherry and cherries. Pour over chicken; cover and bake at 325°F. for 1 hour or until done. Uncover; add sherry and cherries; bake 15 minutes longer. Keep warm, covered, until ready to serve. Serve with fluffy rice. Serves 8.

Florence Stewart

CHICKEN MARBELLA

5 pounds chicken, cut into
  pieces
4 garlic cloves, peeled and
  pureed
½ cup oregano
Salt and pepper
¼ cup red wine vinegar
¼ cup olive oil

½ cup pitted prunes
¼ cup pitted green olives
¼ cup capers
3 bay leaves
1 cup firmly packed brown sugar
1 cup white wine
¼ cup chopped parsley

Marinate chicken overnight in mixture of next 9 ingredients. Arrange chicken in a single layer in large baking dish; cover with marinade. Sprinkle with brown sugar and pour wine around chicken. Bake at 350°F. for 1 hour, basting often. Top with parsley. May be served hot or at room temperature. Serves 10-12.

John Henry Sherman, Jr.

LEMONY CHICKEN CUTLETS

6 chicken breast halves, boned
¼ cup all-purpose flour
½ teaspoon salt
⅛ teaspoon pepper
3 tablespoons or more butter
  or margarine

1 cup water
1 chicken-flavored bouillon cube
3 small lemons, divided
Lemon juice substitute powder
  (optional)

Pound chicken breast halves with meat mallet to ⅛-inch thickness. On waxed paper mix flour, salt and pepper; coat chicken and reserve remaining flour mixture. In 12-inch skillet over medium high heat, cook 3 pieces of chicken in 3 tablespoons butter (add more if necessary) until light brown on both sides. Remove chicken pieces to plate; reduce heat to low. Into drippings in skillet, stir reserved flour mixture; add water, bouillon and juice of 1 lemon, stirring to loosen brown bits. Return chicken to skillet. Thinly slice remaining lemons; place over chicken. Cover and simmer 5-10 minutes or until chicken is tender. Arrange chicken and lemon slices on warm serving platter; sprinkle with lemon juice substitute if desired.

Joyce Moody (Mrs. J. R. III)

CHICKEN MONTEREY JACK

6 tablespoons all-purpose flour,
  divided
1 1¼-ounce package taco
  seasoning mix
4-6 large chicken breasts
1 cup butter or margarine
1 cup crushed tortilla chips
¼ cup vegetable oil

2 tablespoons finely chopped
  onion
¼ teaspoon salt
1 13-ounce can evaporated milk
¼ teaspoon hot pepper sauce
1 cup shredded Monterey Jack
  cheese
¼ teaspoon lemon juice

In a plastic bag combine ¼ cup flour and taco mix. Add 2 pieces of chicken at a time to the bag and shake until coated. Melt butter in 15x10x1-inch baking pan. Roll chicken in butter and then in crushed tortilla chips. Return to pan and bake at 375°F. for 50 minutes. In a saucepan heat oil and cook onion until tender; blend in remaining flour and salt. Add milk and pepper sauce; cook and stir until thick. Add cheese and lemon juice to the sauce. Serve chicken on platter with about 3 tablespoons sauce over each breast. Serve with remaining sauce. Serves 4-6.

Kim Blackwell (Mrs. Ken)

CHICKEN PARMIGIANA

3 whole chicken breasts, split,
    boned and skinned
2 eggs, slightly beaten
1 teaspoon salt
¼ teaspoon pepper
¾ cup fine dry breadcrumbs
⅓ cup vegetable oil

1 15-ounce can tomato sauce
¼ teaspoon dried whole basil
⅛ teaspoon garlic powder
1 tablespoon butter or margarine
½ cup grated Parmesan cheese
2 cups (8-ounces) mozzarella
    cheese

Place each chicken breast on a sheet of waxed paper. Flatten to ¼-inch thickness with meat mallet or rolling pin. Combine eggs, salt and pepper. Dip chicken breasts into egg mixture and roll each in breadcrumbs. Brown chicken in hot oil in a large skillet. Drain on paper towels. Place chicken in greased 13x9x2-inch baking dish. Drain oil from skillet. Combine tomato sauce, basil and garlic powder in skillet. Bring to a boil and simmer 10 minutes; stir in butter. Pour mixture over chicken and sprinkle with Parmesan cheese. Cover and bake at 350°F. for 30 minutes. Uncover and arrange mozzarella slices on top. Bake 10 minutes longer. Serves 6.

Isabel Hall (Mrs. Kent)

CHICKEN-OYSTER-RICE DRESSING

2 cups uncooked rice
6 cups salted water
½ cup butter or margarine
1 large onion, chopped
2 teaspoons thyme

1 pint oysters, drained and
    salted
1 large chicken fryer, cut into
    pieces
Salt and pepper

Boil rice in salted water until all liquid has been absorbed. Add butter and stir. Add onion, thyme and oysters; stir well. Line a 13x9-inch pan with aluminum foil, leaving enough on the ends to cover top of pan. Place rice and oyster mixture in pan, top with chicken pieces, salt and pepper as desired. Bring ends of foil up to cover chicken; bake at 350°F. for 1 hour or until chicken is done. Serves 4-6.

Note: After 1 hour, if the mixture appears too "soupy", uncover and finish baking to desired consistency. This will also brown the chicken. Serve 4-6.

Dale Mckenzie (Mrs. Ted)

BOLOGNESE CHICKEN WITH NOODLES

½ cup butter
½ cup vegetable oil
1 pound fresh mushrooms, sliced
4 boneless chicken breasts,
　halved
Salt and pepper
¾ cup grated Parmesan cheese,
　divided

1 16-ounce container light
　cream or 8-ounces light cream
　and 8-ounces heavy cream
1 teaspoon parsley flakes
1 pound fettucine noodles,
　cooked and drained

Melt butter and oil in large skillet. Sauté mushrooms until brown but still somewhat firm. Remove mushrooms from pan. Add chicken pieces, sprinkle with salt and pepper to taste and cook over low heat until white and firm. Do not overcook! Return mushrooms to pan. Add ¼ cup Parmesan cheese over the chicken. Pour cream over all and add remaining cheese and parsley. Cook over low heat until cream is hot. Serve over fettucine noodles. Serves 4.

Susan Siragusa (Mrs. Robert)

CHICKEN SPAGHETTI

1 large onion, chopped
1 bunch green onions, chopped
1 garlic clove, chopped
4 ribs celery, chopped
½ green pepper, chopped
½ bunch parsley, chopped
2 tablespoons bacon drippings
1 6-ounce can tomato paste
1 16-ounce can tomatoes,
　chopped

Salt and pepper to taste
Sugar to taste
Dash of hot sauce
2 tablespoons Worcestershire
　sauce
1 large chicken fryer, cooked
　boned and diced
1 8-ounce package spaghetti,
　cooked and drained

Sauté vegetables in bacon drippings. Add tomato paste, tomatoes, seasonings and chicken. Simmer for 2 hours. Mixture may be thinned with broth if necessary. Serve over cooked spaghetti. Serves 8.

Jean Pitts (Mrs. Reynolds)

CORNUCOPIA CHICKEN AND ASPARAGUS CRÊPES

6 tablespoons butter
⅓ cup all-purpose flour
1 teaspoon salt
1½ cups chicken broth
1 cup light cream
3 cups cooked, diced chicken
    breast

½ cup toasted slivered almonds,
    divided
16 asparagus spears
16 crepes

Melt butter in a saucepan; stir in flour and salt. Add chicken broth and cream, whisking constantly until sauce is thick. Stir in chicken and ¼ cup almonds. Place an asparagus spear in the center of each crêpe (use 2 spears if you like). Top with some of chicken mixture and roll up. Place in a single layer, seam side down, in a 13x9x2-inch pan. Spoon any remaining chicken mixture over the top of the crêpes and sprinkle with remaining almonds. Bake at 350°F. for about 20 minutes. Serves 8.

Basic Crêpes

1 cup milk
3 eggs, well-beaten

¾ cup sifted all-purpose flour
¼ teaspoon salt

Beat together milk and eggs, add flour and salt and beat until batter is smooth. Preheat an 8-inch iron skillet. Lightly butter the skillet and pour about 2 tablespoons of the batter in. Immediately begin to rotate the pan so that the batter spreads evenly and thinly over the bottom. Turn once. Bake only until light brown. Repeat the procedure until all batter is used. Makes 16 crêpes.

Lida Lewis (Mrs. James)

HOMEMADE CHICKEN PIE

1 cup fresh mushrooms, sliced
¼ teaspoon garlic powder
2 tablespoons butter or margarine
2 tablespoons cornstarch
1½ cups milk
2½ cups cooked chicken, cubed
1 8-ounce can early peas,
    drained

1 2-ounce jar chopped pimento
1 teaspoon salt
¼ teaspoon pepper
1 double crust (10-inch) pastry
    shell, unbaked

Sauté mushrooms sprinkled with garlic powder in butter. Blend cornstarch and milk and add to mushrooms. Cook and stir until mixture thickens and bubbles and continue cooking 1 minute longer. Stir in other ingredients and pour into pastry-lined deep dish pie plate. Top with second crust and seal edges with fork. Cut steam vents in top. Bake at 375°F. for 35 minutes or until browned. Serves 6.

Nell Ennis (Mrs. Powell)

CREAMED CHICKEN ON CORN MEAL WAFFLES

6 tablespoons butter
⅓ cup all-purpose flour
1 teaspoon salt
1½ cups chicken broth

1 cup light cream
3 cups cooked, diced chicken
1 pound fresh mushrooms, sautéed

In a large skillet melt butter; stir in flour and salt. Add chicken broth and cream, whisking constantly until sauce is thick. Stir in chicken and cooked mushrooms. Serve over hot Corn Meal Waffles.

Corn Meal Waffles

1½ cups white corn meal
¼ cup all-purpose flour
½ teaspoon salt
½ teaspoon soda

1 teaspoon baking powder
2 eggs, beaten
2 cups buttermilk
½ cup vegetable oil

In a medium mixing bowl combine corn meal, flour, salt, soda and baking powder and mix well. Beat together the eggs, buttermilk and oil. Add dry ingredients and stir to blend. Bake on a preheated waffle iron. Makes 8 waffles.

Note: Curried fruit or a hot fruit compote is good with this dish. This is always a big hit for brunch.

Lida Lewis (Mrs. James)

173

CHICKEN AND WILD RICE CASSEROLE

2 3-pound chickens
1 cup water
1 cup dry sherry
1½ teaspoons salt
½ teaspoon curry powder
1 medium onion, sliced
½ cup sliced celery
2 6-ounce packages long grain
  and wild rice

1 pound mushrooms
¼ cup butter or margarine
1 cup sour cream
1 10¾-ounce can cream of
  mushroom soup
1 6-ounce can water chestnuts,
  drained and chopped
  (optional)

In a large pot combine first 7 ingredients, cover and simmer 1 hour; strain broth. Refrigerate at once without cooling. When cool, remove chicken from bones and chop chicken. Prepare rice according to directions for firm rice, using broth from chicken as part of the liquid. Sauté mushrooms in butter; combine with chicken and rice, mixing well. Blend in sour cream, soup and water chestnuts. Pour mixture into a large casserole dish, cover and refrigerate overnight if desired. Bake at 350°F. for 1 hour.

Helen Gerhart

CHICKEN YAKI SOBA

1 chicken fryer, cut into pieces
2 tablespoons butter or margarine
Salt
2 carrots, chopped
3 ribs celery, chopped

1 green pepper, chopped
1 medium onion, chopped
2 3-ounce packages instant
  Chinese soup noodles with
  chicken flavor packet

Place chicken pieces in butter in heavy skillet. Salt to taste; cover and cook slowly, turning frequently to prevent sticking. Cook until chicken is very tender (falling off the bone), remove from skillet and spread out in pan to cool for deboning. Place the chopped vegetables into the skillet, cover and cook slowly, about 5 minutes. Add the boned chicken and noodles with flavor packets. Bring to a boil, remove from heat, cover and let stand for 5 minutes. Serves 3-4.

Note: Good with onion-flavored rice crackers.

Ann Bane (Mrs. Curtis)

LUXURY LASAGNA

1 large onion, chopped
2 garlic cloves, crushed
1/3 cup olive oil
1/2 pound chicken livers, chopped
1/2 pound prosciutto, chopped
3 cups chopped cooked chicken
2 15-ounce cans herbed tomato
  sauce
2 6-ounce cans tomato paste
1 cup chicken broth
1 cup dry white wine

1 teaspoon salt
1/2 teaspoon pepper
1/2 teaspoon basil
1/2 teaspoon oregano
1 8-ounce package lasagna
  noodles
1 16-ounce carton ricotta or
  cottage cheese
2 cups grated Parmesan cheese
1/2 pound mozzarella cheese,
  sliced

Sauté onion and garlic in oil until tender. Add chicken livers and sauté until browned. Add prosciutto, chicken, tomato sauce, tomato paste, chicken broth, wine and seasonings. Bring mixture to a boil; cover and simmer for 30 minutes, stirring occasionally. Cook noodles according to package directions; drain. Rinse noodles with cold water; drain. Alternate layers of sauce, noodles, ricotta and Parmesan cheese in a 16x10x3-inch dish or 2 smaller dishes; repeat layers twice. Arrange mozzarella cheese on top. Bake at 350°F. for 30 minutes or until bubbly. Serves 8-12.

Marie Bazemore (Mrs. Eugene)

PARMESAN CHICKEN

1/3 cup Italian seasoned
  breadcrumbs
1/3 cup grated Parmesan cheese
1/2 teaspoon oregano leaves,
  crushed
Generous dash of garlic powder
Generous dash of pepper

1 pound chicken breasts, skinned
  and boned
4 ounces fresh mushrooms
1 10¾-ounce can cream of
  chicken soup
1 cup milk

Combine breadcrumbs, cheese, oregano, garlic powder and pepper; roll chicken in mixture. Arrange chicken in shallow baking pan. Bake at 400°F. for 15 minutes. Meanwhile, slice mushroom tops and sauté. Blend soup and milk and add to mushrooms. Heat until heated through. Turn chicken and bake 15 minutes more. Pour mushroom mixture over chicken and bake until heated through and chicken is done. Serve with rice. Serves 4.

Jennifer Doster (Mrs. Henry)

MEXICAN CHICKEN

2 whole chicken breasts, boned
and skinned
4 3x1-inch slices Monterey
Jack cheese
2 eggs
1 tablespoon grated Parmesan
cheese
1 teaspoon instant chicken
flavored bouillon granules

1 teaspoon chopped parsley
¼ teaspoon pepper
2 tablespoons olive oil
All-purpose flour
1 8-ounce can tomatoes and
green chilies
1 8-ounce carton sour cream
1 4-ounce can ripe olives,
sliced

Cut chicken breasts in half. Make a pocket in each half and put a slice of cheese in each pocket. Beat together the eggs, Parmesan, bouillon granules, parsley and pepper in a shallow bowl. Heat olive oil in heavy skillet. Dip the cheese-stuffed chicken in flour and then in the egg mixture. Place quickly in the hot olive oil and cook until the coating is lightly browned, turning once. Carefully remove from skillet and place in baking dish. (May be refrigerated at this point until ready to use.) Bake at 375°F. for 15-20 minutes (longer if it has been refrigerated). Heat tomatoes and green chilies and serve as sauce for chicken with a dish of sour cream and a dish of ripe olives.

Marise Boyle (Mrs. William)

SHERRY CHICKEN

6 chicken breasts, skinned
Salt and pepper
All-purpose flour
½ cup butter
3 tablespoons olive oil
1 bunch green onions, chopped
1 pound fresh mushrooms, sliced
1 16-ounce carton sour cream

¾ cup sherry
1 teaspoon salt (or more to
taste)
¼ teaspoon white pepper
1 teaspoon basil
2 teaspoons dill
1 garlic clove, crushed
1 bay leaf

Season chicken breasts with salt and pepper and lightly dredge in flour. Place in oil and butter and fry until lightly browned on both sides. Remove from oil and set aside. Place onions and mushrooms in pan drippings and sauté until tender. Add sour cream stirring well. Add sherry and seasonings. Simmer for a few minutes over low heat. Return chicken breasts to mixture and continue cooking for about 1 hour. Serve over hot cooked rice.

Note: Gravy may be thickened with cornstarch dissolved in warm water.

Sherry Knight

SUPREME DE VOLAILLE FARCI

½ pound fresh mushrooms
7 tablespoons butter, divided
½ teaspoon freshly ground pepper
6 chicken breasts, skinned and
  boned
6 whole scallions, finely chopped

4 ounces cooked ham, finely
  chopped
2 tablespoons all-purpose flour
¾ cup dry white wine
2 cups chicken stock

Finely shred mushrooms in food processor; scrape them into a clean kitchen towel and squeeze out and discard all liquid. Melt 4 tablespoons butter over moderately high heat in a 12-inch sauté pan. Sauté shredded mushrooms, quickly lower heat to medium and cook until all the moisture evaporates from them, about 15-20 minutes. Add pepper. Pound chicken breasts to ¼-inch thickness with meat mallet or rolling pin. Add half the scallions to mushrooms and sauté a few minutes (reserve other half for sauce). Add ham to the mushrooms and scallions. Place 2 tablespoons of this mixture in each flattened chicken breast and roll up, tucking in sides and tying if necessary. In sauté pan heat remaining butter until it sizzles. Place the chicken breasts, tucked side down, in the skillet and sauté 4 minutes over medium high heat, turn over and sauté 4 minutes more. Remove browned breasts from pan. Discard all but 2 tablespoons drippings from pan. Remove pan from heat and stir in flour. Place back over heat and cook and stir 2-3 minutes. Remove from heat again, stir in the wine and 1¼ cups chicken stock. Over medium high heat bring to a boil, stirring constantly and adding as much more stock as needed to make sauce desired consistency. (It should be fairly thin.) Add the remaining scallions. Place chicken breasts in sauce and simmer, covered, for 15 minutes.

Verna Burke (Mrs. Les)

CHICKEN BREASTS WITH WINE CASSEROLE

4 whole chicken breasts, boned
  and split
8 4x4-inch slices Swiss cheese
1 10¾-ounce can cream of
  chicken soup, undiluted

¼ cup dry white wine
1 cup herb seasoned stuffing mix
¼ cup melted butter

Arrange chicken in greased 13x9x2-inch baking dish. Top with cheese slices. Combine soup and wine, stir well and spoon over chicken; sprinkle with stuffing mix. Drizzle butter over crumbs. Bake at 350°F. 45-55 minutes. Serves 8.

Hannah Smallwood

CHICKEN ASPARAGUS CASSEROLE

3 8-ounce cans asparagus,
drained and juice of 1 can
reserved
2 10¾-ounce cans cream
of mushroom soup
3 ounces slivered almonds

2 cups 8-ounces shredded Cheddar
cheese
3 hard-cooked eggs, diced
3 cups cooked, diced chicken
1 stack round, buttery crackers
¼ cup butter or margarine, melted

In a large bowl combine reserved asparagus juice with soup. Add almonds, cheese and eggs. Stir in chicken and asparagus and spread mixture in a large casserole dish. Crush crackers and mix with melted butter; spread over top of casserole. Bake at 350°F. for 35-45 minutes until bubbly. May be made ahead of time and refrigerated until ready to bake. Serves 12-15.

Linda Harrison (Mrs. Franklin)

ITALIAN TURKEY BREAST WITH BASIL LINGUINE

1 turkey breast
All-purpose flour
Salt
½ cup butter or margarine

1 tablespoon olive oil
Juice of 1 lemon
½ cup white wine

Cut turkey breast completely off the bone all in one piece. Cut with the grain in ⅛-inch slices, about 2-inches long. Dust filets with flour and salt. Melt butter and olive oil in skillet. Brown each side of filet until golden; remove from pan. Add lemon juice and wine; simmer a few minutes then pour over filets. Serve with Basil Linguine.

Basil Linguine

1 28-ounce can Italian tomatoes
2 tablespoons sweet basil
Salt to taste

1 16-ounce package linguine,
cooked and drained

Chop fine or process tomatoes in food processor. Add basil and salt; simmer 15-20 minutes. Toss linguine with sauce. Serve with turkey breast and its sauce, steamed broccoli and hot bread. Serves 6.

Laura Darnell (Mrs. Douglas)

CORNISH HENS AND RICE

1 6½-ounce package long-grain
  wild rice
2 cups hot water
2 Cornish hens, cleaned and
  halved

Salt and pepper to taste
1 10¾-ounce can cream
  of mushroom soup
1 6-ounce can mushrooms, drained

Pour uncooked rice in bottom of a 3-quart shallow baking dish. Pour hot water over rice. Place cornish hens on top and season with salt and pepper to taste. Sprinkle flavor packet in package of rice over hens. Cover with aluminum foil and bake at 350°F. for 1 hour. Uncover and pour soup and mushrooms over hens; bake uncovered for 15 minutes more. Serves 4.

Marion Collins (Mrs. Charles)

CORNISH HENS WITH SPINACH AND ARTICHOKE DRESSING

Cornish hens, ½ per person
Fresh spinach
1 15-ounce can artichoke hearts,
  drained and cut into eighths
5 ribs celery
1 bunch green onions

Fresh parsley
¼ cup butter or margarine
5 cups breadcrumbs
Chicken broth
Salt and pepper to taste

Thaw hens, rinse and pat dry. Chop fresh spinach, steam and drain well. In food processor chop celery, onions and parsley together. Sauté this in skillet in butter a few minutes. Add spinach and artichokes. Remove from heat, toss with breadcrumbs and moisten as desired with chicken broth. Salt and pepper if desired. Stuff hens fully. Bake, covered, at 350°F. for 1 hour; uncover and bake 15 minutes more. Serve on a bed of fresh spinach or parsley with parsleyed new potatoes and a fruit salad. Very elegant!

Laura Darnell (Mrs. Douglas)

ROCK CORNISH HENS

2 Cornish game hens   4 strips bacon
Salt   ½ cup red wine

Cut hens in half, wash and dry well. Rub inside and out with salt. Cover each with
a strip of bacon and bake at 500°F. for 30 minutes. Reduce heat to 350°F. and
bake 30 minutes more. Add wine and bake 15 minutes longer. Serve with sauce
from pan. Delicious with wild rice. Serves 4.

Ruthie Hunter (Mrs. Charles)

BRAISED DOVE

24 doves   2 tablespoons chopped green
¼ cup salt   pepper
1½ tablespoons red pepper   2 tablespoons chopped parsley
2 tablespoons pepper   2 tablespoons chopped green
¼ cup red wine   onion tops
¼ cup vegetable oil   1 8-ounce can mushrooms
¾ cup plus 2 tablespoons   (optional)
   chopped onions

Season doves inside and out with salt and both peppers. Sprinkle with wine and
refrigerate, covered, overnight. Reserve juices from marinade. Brown doves on all
sides in hot oil in black iron pot. Remove doves from pot and pour off excess oil.
Brown onions and pepper in remaining oil, adding ¼ cup marinade and enough
water to make gravy 1-inch deep in pot. Place doves, breast side down, in gravy,
cover tightly and cook over low heat 3½-4 hours. Add water only if gravy boils
away. Remove doves to heated platter and add chopped parsley and onion tops to
gravy. Add water to make gravy 1-1½-inches deep in pot. Canned mushrooms
may be added now if desired. Serves 6-8.

Helen Arnold (Mrs. J. R.)

DELICIOUS DOVES AND MUSHROOMS

8 dove breasts
Salt
Pepper
Garlic salt
⅓ cup butter or margarine
¾ cup sliced mushrooms

3 tablespoons dry sherry
2 tablespoons Worcestershire
  sauce
1 tablespoon lemon juice
1 tablespoon all-purpose flour
½ cup light cream

Sprinkle doves with salt, pepper and garlic salt. Brown in melted butter with mushrooms. Add sherry, Worcestershire and lemon juice. Cover tightly and simmer very slowly 15-20 minutes. Remove doves from skillet; blend in flour and then cream to make gravy. Serve doves with gravy over a bed of rice. Serves 2-4.

Anda Gagnet (Mrs. Ted)

DOVES IN WINE

6 dove breasts
1 cup red wine
Salt
Pepper

3 tablespoons butter or bacon
  drippings
1 cup hot water

Marinate dove breasts in wine for ½ hour. Salt and pepper breasts and brown on both sides in butter or bacon drippings in a heavy iron skillet. When brown, pour in hot water and the wine left over from marinating. Cover skillet and bake at 350°F. for 1 hour or until doves are tender. Serve with wild rice or rice pilaf. Serves 2-3.

Joseph W. Smith III

SIMPLY DELICIOUS DOVE

16 dove breasts
4 teaspoons garlic salt

8 slices bacon, cut in half

Wash dove breasts; sprinkle each breast generously with garlic salt and wrap with ½ strip of bacon. Secure bacon with a toothpick. Cook over hot coals on grill to desired doneness. Excellent with wild rice....or without! Serves 4.

Ruthie Hunter (Mrs. Charles)

DOVE PIE

24 fresh or frozen whole doves,
  cleaned
1-1½ quarts water
1 teaspoon salt
1 teaspoon red pepper
1 pound fresh mushrooms

6 hard-cooked eggs, sliced
3 10¾-ounce cans cream
  of chicken soup, undiluted
Dash of Worcestershire sauce
Pie pastry
1 beaten egg

In a heavy Dutch oven cook doves in water to which salt and pepper have been added and cook until tender. Remove doves from the broth and arrange in a casserole dish alternating doves, mushrooms and sliced hard-cooked eggs in layers. Mix soup with 3 cups dove broth and Worcestershire; pour over casserole. Cover with a thin pie pastry. Make a few slits in the top and brush with beaten egg. Bake at 350°F. for 30-45 minutes until pie is hot and crust is light brown. This is a delicious way to serve doves for a buffet luncheon or brunch. Serves 8-10.

Helen Arnold (Mrs. J. R.)

DUCK CASSEROLE

2 ducks
1 whole onion
2 ribs celery
1 6½-ounce package long-grain
  and wild rice
½ cup butter
½ cup chopped onion
¼ cup all-purpose flour

1 6-ounce can mushrooms
1½ cups duck broth
1½ cups light cream
1 tablespoon chopped parsley
1½ teaspoons salt
¼ teaspoon pepper
1 4½-ounce package slivered
  almonds

Boil ducks for 2 hours with whole onion and celery. Cook rice according to package directions; set aside. In deep skillet melt butter; sauté chopped onion, stir in flour. Add mushrooms and broth. Add cream, parsley, salt, pepper and rice. Debone duck and add to other ingredients. Place in 2-quart casserole; sprinkle with almonds. Bake at 350°F. for 25 minutes. Serves 6-8.

Bess Hooks (Mrs. H. J.)

EASY DUCK

2 ducks
Salt
Pepper

2 10½-ounce cans French onion
soup

Clean ducks and place in roaster. Salt and pepper ducks; pour soup over ducks. Bake, covered, at 400°F. for 1 hour. Recipe may be easily halved or doubled. Serves 4-6.

Joyce Moody (Mrs. J. R. III)

GRILLED DUCK BREASTS

4 duck breasts, skinned and
   boned
Salted water

16 slices bacon, cut in half
2 cups Italian salad dressing
⅔ cup red wine

Cut each breast half into 4 pieces. Soak in salted water for 1 hour; drain. Wrap each piece in ½ strip bacon. Marinate in mixture of salad dressing and wine for 3-4 hours. Grill over hot coals for 8 minutes, turning once. Remove bacon and serve. Serves 4-6.

David Scott

BAKED QUAIL WITH MUSHROOMS

⅓ cup plus 5 tablespoons
   all-purpose flour, divided
1 teaspoon salt
½ teaspoon pepper
6 quail, cleaned

10 tablespoons butter, divided
½ pound fresh mushrooms, sliced
2 cups chicken broth
½ cup sherry
Hot cooked rice

Combine ⅓ cup flour, salt and pepper. Dredge quail in flour mixture; set aside. Melt 2 tablespoons butter in a large skillet; add mushrooms and sauté 4 minutes. Remove mushrooms from skillet; set aside. Melt remaining butter is skillet; brown quail on both sides. Remove quail to 1½-quart casserole. Add remaining flour to drippings in skillet; cook 1 minute, stirring constantly. Gradually add chicken broth and sherry; cook over medium heat, stirring constantly, until gravy is thick and bubbly. Stir in mushrooms. Pour mushroom gravy over quail. Cover and bake at 350°F. for 1 hour. Serve over rice. Serves 6.

Louverne Barron (Mrs. Dempsey)

FLORIDA QUAIL

3 tablespoons all-purpose flour
Celery salt
Salt
Pepper
7-9 quail
10 tablespoons butter or
    margarine, divided

2½ cups sliced mushrooms
1 cup consommé
1 cup dry red wine
⅓ cup orange juice

Season flour with celery salt, salt and pepper, Dredge quail in flour mixture and sauté in 6 tablespoons butter in large skillet. In separate skillet sauté mushrooms in remaining butter; pour over quail. Add consommé and red wine. Cover and cook slowly over low heat for 20-30 minutes. Stir in orange juice and heat. Serve over bed of rice. Serves 7-9.

Anda Gagnet (Mrs. Ted)

FRIED QUAIL

6 whole quail, cleaned and split
    down the back
Salt and pepper

Self-rising flour
Vegetable oil

Sprinkle quail with salt and pepper. Dip in flour. In a heavy cast-iron skillet heat oil to 350°F. Fry quail until brown on both sides (at least 5 minutes); drain well. Place quail on hot platter garnished with lemon slices and parsley. Serve with wild rice casserole. Serves 6.

Henry C. Smallwood

RANCH STYLE CREAM QUAIL

12 quail, dressed
Salt and pepper
2 cups butter or margarine

4 cups sweet cream
1-1½ cups toasted breadcrumbs

Season quail with salt and pepper. Place in large skillet and simmer slowly in butter until tender. Add cream and continue simmering until done. Remove quail to platter; sprinkle with breadcrumbs. Pour cream gravy over all. Serves 8-10.

Ruth Lark (Mrs. William E.)

MARINATED BARBECUED VENISON STEAKS

1 10½-ounce can French onion
   soup
½ cup catsup
¼ cup butter or margarine
Several drops of hot pepper
   sauce

¼ teaspoon salt
¼ teaspoon garlic powder
¼ teaspoon pepper
Venison tenderloin, cut into
   1¼-inch filets
Bacon slices

Combine soup, catsup, butter and seasonings in saucepan; bring to a boil, simmer 10 minutes, stirring occasionally. Cool sauce. Wrap venison filets with bacon slices. Marinate venison in sauce 6-8 hours. Cook steaks over hot coals, basting with marinade. Serves 4-6.

Note: This marinade removes any wild taste and tenderizes the venison.

Ted Gagnet

VENISON BITES

Venison (tenderloin is best)
Meat marinade with tenderizer
Dale's® Steak Sauce
Seasoned salt

Pepper
All-purpose flour
Vegetable oil

Debone venison; soak several hours in cold water (until meat loses most of its bloody look). Drain. Soak 15 minutes in meat marinade (add extra tenderizer if desired); drain. Cut meat into bite-size chunks. Soak 1-2 hours in steak sauce, diluted with a little water; drain. Season with salt and pepper, coat with flour. Fry in hot oil in skillet until evenly browned. Don't overcook or it will be dry and tough. Serves 4-6.

Pat and Willis Holley

VENISON STEW

1½ pounds venison, cut into
  1½-inch cubes
3 tablespoons all-purpose flour
1 teaspoon salt
½ teaspoon pepper
½ teaspoon garlic powder
¼ cup vegetable oil
1 onion, chopped

1 10½-ounce can beef consommé
Water
2 teaspoons brown sugar
3 ounces bourbon whiskey
1½ pounds vegetables (onions,
  carrots, celery, potatoes),
  cut into chunks

Trim all fat from venison, Combine flour, salt, pepper and garlic powder in paper or plastic bag; shake well to mix seasonings. Put meat into the bag and shake again to coat each cube with seasoned flour. Heat oil in Dutch oven; brown the chopped onion then add the venison and brown each piece on all sides. Add consommé and enough water to cover meat. Bring to a boil and immediately reduce heat to simmer. Sprinkle in brown sugar and pour in bourbon. Cover and simmer for 1 hour. (Water may be added if too much liquid evaporates.) Add vegetables and simmer for 1 more hour. Stir once or twice. Serve with tossed green salad and French rolls. Serves 4-6.

Joseph W. Smith III

VENISON BURGUNDY

1½ cups sliced onion
½ cup vegetable oil
2½ pounds venison, cut into
  cubes
¼ cup all-purpose flour
1 cup burgundy
¾ cup water

1 10½-ounce can beef broth
Pinch of thyme
Pinch of marjoram
½ teaspoon salt
¼ teaspoon freshly ground pepper
1 pound sliced mushrooms

Sauté onion in hot oil in large, heavy skillet; remove onion. Dredge venison in flour; brown in the oil. Stir in liquids and seasonings; bring to a boil. Cover and simmer 2 hours, stirring occasionally. Add the mushrooms and cooked onions the last 30 minutes of cooking. Serve over bed of rice. Serves 4-6.

Ted Gagnet

VENISON VIENNA

Marinade

1 cup dry red wine
2 cups water
5 crushed juniper berries
¼ teaspoon thyme

2 bay leaves
1 cup coarsely chopped onions
½ teaspoon finely chopped garlic
½ teaspoon freshly ground pepper

In a large shallow glass, stainless-steel or enameled baking dish, combine all ingredients. Add the cutlets and moisten thoroughly with the marinade. Marinate the cutlets for 2 hours at room temperature or 4 hours in the refrigerator. Remove the cutlets and strain and reserve the marinade.

Cutlets

12 4-ounce cutlets, about
⅜-inch thick, cut from a
boned saddle of venison
½ teaspoon salt

Freshly ground pepper
All-purpose flour
3 tablespoons butter or margarine
2 tablespoons lard

Pat the cutlets dry with paper towels and sprinkle with salt and a few grindings of pepper. Dip them in flour and vigorously shake off the excess. In a heavy 10-12 inch skillet, heat the fat over medium heat. When the foam subsides, add the cutlets, a few at a time, cooking over high heat for 2-3 minutes on each side or until they are well browned. Arrange them on a heated platter and pour off all but a thin film of fat from the skillet.

Sauce

1 cup heavy cream
2 tablespoons red currant jelly

½ teaspoon fresh lemon juice
Salt

Pour ¾ cup of marinade through a strainer into the skillet. Bring it to a boil and boil about half of it away while scraping in any brown bits that cling to the bottom and sides of the skillet. Return the cutlets to the skillet and simmer over low heat for 5 minutes, basting every 2-3 minutes. Remove cutlets and arrange them on a heated serving platter. Stir the cream, jelly and lemon juice into the skillet. Simmer until the jelly dissolves, stirring almost constantly. Taste the sauce for seasoning, then pour it over the cutlets and serve. Serves 12.

Rowlett W. Bryant

ROAST PHEASANT

1 pheasant
Salt
Pepper
Stuffing of your choice or wild
   rice
Bacon strips
Bay leaves
Lemon slices

Celery leaves
Onion slices
½ cup white wine or vermouth
1 cup chicken stock
Boiled giblets
All-purpose flour or cornstarch
1 cup cream (optional)

Season each bird with salt and pepper inside and out. Fill cavity with stuffing of your choice or wild rice. Cover each pheasant with bacon strips and place on rack in roaster. Arrange bay leaves, lemon slices, celery leaves, onion slices and more bacon strips around bird. Add wine and chicken stock. Cover and cook 1 hour at 350°F. Uncover and return to oven to permit skin to brown, basting often with pan juices. Remove pheasant to heated platter and remove bay leaves and lemon slices from roaster. Add giblets to pan juices in roaster; thicken with flour or cornstarch to make gravy. Add cream just before serving if desired. Serves 2-4.

Dee Redding (Mrs. Ben)

CAPON AU COGNAC

4 capon breasts
6 tablespoons butter
Salt and pepper
3-4 chopped shallots or green
   onions

2 egg yolks
1 cup light cream
¼ cup cognac

Wash capon breasts and dry thoroughly. Brown in butter turning to color evenly. Season with salt and pepper to taste and add chopped shallots. Cover and cook over low heat for 5-10 minutes or until tender. Remove to a hot platter and keep warm. Continue cooking shallots until soft, adding more butter if necessary. Beat egg yolks and stir cream into them. Place pan over hot water or very low flame; add cream and egg mixture and cook gently, stirring until thick and smooth. Correct seasoning. Pour cognac over breasts, ignite cognac and when flames die out, add the cream sauce and serve. Serves 4.

Caroline Ireland (Mrs. Charles W.)

CORNISH HEN GRILLING SAUCE

½ cup unsalted butter
  (no substitute)
4 tablespoons fresh lemon juice
¼ teaspoon angostura bitters
1 teaspoon orange extract or
  1 tablespoon orange flavored
  liqueur

½ teaspoon hot pepper sauce
½ teaspoon freshly ground pepper
2 teaspoon grated orange rind
3 tablespoons dark molasses
2 tablespoons brown sugar

Combine all ingredients well; cook until well heated, stirring frequently. Coat hens with sauce before grilling and continue basting while slow cooking. Makes enough for 4 hens.

Bonnie Mohammad (Mrs. Mo)

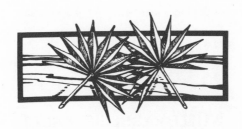

BAR-B-Q SAUCE

4 cups water
10 bay leaves
2 cups chopped onions
5 garlic cloves
5 tablespoons prepared mustard
2 lemons, squeezed
5 tablespoons soy sauce
1 cup steak sauce

1 cup vegetable oil
2 cups vinegar
2 tablespoons salt
2 tablespoons pepper
4 tablespoooons liquid smoke
2 cups catsup
3 tablespoons brown sugar

Combine first 13 ingredients in a large saucepan; simmer for 2 hours. Add catsup and brown sugar and simmer 1 hour longer. Makes 1 gallon.

Rowlett W. Bryant

J.P.'S BARBECUE SAUCE

1 32-ounce bottle catsup
2 tablespoons Worcestershire
  sauce

½ cup sugar
2 tablespoons liquid smoke
2 tablespoons wine vinegar

Combine all ingredients; bring to a boil and simmer until sauce reaches desired consistency.

Rachel Cowan (Mrs. John)

CURRANT JELLY SAUCE

½-1 12-ounce jar currant jelly
⅓ cup Worcestershire sauce

½ cup butter

Combine all in top of double boiler, simmer for 15 minutes, serve with duck.

Bess Hooks (Mrs. H. J.)

WHITE BARBECUE SAUCE

1½ cups mayonnaise
½ cup lemon juice
¼ cup sugar
¼ cup vinegar

¼ cup Worcestershire sauce
4 teaspoons salt
⅛ cup pepper

Mix all ingredients together well and let stand at room temperature at least 15 minutes before using. Use as basting sauce while cooking and pour leftover sauce over meat to serve. Good over chicken.

Jane Bolinger (Mrs. Larry)

MEATS

Sandpipers—Dodging in and out of the tide, busy sandpipers scurry for morsels of food.

MEATS

TENDERLOIN OF BEEF STROGANOFF WITH WILD RICE

6 slices beef tenderloin, about
   1-inch thick
⅓ cup butter or margarine
1 carrot, finely chopped
½ cup finely chopped celery
1 tablespoon finely chopped onion
½ teaspoon dill seed

3 tablespoons all-purpose flour
1 10½-ounce can beef broth
1 tablespoon catsup
¼ cup Sauterne wine
½ cup sour cream
4½ cups cooked wild rice

Sauté beef slices in butter until medium rare. Place on a platter and keep warm. To pan drippings add carrots, celery, onion, and dill. When vegetables are tender, stir in flour. Gradually stir in beef broth, catsup and wine. Cook over low heat, stirring constantly, until sauce bubbles and thickens. Press sauce through a sieve or whirl in a blender. Reheat and stir in sour cream. Do not boil. Spoon sauce over meat slices which have been placed over hot cooked wild rice. Serves 6.

Richard Youd

STUFFED TENDERLOIN

1 whole beef tenderloin, trimmed
   of fat
Salt and pepper to taste

Seasonings of your choice to taste
3 quarts water
2 pounds thick king crab legs

With sharp knife, slit tenderloin halfway through on 1 side. Season to taste. Bring water to a boil; add crab legs. Return to a boil and immediately drain. When cool, carefully remove meat from shell, trying to keep meat in solid strips. Place crabmeat along opening in loin, close loin and wrap in kitchen string several places. Cook stuffed loin 40 minutes at 325°F. for medium rare. Slice and serve. Serves 6-8.

Salie Cotton (Mrs. Philip)

PERFECT MEDIUM RARE PRIME RIB

1 7-8 pound standing rib roast,   Freshly ground pepper
  at room temperature

Place roast in shallow roasting pan. Bake, uncovered, at preheated 375°F for 30 minutes. Turn oven off and leave roast in oven for 3-4 hours. Return oven to 350°F and roast for 30 minutes more. Season with pepper after cooking or your favorite sauce.

Jeanette Chapman (Mrs. Joseph)

FILLET OF BEEF WITH SOUR CREAM SAUCE

1 3-pound fillet or eye of round   4 whole allspice
  roast, rolled and tied   2 bay leaves
½ pound onions, sliced   1 teaspoon salt
1 cup diced celery   Freshly ground pepper
⅔ cup diced carrots   ¼ teaspoon thyme
1 cup diced parsnips   1 tablespoon melted butter or
¼ cup diced bacon   margarine
8 peppercorns   2 cups beef or chicken stock

The Sauce

1 tablespoon lemon juice   2 tablespoons flour
2 cups sour cream

Place beef, vegetables and seasonings in casserole. Drizzle butter over casserole. Marinate for 24 hours. Bake fillet, and vegetables uncovered, for 25-30 minutes at 450°F., turning meat once. Lower heat to 350°F. Bring stock to a boil and pour into casserole; bake 1 hour longer, turning meat occasionally. Add more stock if needed. Place meat on platter and keep warm. Strain remaining contents of casserole; return to casserole. Simmer strained liquid over medium heat; add 2 tablespoons to sour cream then beat in flour with whisk. Stir mixture into casserole. Cook 3-4 minutes without boiling. Add lemon juice; taste for seasoning. Serve the beef sliced and sauce in a separate dish.

Ruth Lark (Mrs. William E.)

BOLICHI

1 ¼-pound slice of ham
1 8-ounce piece of pepperoni
1 small green pepper
1 medium onion
2 ribs celery
Salt and pepper

Oregano
Basil
Worcestershire sauce
1 (3-4 pound) eye of round or
 tenderloin roast

In meat grinder or food processor chop ham, pepperoni and vegetables. Season and stuff roast (cut across grain of roast). Roll meat in remaining stuffing. Wrap in foil and roast at 350°F for 2 hours. Open foil to brown. Make gravy with drippings and pour over roast. Best sliced when cool; gravy may be heated to rewarm meat.

Mrs. James Fuller Holly, Jr.
Orlando, Florida

MARINATED BEEF TENDERLOIN

1 5-pound beef tenderloin,
 trimmed of fat

Marinade (recipe below)

Place tenderloin in a large baking dish; pour marinade over top and cover tightly. Refrigerate at least 2 hours or overnight, turning after 1 hour and occasionally during marinating time. Uncover tenderloin, place dish on bottom rack of oven (do not drain marinade). Broil 20 minutes on each side. Cover and bake at 350°F. for 10-15 minutes. Garnish with endive and cherry tomatoes, if desired.

Marinade

½ cup burgundy wine
¼ cup olive oil
¼ cup soy sauce
1 tablespoon dried parsley flakes

1 tablespoon paprika
⅓ cup tarragon vinegar
1½ teaspoons seasoned salt

Combine all ingredients in a small bowl and mix well. Makes about 1½ cups.

Helen Kruse (Mrs. Foster H.)

BOEUF AUX CHAMPIGNONS A LA CRÈME

4 tablespoons butter or margarine, divided
2 tablespoons vegetable oil, divided
½ pound fresh mushrooms, sliced
4 green onions, finely chopped
Salt and pepper to taste

2 pounds flank steak, partially frozen
¼ cup dry white vermouth
1 cup beef stock
1 cup whipping cream
2 teaspoons cornstarch
Fresh parsley

Heat 2 tablespoons butter and 1 tablespoon oil in skillet; add mushrooms and sauté 4-5 minutes to brown. Add green onions and cook for 1 minute longer, seasoning with salt and pepper; set aside. Cut partially frozen meat into pieces and slice. Heat remaining butter and oil in skillet in which mushrooms were cooked and brown a few pieces of meat at a time. Meat should remain rare. Set aside as the meat is cooked. Pour vermouth and beef stock into hot skillet and reduce liquid to about ⅓ cup. Beat in cream and cornstarch (blended with 1 tablespoon cream) with a wire whisk; simmer 1 minute, add the mushrooms and simmer 1 minute more. Season beef lightly with salt and pepper and return to skillet with any juices that may have escaped; stir gently to combine. Correct seasoning. When ready to serve, reheat slowly, but do not overdo it. Serve over rice or noodles garnished with parsley.

Ruth Lark (Mrs. William E.)

STEAK WITH CHICKEN LIVERS

4 ounces, about ½ cup, chicken livers
2 tablespoons butter or margarine
¼ cup chopped green onion
1 cup sliced fresh mushrooms

½ cup dry white wine
¼ teaspoon salt
Dash of pepper
1 2-2½-pound beef sirloin steak, cut 1-1½-inches thick

Slice chicken livers and quickly cook in hot butter in skillet; remove from pan. In same skillet cook onion until almost tender; add mushrooms and cook 1-2 minutes more. Return livers to skillet. Stir in wine, salt and pepper. Keep warm; do not boil. Grill steak over medium heat, turning once (20-25 minutes for medium rare). Spoon some of the chicken liver mixture over steak. Garnish with parsley and red hot peppers.

Ann Aldrich Logue

MARINATED FLANK STEAK

½ cup soy sauce
6 tablespoons honey
¼ cup red wine vinegar
1 tablespoon garlic powder

1 tablespoon ground ginger
1½ cups vegetable oil
2 green onions, finely chopped
2 1½-pound flank steaks

Combine first 7 ingredients and pour over scored flank steaks. Let stand at room temperature 4 hours or in refrigerator overnight. Broil or grill 6 minutes on each side for medium rare. Slice on diagonal before serving. Serves 6-8.

Anne Hull
Nancy Boyd (Mrs. James)

WINE PEPPER STEAK

1½ pounds beef tenderloin tips or
   sirloin steak, cut into thin
   strips
¼ cup vegetable oil
1 large green pepper, cut into
   strips
1 large onion, thickly sliced
¼ cup burgundy wine

2 tablespoons soy sauce
½ teaspoon sugar
1 10½-ounce can beef broth
1 tablespoon cornstarch dissolved
   in ¼ cup water
1 4-ounce can mushrooms, drained
¼ teaspoon salt
¼ teaspoon pepper

Brown meat quickly in oil; remove from pan. In same pan sauté pepper and onion lightly. Add meat and other ingredients; heat thoroughly. Serve over rice. Serves 5-6.

Sara Sweat (Mrs. Emerson)

GARLIC PEPPER STEAK

Marinade

¼ cup vegetable oil
2 tablespoons lemon juice
2 tablespoons soy sauce
2 tablespoons chopped onion

1 garlic clove, crushed
1 teaspoon coarsely ground pepper
1 teaspoon celery salt
1 lean flank steak

Mix ingredients for marinade and marinate steak at least 6 hours or overnight. Drain and broil 3-4 inches from heat 5 minutes on each side for medium rare.

Elizabeth Pope (Mrs. Harold)

ONION-STUFFED STEAK

2 1¼-1½-pound porterhouse steaks,
    cut 1½-inch thick
½ cup chopped onion
1 large garlic clove, minced
3 tablespoons butter or margarine,
    divided

Dash of celery salt
Dash of pepper
¼ cup dry red wine
2 tablespoons soy sauce
1 cup sliced fresh mushrooms

Slash fat edges of steak at 1-inch intervals being careful not to cut into meat. Slice pockets in each side of meat, cutting almost to the bone. In a skillet cook onion and garlic in 1 tablespoon butter; add celery salt and pepper. Stuff pockets with onion mixture; close with skewers. Mix wine and soy sauce; brush on steaks. Grill over medium hot heat for 15 minutes; brush often with soy mixture. In small skillet cook mushrooms in remaining 2 tablespoons butter until tender. Slice steak across grain; pass mushroom sauce. Serves 4.

Ann Aldrich Logue

SPIZZADETZA

1 bunch fresh parsley
1 3-pound flank steak or sirloin
    steak
4 tablespoons olive oil, divided
1 pound fresh mushrooms, sliced

2 or more garlic cloves, minced
Salt and pepper to taste
1-2 cups water
Cooked spaghetti
Freshly grated Parmesan cheese

Wash parsley; leave each sprig whole but remove stalks; set aside. Partially freeze steak, cut into thin strips against the grain; set aside. In a heavy pot heat 2 tablespoons olive oil until it smokes. Add steak a little at a time and brown very well. Add mushrooms and garlic; sauté a few minutes. Add all the fresh parsley and salt and pepper. Stir 1 minute and add water and remaining 2 tablespoons olive oil. Cook over low heat for at least 3-4 hours, adding water and oil if needed (it will probably take 2-3 cups of water). Serve over spaghetti with lots of cheese and a salad and bread. Serves 4-6.

Laura Darnell (Mrs. Douglas)

PEPPER STEAK

1 pound sirloin
2 tablespoons butter or margarine
1 tablespoon paprika
1½ cups beef broth
1 cup chopped onions

2 green peppers, chopped
2 tablespoons cornstarch
¼ cup water
¼ cup soy sauce
2 tomatoes, cut in wedges

Slice meat crosswise of grain into thin strips, brown in butter; sprinkle with paprika. Add beef broth, cover and simmer 30 minutes. Stir in onions, green peppers and cook, covered, 5 minutes. Blend cornstarch, water and soy sauce; stir into mixture until clear and thick, about 2 minutes. Add tomatoes and stir gently. Serve over rice or thin noodles. Serves 6

Sharon Mathews (Mrs. Marion)

BEEF CANTONESE WITH GINGER RICE

¼ cup soy sauce
¼ cup cooking sherry
2 tablespoons sugar
¼ teaspoon cinnamon
2 pounds beef chuck, cut into
   ½-inch cubes

1½ cups water
2 tablespoons cornstarch
2 tablespoons cold water

Mix soy sauce, sherry, sugar, and cinnamon; marinate beef in mixture for 1 hour, stirring occasionally. Add 1½ cups water, cover and simmer (do not boil) for 1 hour until tender. Blend cornstarch and 2 tablespoons cold water, add to meat mixture and cook and stir until thickened. Serve over Ginger Rice (recipe below).

Ginger Rice

½ cup chopped green onions
3 tablespoons vegetable oil
2 tablespoons finely diced candied
   ginger

4 cups hot cooked rice

Cook green onions in hot oil for 1 minute. Add ginger and hot cooked rice; toss lightly.

Laura Darnell (Mrs. Douglas)

STEAK PARMIGIANA

½ cup all-purpose flour
½ cup shredded Cheddar cheese
(may need more)
6 serving size pieces of lean
cubed steak
1 egg, beaten
½ cup vegetable oil
1 6-ounce can tomato paste

1 garlic clove, minced
Salt and pepper to taste
2 cups boiling water
1 8-ounce package mozzarella
cheese
Hot cooked noodles, tossed with
poppy seeds and butter

Combine flour and Cheddar cheese; set aside. Dip steak into egg and coat with flour mixture; brown in hot oil. Place meat in a 2-quart baking dish. In same skillet used for meat, sauté onion in oil; stir in tomato paste, garlic, salt, pepper and hot water. Simmer for 10 minutes. Pour sauce over steaks and top with mozzarella cheese. Bake, covered, for 1 hour at 350°F. Serve over hot buttered noodles that have been tossed with poppy seeds.

Helen Hindsman (Mrs. Gordon)

BEEF SCALOPPINI MARSALA

2 ¾-pound beef top round
steaks, ¼-inch thick
1 egg
3 tablespoons milk
1¼ cups dry breadcrumbs
¼ cup grated Parmesan cheese
1 teaspoon salt
⅛ teaspoon pepper

¾ cup or more butter or margarine
1 garlic clove, sliced
¾ cup water
2 teaspoons all-purpose flour
½ cup Marsala wine
¼ cup minced parsley
1 beef bouillon cube

Pound each steak to ⅛-inch thickness. Cut into 4x2-inch pieces. In pie plate beat egg with milk. On waxed paper combine breadcrumbs, Parmesan, salt and pepper. Dip meat in egg mixture and coat with crumb mixture. In a skillet melt 2 tablespoons butter; cook garlic and meat until lightly browned. Discard garlic and remove meat; melt more butter in skillet. Mix water and flour and add Marsala, parsley, bouillon and cook until thickened; add meat and bake at 350°F. for ½ hour.

Lorraine Koenigs
Pella, Iowa

BEEF STIR FRY

½ pound round steak, partially
   frozen for easy slicing
2 tablespoons soy sauce
2 teaspoons sherry
8 teaspoons vegetable oil, divided
½ teaspoon sugar

Dash of ginger
½ cup sliced carrot
2 green onions, chopped
1 10-ounce package frozen Chinese
   pea pods
1 cup sliced fresh mushrooms

Thinly slice steak; set aside. Combine soy sauce, sherry, 2 teaspoons oil, sugar, ginger and pour over meat slices. Marinate for 10 minutes. Heat remaining 2 tablespoons oil in wok or skillet. Add vegetables and stir-fry for about 2 minutes until tender-crisp. Remove vegetables and set aside. Quickly stir-fry meat, about 30 seconds. Return vegetables to pan and toss with meat. Serve immediately over cooked rice. Serves 2.

Anne Hull

STEAK KABOBS

2 pounds round or sirloin steak,
   1½-inches thick
Meat tenderizer
½ cup dry white wine
½ cup catsup
1 tablespoon prepared mustard
1 tablespoon Worcestershire sauce
1 garlic clove, minced
½ teaspoon whole rosemary
2 tablespoons firmly packed brown
   sugar

2 tablespoons vinegar
12 cherry tomatoes
1 4-ounce can mushroom caps,
   drained, or fresh mushrooms
1 green pepper, cut into 1½-inch
   strips
1 1-pound can boiled whole onions
   or fresh onions quartered

Cut meat into 1½-inch cubes; sprinkle with meat tenderizer (for round steak only) as directed on package. Marinate meat in mixture of next 8 ingredients and refrigerate for several hours. Put meat and vegetables alternately on skewers. Brush with marinade. Place on grill for 8-10 minutes, turning frequently. Heat remaining marinade and serve with kabobs. Serves 4-6.

Forrest Stewart (Mrs. Richard)

BEEF WITH CHINESE BROCCOLI

Vegetable oil
1 pound sirloin steak, cut into
thin strips
1 10-ounce package frozen
broccoli cuts, thawed
2 teaspoons soy sauce
½ teaspoon sugar

Dash of pepper
2 tablespoons sherry
1 teaspoon grated ginger
1 garlic clove, finely chopped
½ cup chicken broth
1 tablespoon cornstarch
1½-2 cups water

Heat a little oil in skillet; stir-fry meat then remove meat. Add a little more oil and broccoli; combine seasonings and chicken broth and add to pan. Cook until broccoli is tender. Add beef; thicken with cornstarch and water. Serves 5.

Martha Coleman White

STROGANOFF STEAK SANDWICH

⅔ cup beer
⅓ cup vegetable oil
1½ teaspoons salt, divided
¼ teaspoon garlic powder
¼ teaspoon pepper
2 pounds flank steak, 1-inch thick

2 tablespoons butter or margarine
½ teaspoon paprika
4 cups sliced onions
12 slices French bread, toasted
1 cup sour cream, warmed
½ teaspoon prepared horseradish

Combine beer, oil, 1 teaspoon salt, garlic powder and pepper. Pour over steak. Cover and refrigerate overnight or let stand at room temperature; drain. Broil 3 inches from heat for 5-7 minutes each side for medium rare. In saucepan, melt butter; blend in paprika and remaining salt. Add onion, sauté until tender but not brown. Thinly slice meat on the diagonal across grain. Arrange some meat slices over 2 slices of bread for each serving. Top with onions. Combine sour cream and horseradish and spoon on top of each sandwich. Serves 6.

Terry Rissier (Mrs. Henry)
Naperville, Illinois

PÂTÉ EN CROÛTE

Pastry

3 cups all-purpose flour
1½ teaspoons salt
1¼ cups frozen butter

¼ cup frozen vegetable shortening
½-¾ cup ice water

Place flour and salt in work bowl of food processor; process 2-3 seconds. Add butter and shortening which have been cut into ½-inch pieces. Process 2-3 seconds until butter is just cut in. Add ½ cup ice water. Turn machine on; if mixture seems dry, add more water by tablespoons. Process until dough just begins to mass on the blades. Chill 2 hours.

Filling

1 garlic clove, peeled
1 large onion, quartered
3 large ribs celery
1 large green pepper
1½ pounds extra lean beef

1 pound mild sausage
1 6-ounce can tomato paste
2 teaspoons salt
Pepper to taste

Place steel blade in work bowl of food processor. With machine running, drop in garlic and process until minced. Add onion and chop finely; transfer to mixing bowl. Chop celery and green pepper finely; add to onion. Chop meat in 2 batches, not too finely. Add to vegetables; add remaining ingredients to mixing bowl and mix thoroughly.

To assemble

Roll dough into a rectangle. Place filling in center of pastry; fold ends over, then fold sides over top. Pinch edges to seal. Place on ungreased baking sheet, seam side down. Decorate with pastry scraps and pierce 2 or 3 holes in the top of the loaf to allow steam to escape. Brush with beaten egg. Bake at 425°F. for 30 minutes; reduce heat to 325°F. and bake 1 hour longer or until meat thermometer registers 165°F. Let stand 15 minutes before serving.

Hannelore Holland (Mrs. William)

BUSY DAY BARBECUE

3 cups shredded cooked beef
½ cup chopped celery
1 medium onion, chopped
2 tablespoons butter or margarine
2 tablespoons vinegar
2 tablespoons firmly packed brown
 sugar

1 cup catsup
½ teaspoon prepared mustard
4 teaspoons lemon juice
½ teaspoon red pepper (optional)
½ cup water
Salt and pepper to taste

Sauté beef, celery and onion in butter; set aside. In another pan combine remaining ingredients and bring to a boil. Add to meat mixture and simmer slowly for 1 hour. Very good on toasted hamburger buns.

Jean Lee (Mrs. Gary)

EASY-WAY SAUERBRATEN

1 3-pound boneless chuck roast
½ cup wine vinegar
1 bay leaf, crumbled
1 garlic clove, minced or crushed

Dash of pepper
1 1⅛-ounce package onion soup
 mix
2-4 ginger snaps, crushed

Arrange a large sheet of heavy-duty aluminum foil in a shallow baking pan. Place meat in center of foil. Pour vinegar over roast, sprinkle with bay leaf, garlic and pepper. Bring foil up over meat, overlapping it; let stand at room temperature for 30 minutes. Open foil and sprinkle with onion soup mix, coating all sides. Close foil, sealing edges with a double fold. Bake at 325°F. for 3 hours. Remove from oven; transfer meat to serving platter or carving board. Strain drippings into a saucepan, skim off fat. To make gravy add crushed ginger snaps to drippings; cook until smooth and thick, stirring constantly. Serve gravy over roast. Serves 6-8.

Karon Wakstein (Mrs. Gary)

PICADILLO

2 medium onions, diced
2 large green peppers, diced
2 garlic cloves, minced or
½ teaspoon garlic powder
2 tablespoons olive oil
1½ pounds ground beef
¼ teaspoon oregano
½ teaspoon salt
¼ teaspoon pepper
½ teaspoon celery salt

2 tablespoons Worcestershire sauce
1 8-ounce can tomato sauce
1 16-ounce can whole tomatoes,
broken up
1 4-ounce jar pimento stuffed
olives, drained
½ cup raisins or to taste
1 10-ounce package yellow rice,
cooked according to package
directions

In large skillet sauté onion, peppers and garlic in oil; remove and set aside. Sauté ground beef in same skillet; drain well. Return vegetable mixture to beef, add all remaining ingredients except rice, and simmer, covered for 30 minutes. Serve over cooked yellow rice. May be made ahead. Serves 6.

Karon Wakstein (Mrs. Gary)

ITALIAN MEATLOAF

2 pounds ground beef
½ teaspoon thyme
10 tablespoons fine dry
breadcrumbs, divided
1 egg
1 4-ounce can sliced mushrooms,
drained and liquid reserved
Water (optional)

½ teaspoon garlic powder
⅔ teaspoon salt
5 slices bacon
1 teaspoon parsley flakes
⅔ teaspoon oregano
1 medium onion, diced
1 cup shredded mozzarella cheese
2 15-ounce can tomato sauce

In a bowl combine ground beef, thyme, breadcrumbs, egg, ½ cup reserved mushroom liquid (add water to make ½ cup if necessary), garlic powder and salt. Mix thoroughly, cover and refrigerate until needed. In a small skillet fry bacon; drain and reserve bacon fat and crumble bacon. Put meat mixture in a 12x8-inch rectangle on a sheet of waxed paper. Drizzle reserved bacon fat over meat. Sprinkle meat with garlic powder, salt, parsley, oregano and 2 tablespoons breadcrumbs. Leaving a ½-inch border, scatter crumbled bacon, onion, mushrooms and cheese over meat. Starting with short side and using the waxed paper as a guide, roll up meat jelly-roll style to contain mixture. Place roll, seam side down, in a 13x9x2-inch pan. Pour tomato sauce over meat roll. Bake at 350°F. for 30 minutes. Cover with foil and bake 30 minutes more. Serves 6-8.

Kim Blackwell (Mrs. Ken)

CALIFORNIA MEAT AND VEGETABLE DISH

3 ribs celery, chopped
1 green pepper, chopped
2 medium zucchini, chopped
1 large onion, chopped

2-3 pounds blade cut chuck roast
  or stew beef, cubed
2 15-ounce cans tomatoes
Buttered noodles

Place vegetables with meat in a large pan or Dutch oven. Cover and cook 2½ hours at 325°F. Near end of the cooking time, add canned tomatoes; serve with buttered noodles.

Judith Laird (Mrs. Richard)

BEEF MEXICANA
Quick and easy.

1 large onion, chopped
2 tablespoons vegetable oil
1 pound ground beef
2 8-ounce cans tomato sauce
1 16-ounce can whole kernel corn,
  drained

¾ teaspoon salt
⅛ teaspoon pepper
Chili powder to taste

Sauté onion in skillet with oil. Add ground beef and brown lightly, stirring to break it up. Add tomato sauce, corn and seasonings. Cover and simmer 20-30 minutes. Serve with cooked rice and slices of green pepper.

Bette Vetland (Mrs. Ted)

BURRITO PIE

¼ cup vegetable oil
4 8-inch flour tortillas
½ pound ground beef
1 small onion, diced
½ teaspoon garlic salt
1 4-ounce can green chilies,
  drained and chopped

1 8-ounce can refried beans
⅓ cup mild taco sauce
2 cups shredded Monterey Jack
  cheese
1 cup shredded Cheddar cheese
1 cup shredded lettuce
1 large tomato, diced

In a small skillet heat oil and lightly brown tortillas, 1 at a time; set aside. Cook ground beef and onion until browned then remove from heat. Stir in garlic, chilies, beans and taco sauce. In a 9-inch pie plate place 1 tortilla, top with ¼ of meat mixture and ¼ of cheese; repeat with remaining tortillas. Bake at 350°F. for 30 minutes. Sprinkle with shredded lettuce and diced tomato. Serves 6.

Sharon Mathews (Mrs. Marion)

CHILI-BREAD MIXER

2 pounds ground beef
Salt
1½ tablespoons chili powder
1 4-ounce can green chilies
1 1⅜-ounce package onion
  soup mix

1 8-ounce can tomato sauce
1 cup beer
1 20-ounce can kidney beans,
  drained
1 8½-ounce package cornbread mix
1 cup shredded Cheddar cheese

Brown ground beef in skillet; add salt to taste. Drain excess grease. Add chili powder, chilies, soup mix that has been mixed with tomato sauce and beer. Simmer for about 20 minutes; add kidney beans. Prepare cornbread mix according to package directions; add cheese. Spoon onto ground beef mixture and bake, uncovered, at 400°F. for 20 minutes or until golden. May be prepared and served in cast iron skillet. May also be prepared ahead of time, adding cornbread mixture to warmed mixture at the last minute. Let stand for easy serving.

Nancy Wyatt (Mrs. Terrance)

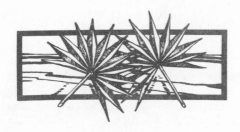

ENCHILADAS

1½ pounds ground beef
1 onion, chopped
1 7½-ounce can beef taco filling
2 10-ounce cans mild or hot
  enchilada sauce

3-4 cups shredded Monterey Jack cheese
10-12 flour tortillas

Brown meat and onion; drain. Add taco filling, 5 ounces (½ can) sauce, and about half the cheese. Heat until cheese melts and ingredients are well-blended. To assemble enchiladas, pour some sauce into a plate and dip tortillas into sauce. Put a little meat mixture on tortilla and roll. Place rolled tortillas into a greased baking dish. Pour remainder of sauce over tortillas and cover with remaining cheese. Bake at 325°F. for 25 minutes. May be made ahead of time. Serves 10.

Barbara Almond (Mrs. Donald J.)

EASY CHILI ENCHILADAS
A quick dish!

14 frozen tortillas
3 16-ounce cans chili without
  beans

2 large onions, chopped
2 cups shredded Cheddar cheese

Steam tortillas until they are pliable. Spread about 2 tablespoons chili on each tortilla. Add about 1 teaspoon onion and 1 teaspoon cheese on top of chili and roll up. Place filled tortillas in a large baking dish. Cover with remaining chili and bake at 350°F. for 20 minutes; remove from oven and sprinkle with cheese. Bake another 15 minutes or until cheese is bubbly. Serves 6-8.

Ann Bane (Mrs. Curtis)

BRISKET

1 beef brisket
½ cup soy sauce
½ cup Worcestershire sauce
¾ bottle liquid smoke, divided
Salt

Pepper
Garlic salt
⅔ bottle hickory smoked barbecue
  sauce

Marinate brisket in mixture of soy sauce, Worcestershire, ½ bottle liquid smoke, salt, pepper and garlic salt to taste for 24 hours, turning after 12 hours. Drain and place, fat side down, in pan. Add barbecue sauce and ¼ bottle liquid smoke. Bake, covered, at 350°F for 3½ hours, turning after 2½ hours; increase temperature to 375°F. for 45 minutes more.

Amy Armstrong (Mrs. Larry)

SUPER EASY BRISKET

1 beef brisket
Salt and pepper
1 1⅛-ounce package onion soup
  mix

½ 12-ounce bottle chili sauce
1 12-ounce can beer

Salt and pepper brisket; place in baking pan. Sprinkle onion soup mix over meat. Add chili sauce and ½ the beer on top of meat; the other half around meat. Cover with foil. Bake at 325°F. 4-5 hours. Slice on diagonal and serve with pan gravy.

Patricia Kiernan (Mrs. Don E.)

MOUSSAKA

Meat Sauce

2 tablespoons butter or margarine, divided
1 cup finely chopped onion
1½ pounds ground beef chuck or lamb
1 garlic clove, crushed
½ teaspoon dried oregano leaves

1 teaspoon dried basil leaves
½ teaspoon cinnamon
1 teaspoon salt
Dash of pepper
2 8-ounce cans tomato sauce
4 4-ounce eggplants

In a 3½-quart Dutch oven melt 2 tablespoons butter; sauté onion, ground beef and garlic, stirring until brown, about 10 minutes. Add herbs, spices, tomato sauce; bring to a boil, stirring. Reduce heat, simmer uncovered for ½ hour. Cut unpared eggplant in half lengthwise; slice crosswise ½-inch thick. Place in bottom of a broiler pan, sprinkle lightly with salt and brush lightly with remaining melted butter. Broil 4 inches from heat, 4 minutes per side or until golden brown.

Cream Sauce

2 tablespoons butter or margarine
2 tablespoons all-purpose flour
½ teaspoon salt

Dash of pepper
2 cups milk
2 eggs

In medium saucepan melt butter. Remove from heat; stir in flour, salt and pepper. Add milk gradually. Bring to a boil, stirring, until mixture is thickened. Remove from heat. In small bowl beat eggs with wire whisk. Beat in some hot cream sauce mixture, return mixture to saucepan; mix well and set aside.

Casserole

Meat Sauce
½ cup grated Parmesan cheese, divided
½ cup shredded Cheddar cheese, divided

2 tablespoons dry breadcrumbs
Cream Sauce

In bottom of a shallow 2-quart baking dish, layer half of eggplant, overlapping slightly; sprinkle with 2 tablespoons Parmesan and 2 tablespoons Cheddar cheese. Stir breadcrumbs into Meat Sauce; spoon evenly over eggplant in casserole; then sprinkle with 2 tablespoons each Parmesan and Cheddar cheese. Layer rest of eggplant slices, overlapping as before. Pour Cream Sauce over all. Sprinkle top with remaining cheese. Bake at 350°F. for 35-40 minutes or until golden brown, and top is set. If desired, brown top a little more under broiler for 1 minute. Cool slightly to serve. Cut into squares. May be baked a day ahead, refrigerated and reheated in time for serving. Serves 12.

Georgia Dake (Mrs. James L.)

ITALIAN STUFFED PEPPERS

1 pound ground beef
½ teaspoon garlic salt
Salt and pepper
2 10-ounce cans tomato puree
1 cup thinly sliced celery
1 cup thinly sliced green onions

1 cup cooked rice
1 egg
8-10 green peppers
Buttered bread crumbs (recipe
  below

Brown ground beef; add garlic salt and salt and pepper to taste. Add tomato puree, celery and green onion; simmer for 20 minutes. Then add cooked rice to meat sauce. Beat egg slightly and add to mixture; set aside. Clean green peppers-cut tops off and remove seeds. Place peppers in boiling water and cook 5 minutes; drain immediately and cool. Stuff peppers with meat mixture and top with Buttered Breadcrumbs. Bake at 425°F. for 15-20 minutes.

Buttered Breadcrumbs

1 cup breadcrumbs
¼ cup melted butter or margarine

½ teaspoon garlic salt
2 teaspoons parsley

Toss together all ingredients; set aside.

Ann Russo (Mrs. Bruno)

MOLASSES BEEF STEW

3 tablespoons all-purpose flour
1 teaspoon salt
½ teaspoon celery salt
¼ teaspoon pepper
½ teaspoon ground ginger
3 pounds beef chuck or stew beef,
  cubed
2 tablespoons vegetable oil

1 15-ounce can tomatoes
3 medium onions, sliced
⅓ cup red wine vinegar
½ cup molasses
½ cup water
6-8 cooked carrots
½ cup raisins
Hot cooked rice

Combine first 6 ingredients in a bag; shake to coat beef, brown beef in oil. Add next 5 ingredients; bring to a boil, cover and simmer 2 hours. Add carrots and raisins, heat through. Serve over rice. Good with corn bread.

Mimi Bozarth (Mrs. John)

MANICOTTI

Tomato Sauce

⅓ cup chopped onion
½ cup chopped green pepper
8 ounces fresh mushrooms, sliced
2 garlic cloves, minced
1 tablespoon olive oil
½ pound mild sausage
½ pound ground round steak
1 15-ounce can tomatoes,
   undrained
1 6-ounce can tomato paste
⅜ cup red wine

1 tablespoon parsley, minced
1½ teaspoons salt
½ teaspoon vinegar
½ teaspoon chili powder
½ teaspoon oregano
½ teaspoon pepper
¼ teaspoon Italian seasoning
¼ teaspoon cinnamon
Dash of curry powder
½ bay leaf

Sauté onion, green pepper, mushrooms and garlic in oil in heavy skillet. In separate pan cook sausage and ground round; drain well and add to vegetables with remaining ingredients; mix well and simmer 2 hours.

Cheese Filling

3 cups large curd cottage cheese
2 cups shredded mozzarella
   cheese
¾ cup freshly grated Parmesan
   cheese

2 eggs
1 tablespoon minced parsley
½ teaspoon oregano
Salt and pepper to taste

Mix cheeses, eggs, parsley, oregano and salt and pepper. Blend well and set aside.

Noodles

1 package manicotti shells
1 tablespoon salt

5 quarts water

Slowly add manicotti shells to rapidly boiling, salted water. Cook 6 minutes until half done. Rinse in cold water and hold in water to prevent noodles from sticking together. Stuff shells quickly with cheese filling. Cover the bottom of a 13x9-inch pan with some of the Tomato Sauce and arrange stuffed shells in a single layer over sauce. Cover the shells with remaining sauce. Sprinkle additional Parmesan cheese on top if desired and bake, covered, at 325°F. for 45-60 minutes.

Mary Louise Moyer (Mrs. Walter)
Pensacola, Florida

211

BAKED PASTITSIO

Meat Sauce

2 pounds lean ground beef chuck	1 cup boiling water
¼ cup butter or margarine	2 teaspoons cinnamon
2 large onions, finely chopped	Salt and pepper to taste
1 6-ounce can tomato paste	2 eggs, well-beaten

Sauté ground beef over high heat for 15 minutes. Add butter and onions, continue to brown for 15 minutes, stirring often. Blend tomato paste with water. Add to meat mixture with cinnamon. Salt and pepper to taste. Cover and cook 15 minutes over medium heat. Add more water if needed. Uncover and cook 10 minutes until thick, stirring occasionally. Skim off as much collected fat as possible and discard. Remove from heat and cool. Add well-beaten eggs and mix well.

Pastitsio

1½ pounds thin spaghetti	1 10-ounce package sharp
Boiling water	Cheddar cheese, shredded
Salt	Meat Sauce (recipe above)
½ cup butter or margarine,	Cream Sauce (recipe below)
melted	Cinnamon
2 eggs, well beaten	

Cook spaghetti in rapidly boiling water for 10 minutes. Drain well in colander. Put spaghetti in bowl, add melted butter and beaten eggs. Mix thoroughly. Arrange half the spaghetti in bottom of an 11x14-inch baking dish. Sprinkle with half the cheese; spread and pat firmly Meat Sauce over this. Arrange remaining spaghetti over Meat Sauce and sprinkle with remaining cheese; top with Cream Sauce. If desired, add more cheese and sprinkle lightly with cinnamon.

Cream Sauce

6 tablespoons butter or	3 cups heated milk
margarine	Salt to taste
¼ cup all-purpose flour	2 eggs, well-beaten

Melt butter in top of a double boiler; blend in flour and gradually add heated milk. Stir until mixture is smooth and thick. Salt to taste. Add beaten eggs very slowly, stirring so they won't cook. Spread sauce over Pastitsio.

Bake at 400°F. for 30 minutes. Cool for 15 minutes before serving. Cut into squares. Serves about 16.

Eleanor Lewis (Mrs. Mack)

REUBEN CASSEROLE

1 27-ounce can sauerkraut,
well-drained
1 large tomato, sliced
¼ cup thousand island salad
dressing

2 cups corned beef, sliced or
cubed
2 cups Swiss cheese, shredded
¼ cup crushed croutons or crackers
¼ teaspoon caraway seed (optional)

In a 8 or 9-inch square baking dish, layer ingredients in order given. Bake, un-covered, at 425°F. about 20 minutes or until hot and bubbly. May microwave on high power 10-12 minutes until bubbly. Double and bake in 13x9-inch pan.

Annette Trujillo (Mrs. Pat)

REUBEN ON RYE

2 packages corned beef, slivered
3 cups Swiss cheese, shredded
1 10½-ounce can sauerkraut,
drained
½ cup bottled oil and vinegar
salad dressing

1 tablespoon caraway seeds
1 teaspoon dark mustard
Seasoned rye crackers or
toasted rye bread

Stir together corned beef, cheese, sauerkraut and remaining ingredients except bread. Heat until bubbly hot, about 15 minutes. Serve in chafing dish with seasoned rye crackers or on toasted rye bread. If desired, top with crushed potato chips. Serves 4-6.

Frances Mozley (Mrs. Hugh)
Nancy Wyatt (Mrs. Terrance)

COMPANY SCRAMBLED EGG CASSEROLE

1 cup cubed ham
7 tablespoons butter or margarine,
  divided
1 dozen eggs, beaten

Cheese Sauce (recipe below)
2¼ cups bread cubes
Paprika

Sauté ham in 3 tablespoons butter. Add eggs and cook over medium heat until set. Stir in Cheese Sauce. Place eggs in greased 13x9x2-inch glass baking dish. Combine remaining melted butter and bread cubes. Spread over egg mixture. Sprinkle with paprika. Cover and chill overnight. Uncover and bake at 350°F. for 30 minutes.

Cheese Sauce

2 tablespoons butter or margarine
2½ tablespoons all-purpose flour
½ teaspoon salt

⅛ teaspoon pepper
2 cups milk
1 cup shredded Cheddar cheese

Melt butter over medium heat. Blend in flour, salt, and pepper; cook 1 minute. Gradually add milk. Cover over medium heat until thickened, stirring constantly. Add cheese and continue stirring until cheese melts. Serves 8-10.

Jean Pitts (Mrs. Reynold E.)

QUICHE CORDON BLEU

½ pound bacon, cooked crisp and
  crumbled
3 ounces ham
1½ cups diced or shredded Swiss
  cheese
1 10-inch baked pastry shell,
  cooled
4 eggs, well-beaten

1 cup whipping cream
1 cup light cream
1 tablespoon all-purpose flour
¾ teaspoon salt
Dash of nutmeg
Dash of white pepper
4 green onion tops, diced and
  sautéed

Alternate bacon, ham and cheese in pastry shell. Combine eggs, cream and remaining ingredients; pour into pastry shell. Bake at 375°F. for 10 minutes; reduce heat to 350°F. and bake about 30 minutes or until firm.

Mrs. James Fuller Holly, Jr.
Orlando, Florida

CHEDDAR SWISS HAM QUICHE

½ cup diced green pepper
1 medium onion, diced
2 tablespoons butter or margarine
1 cup sliced mushrooms (optional)
2 tablespoons dry breadcrumbs
1 cup shredded Cheddar cheese
½ cup shredded Swiss cheese
½ cup chopped ham (optional)
Bacon, cooked and crumbled
    (optional)

5 eggs
½ cup mayonnaise
½ cup light cream
2 tablespoons minced parsley
1 teaspoon Dijon mustard
½ teaspoon salt
¼ teaspoon pepper
1 9-inch baked pastry shell,
    cooled

Sauté onion and green pepper (and mushrooms, if using) in butter until onion is tender. Sprinkle breadcrumbs in bottom of pastry shell. Add cheeses and optional ingredients if desired. Mix remaining ingredients until blended. Pour into pastry shell; bake at 375°F. for 30-35 minutes or until a knife inserted in center comes out clean. May be frozen.

Karon Wakstein (Mrs. Gary)

HOT HAM AND CHEESE SANDWICHES

12 slices bread, white or whole
    wheat
Butter or margarine
½ pound diced ham
½ pound shredded sharp Cheddar
    cheese

4 eggs, separated
3 cups milk
Salt and pepper to taste

Remove crusts from bread; butter one side of each slice. Lay 6 bread slices, buttered side down in a 13x9x2-inch baking dish that has been sprayed with non-stick coating. Sprinkle evenly with the ham followed by the cheese. Top with remaining 6 slices of bread, buttered side up. Beat together egg yolks and milk. Beat egg whites until stiff, fold into milk mixture. Pour over assembled sandwiches slowly, allowing the mixture to soak in. Cover and refrigerate overnight. Remove from refrigerator 45 minutes prior to baking. Bake, uncovered, at 350°F. for 45 minutes or until golden brown. Freezes well. Serves 6.

Variation: If in a hurry, omit crust removal, beat whole eggs with milk-not quite as pretty but tastes just as good!

Henryetta Groce (Mrs. A.L)

HAM RING

2 tablespoons butter or margarine
½ cup minced onion
1 cup finely diced celery
1 pound ground cooked ham
1 pound ground pork, uncooked

2 eggs
½ cup mayonnaise
2 tablespoons prepared mustard
2 cups soft breadcrumbs

Melt butter in skillet and add onion and celery. Cook until tender. Combine with remaining ingredients in a large bowl; mix thoroughly. Press into a 6½-cup oiled ring mold. Unmold into shallow baking pan. Bake at 375°F. for 1 hour. Top with sauce if desired. Serves 6-8.

Optional Sauce

1 10¾-ounce can cream of
mushroom soup

1 cup shredded sharp Cheddar cheese
⅓ cup milk

Combine soup and milk in a saucepan; heat and stir in cheese until melted.

Patricia Speh (Mrs. Charles)
Buckinghamshire, England

ROAST LEG OF LAMB WITH HERBS

1 6-pound oven-ready leg of lamb
   roast
2 small garlic cloves
½ teaspoon thyme leaves, crushed
1 teaspoon rosemary leaves, crushed
1 teaspoon salt
½ teaspoon freshly ground pepper
2 tablespoons all-purpose flour

¼ cup tarragon vinegar
½ cup water
2 or more medium onions, peeled
   (leave whole)
2 carrots, scraped and sliced
2 ribs of celery
1 cup dry red wine

Place lamb in roasting pan. Cut garlic into slivers and insert randomly into lamb using point of sharp knife. Mix together thyme, rosemary, salt, pepper and flour; rub this mixture well into lamb. Pour mixture of tarragon vinegar and water over lamb. Roast for 1 hour at 350°F; lower temperature to 300°F. Remove from oven, scatter vegetables around and under lamb. Pour wine over all; return to oven, continue roasting for about 1¼ hours. Baste several times during final roasting. Discard celery; serve remaining vegetables around meat. May be served with mint jelly. Serves 8.

Ann Cook Humphreys

LAMB WITH HERBS

4 thick lamb chops
1 tablespoon vegetable oil
2 tablespoons unsalted butter or
  margarine
½ teaspoon fresh basil

½ teaspoon chives
½ teaspoon rosemary
2 cups heavy cream
Salt and freshly ground pepper

Sauté the chops in a large heavy skillet with oil and 1 tablespoon butter for 2-3 minutes per side. (Cook 4-5 minutes if chops are large and thick.) Set aside on warmed platter. Sauté basil, chives and rosemary in remaining 1 tablespoon butter for ½ minute. Add cream and reduce to ½ volume. Season to taste with salt and freshly ground pepper. Pour over lamb and serve at once. Serves 4.

Dee Redding (Mrs. Ben)

BARBECUED PORK ROAST

1 5-pound pork shoulder roast
½ cup catsup
1 10¾-ounce can tomato soup,
  undiluted
½ cup sugar
1⅓ cups water

⅓ cup vinegar
10 bay leaves
10 whole cloves, or 1 tablespoon
  ground cloves
Salt and pepper to taste

Place pork roast in a broiler pan lined with foil; bake at 325°F. about 3½ hours. Combine remaining ingrediets to make a sauce. Drain all fat from pan, add the sauce and bake until sauce thickens, basting frequently. Serves 8.

Wanda Maitland (Mrs. William W.)

MARINATED BONELESS PORK

1 3-3½ pound boneless pork butt
2 tablespoons hoisin sauce
¼ cup catsup
¼ cup sugar

1 teaspoon salt
1 tablespoon soy sauce
¼ teaspoon saltpeter

Cut pork butt into 4x2x1-inch strips. Mix remaining ingredients and rub over pork pieces. Marinate at least 4 hours or overnight. Line roasting pan with foil and place pork on roasting rack. Roast at 375°F. about 45 minutes, turning once or twice during baking.

Rose Marie LeBarr

PORK TENDERLOIN SCALLOPS

1 1½-pound pork tenderloin, cut
  into ½-inch slices
All-purpose flour
2-3 tablespoons butter or
  margarine
1 beef bouillon cube

½ cup water
½ cup white wine
Salt and pepper

Flour pork slices lightly and sauté in butter over medium high heat about 3 minutes per side. Reduce heat and add bouillon dissolved in water and wine. Simmer for about 10-15 minutes over low heat. Season as desired with salt and pepper. Serves 4.

Laurie Combs (Mrs. Sam)

MARINATED GRILLED PORK CHOPS

8-10 boneless pork chops
Hickory smoked salt
Lemon and pepper seasoning
Garlic powder
¼ cup red wine vinegar

3 tablespoons water
½ cup vegetable oil
1 1⅜-ounce package Italian
  salad dressing mix

Sprinkle both sides of pork chops lightly with hickory smoked salt, lemon and pepper seasoning and garlic powder. Combine vinegar, water, oil and salad dressing mix and shake well. Place pork chops in baking dish and cover with marinade sauce. Marinate at least 2 hours or overnight in refrigerator. Cook slowly on grill, about 45 minutes turning occasionally and basting with marinade.

Linda Harrison (Mrs. Franklin)

GRILLED BOSTON BUTT

1 Boston Butt
¼ cup salt

¾ cup vinegar

Mix salt and vinegar together to use as a baste. Cook 30 minutes per pound over indirect heat on grill. Baste often.

Twedell Wilson (Mrs. Kyser)

PORC EN BALON

Adapted from an old English recipe.

1 4-pound blade of pork, boned

Stuffing

4 ounces bulk sausage
2 ounces cooked ham, cut in
   match sticks
1 rib celery, finely chopped
Yolks of 3 hard-cooked eggs,
   mashed

2 gherkin pickles
1 teaspoon dried sage
Juice and rind of 1 lemon
Salt and pepper to taste

In a bowl mix all ingredients well; stuff the boned pork with mixture, secure with skewer and string. Roast at 375°F. for 30 minutes per pound. Serve with sauce. Serves 8.

Sauce

3 ounces onion, finely chopped
1 teaspoon dried sage
½ ounce butter or margarine
2 teaspoons whole-grain mustard

1 handful chopped parsley
Juice and grated rind of 2 oranges
10 ounces chicken stock
Salt and pepper

Cook the onion and sage gently in the butter until onion is soft. Add mustard, parsley, orange juice and rind and stock. Bring to a boil and simmer for 2-3 minutes; season with salt and pepper.

Patricia Speh (Mrs. Charles)
Buckinghamshire, England

QUICK ROAST PORK

1 1½-pound pork tenderloin
2 tablespoons soy sauce
2 tablespoons hoisin sauce
2 tablespoons vegetable oil

1 teaspoon salt
1½ teaspoons sugar
2 tablespoons butter or margarine

Marinate tenderloin in soy sauce, hoisin sauce, oil, salt and sugar for at least 2 hours in refrigerator. Place meat on roasting rack at 500°F. for 9 minutes. Turn meat, roast 9 minutes more. Slice meat across the grain into thin slices. Add butter to pan drippings. Drizzle over meat.

Somethin's Cooking Cooking School

ROAST HOLIDAY TENDERLOIN OF PORK

Pork Tenderloin
All-purpose flour
Butter or margarine
Rosemary

Salt
Pepper
Garlic salt or garlic powder
Cumberland Sauce (recipe below)

Lightly flour tenderloin and brown in sauté pan with melted butter to sear in natural juices of meat. Remove from pan and place on rack in baking pan. Top with seasonings and bake at 350°F. as necessary until pork is done. Remove from oven and allow to cool slightly before slicing. Slice tenderloin into thin medallions and top with ribbon of Cumberland Sauce.

Cumberland Sauce

Grated rind of 2 lemons plus juice
   to taste
Grated rind of 2 oranges plus
   juice to taste
2 tablespoons powdered sugar

2 tablespoons Dijon
   mustard
1 cup melted red currant jelly
2 tablespoons port wine
Water (optional)

Combine and blend well all ingredients except water. If the jelly is too stiff, it may be diluted over heat with 1-4 tablespoons of hot water. When sauce has right consistency, lace a ribbon of sauce over sliced tenderloin. Serve at once.

Robert Neubert

LEMON PORK CHOPS AND RICE
Quick and easy.

6 pork chops
Garlic salt
Seasoned salt
Coarsely ground pepper

2 tablespoons vegetable oil
1 lemon, sliced
Water
1¼ cups raw rice

Sprinkle pork chops on both sides with seasonings and brown well in oil. Place lemon slices on tops of pork chops, add water to cover. Simmer about 35 minutes. Remove pork chops from skillet leaving 3 cups liquid in pan. Lemon slices should also remain. Add rice, cover and simmer for 25-30 minutes. Pork chops may be returned to skillet for reheating. Serves 3-4.

Carol Mizell (Mrs. Herb)

PORK CHOP DINNER

4-6 pork chops
Seasoned all-purpose flour
2-3 tablespoons vegetable oil
2 garlic cloves
1 onion, chopped
Salt and pepper to taste
Parsley to taste

Italian seasoning (optional)
1 15-ounce can tomatoes
1 16-ounce can sweet peas
½ pound cooked vermicelli or
    4 medium potatoes, peeled and
    cubed

Dredge pork chops in seasoned flour. Brown in oil in electric skillet or Dutch oven; set aside. Add garlic, onion, seasonings and tomatoes, scraping bottom of skillet. Break up tomatoes and simmer a few minutes. Return chops to skillet, baste with sauce and simmer 1-1½ hours, tightly covered. Check occasionally and add water if needed. The last 15 minutes add drained peas and potatoes if used. Salt slightly. Simmer until potatoes are tender. If using spaghetti, spoon sauce over it, top with a chop and sprinkle with Parmesan or mozzarella cheese. Serve with Italian bread for a complete meal. Serves 4-6.

Laura Darnell (Mrs. Douglas)

PORK CHOPS WITH CALVADOS SAUCE

6 loin pork chops, 1-inch thick
Salt and pepper to taste
6 tablespoons lightly salted
    butter or margarine
½ pound Gruyere cheese, shredded

3 tablespoons Dijon mustard
8 tablespoons whipping cream, divided
6 tablespoons calvados or
    applejack brandy
Finely chopped parsley to garnish

Season pork chops with salt and pepper. Melt butter in a skillet, add chops and brown on both sides. Save drippings. Place chops in a covered casserole and bake for 45 minutes at 350°F. Meanwhile mix cheese, mustard and 3 tablespoons cream. Spread this mixture on chops. Run chops with cheese under a preheated broiler until the top is lightly browned. Cook briefly over medium heat, scraping up all bits in the bottom of the skillet. Lower heat to simmer, add remaining cream and simmer for 3-5 minutes. Pour sauce over chops, garnish with parsley and serve.

Genie Lloyd (Mrs. Rayford, Jr.)

PORK CHOPS PARMESAN
Easy family recipe

1½ cups herb-seasoned stuffing mix
⅓ cup freshly grated Parmesan
  cheese
2 tablespoons minced parsley
½ garlic clove, minced

1 teaspoon salt
⅛ teaspoon pepper
6-8 center cut pork chops,
  ¾-inch thick
½ cup butter or margarine, melted

Mix together stuffing mix, Parmesan, parsley, garlic, salt and pepper. Dip pork chops in melted butter then in crumb mixture to coat well. Arrange on foil in pan, drizzle remaining melted butter over pork chops. Bake, uncovered, at 350°F. for 55-60 minutes. Adjust cooking time if chops are thinner.

Anda Gagnet (Mrs. Ted)

HAWAIIAN PORK CHOPS

6 pork chops, trimmed of fat
1 tablespoon all-purpose flour
1 teaspoon salt
Dash of pepper
2 tablespoons wine vinegar
½ cup pineapple syrup

¼ cup catsup
1 small onion, quartered
1 green pepper, cut into 1-inch
  squares
5 slices pineapple, cut into
  wedges

Coat meat with mixture of flour, salt and pepper. Brown chops in a greased skillet. Combine remaining ingredients; pour over the chops in skillet. Cover and simmer 45 minutes or until done. Serve with rice. Serves 6.

Bette Vetland (Mrs. Ted)

TEXAS STYLE RIBS

1 8-ounce can tomato sauce
2 tablespoons firmly packed dark
  brown sugar
2 tablespoons red wine vinegar
1 tablespoon Dijon mustard

1 garlic clove, minced
1 teaspoon Worcestershire sauce
⅛ teaspoon ground red pepper
4-6 pounds beef or pork ribs

Mix all ingredients except ribs in saucepan and simmer 10 minutes over moderately low heat; cool. Brush ribs with sauce and let stand at room temperature 1-2 hours. Cook on barbecue grill, covered, for 1 hour, turning once or twice and brushing with any extra sauce. Serves 4-6.

Anne Hull

COUNTRY RIBS WITH LUAU GLAZE

3 pounds country-style pork ribs
⅓ cup sugar
1½ tablespoons cornstarch
1 teaspoon salt
½ teaspoon ground ginger

¼ teaspoon pepper
⅔ cup water
⅓ cup lemon juice
¼ cup soy sauce
¼ cup Worcestershire sauce

Line a baking pan with foil and place ribs on rack over the foil. Bake ribs at 350°F. for 10 minutes, turn and bake 10 minutes more. While ribs bake, prepare the glaze. Mix sugar, cornstarch, salt, ginger and pepper in a small saucepan; stir in remaining ingredients. Cook over medium heat, stirring constantly, until mixture thickens and begins to simmer. Simmer 3 minutes, stirring frequently, then remove from heat. Brush ribs with a light coating of the glaze. Bake 50 minutes more, turning ribs and brushing lightly with the glaze about every 10 minutes until richly glazed.

Ann Bane (Mrs. Curtis)

DENVER SPAGHETTI

6 ounces spaghetti
2 eggs, beaten
¼ cup Parmesan cheese
1 8-ounce carton sour cream
1 6-ounce can tomato
   paste

2 tablespoons butter
½ cup chopped onion
1 pound Italian sausage
1 cup water
4 ounces mozzarella cheese
   cut in strips

Break 6 ounces spaghetti and cook according to package directions. Drain spaghetti; while warm combine spaghetti, 2 beaten eggs and ¼ cup Parmesan cheese. Place spaghetti mixture in a 10-inch greased pie plate.

Melt 2 tablespoons butter in a sauce pan. Add ½ cup chopped onions and sauté. Remove onions from heat. Combine ½ cup onions and 8 ounces sour cream. Spoon sour cream mixture over spaghetti. Remove casing from 1 pound Italian sausage. Crumble in sauce pan and brown. Drain grease. Add 1 6-ounce can tomato paste and 1 cup water. Simmer 10 minutes. Spoon this mixture over sour cream. Bake in 350°F. oven for 25 minutes. Remove from oven and arrange 4 ounces mozzarella cheese spoke fashion on top. Return to oven and let cheese melt. Serves 4-6.

Debbie Lane
Tucson, Arizona

SPAGHETTI CARBONARA

1 pound bacon, cut into pieces
1 1-pound package spaghetti
Salt and pepper to taste

1 teaspoon parsley flakes
¾ cup Parmesan cheese
6 eggs

Fry bacon and set aside. Cook spaghetti according to package directions. In a mixing bowl add salt, pepper, parsley and Parmesan to eggs and beat well. Drain cooked spaghetti and toss with bacon in pan with bacon drippings. Add egg-cheese mixture and toss again. Sprinkle with additional cheese. Serves 4.

Susan Siragusa (Mrs. Robert)

LASAGNA

1½ pounds sweet Italian sausage
1 garlic clove, crushed
1 20-ounce can Italian tomatoes
1 6-ounce can tomato paste
1 1⅛-ounce package onion soup
   mix
1 teaspoon salt
½ teaspoon basil

⅛ teaspoon pepper
½ package lasagna noodles
   (9 noodles)
1 tablespoon olive oil
2 eggs
4 cups ricotta or cottage cheese
4 cups shredded mozzarella cheese
½ cup grated Parmesan cheese

Remove sausage from casings, combine with garlic and just enough water to cover in a skillet; simmer 10 minutes or unti liquid evaporates; set aside. Break up tomatoes with a fork, combine with tomato paste, onion soup mix, salt, basil and pepper in a medium saucepan; cover and simmer 1 hour or until slightly thick; stir in sausages. Slide lasagna noodles, 1 at a time, so as not to break, into a large kettle of boiling salted water. Add olive oil (this keeps noodles from sticking). Cook until tender (not soft); drain, cover with cold water. Beat eggs and stir into ricotta or cottage cheese. Line bottom of an oiled 13x9x2-inch baking dish with noodles. Cover with ⅓ ricotta mixture, tomato sauce, mozzarella and Parmesan. Repeat to make 2 more layers. Bake at 350°F. for 30 minutes or until bubbly. Let stand about 15 minutes; cut into serving portions; lift out with a wide spatula. Leftovers may be frozen and reheated for another time. Serves 8 generously.

Chuck Braud

GINGER ALE SPAGHETTI SAUCE

1 pound ground beef
1 small onion, chopped
1 6-ounce can tomato paste
1 8-ounce can tomato sauce
1 15-ounce can stewed tomatoes

Pinch of oregano
1 cup ginger ale
⅓ teaspoon fennel
⅓ teaspoon basil
1 tablespoon parsley

Brown ground beef and onion; add other ingredients and simmer for 1 hour. Serve over cooked spaghetti. Serves 4.

Eunice Dake (Mrs. Gordon L.)
Mt. Dora, Florida

GARBAGE QUICHE

1 9-inch unbaked pastry shell
½ pound sausage, cooked and
  drained
Sliced mushrooms
Thinly sliced green pepper rings
Thinly sliced onion rings

Sliced tomatoes
Anything else you may have
3 eggs, beaten
1 cup milk or light cream
Shredded cheese of your choice

In an unbaked pastry shell layer all but eggs, milk and cheese. Mix together eggs and milk and pour over layers. Top with shredded cheese of your choice. Bake at 350°F. for 45 minutes on bottom shelf of oven.

Penny Quantz

SAUSAGE QUICHE

¾ pound pork sausage
½ cup chopped onion
⅓ cup chopped green pepper
1½ cups shredded sharp cheese
1 tablespoon all-purpose flour
1 10-inch deep dish pastry shell

2 eggs, beaten
1 cup evaporated milk
1 tablespoon parsley flakes
¾ teaspoon seasoned salt
¼ teaspoon garlic
¼ teaspoon pepper

Cook sausage in a skillet; remove sausage and drain on paper towels. Sauté onion and pepper in sausage drippings. Combine cheese and flour; add sausage, pepper and onion. Spread in pastry shell. Combine remaining ingredients and pour over pastry shell. Bake on a cookie sheet for 40-55 minutes at 375°F. until browned and filling is set.

Milton Acton

WILD RICE CASSEROLE

1 cup chopped onion
1 cup chopped celery
½ green pepper, chopped
2 tablespoons butter or margarine
1 cup cooked wild rice
2 tablespoons soy sauce

1 10¾-ounce can cream of
  mushroom soup
1 10¾-ounce can cream of
  chicken soup
1 pound bulk sausage, browned and
  drained

Sauté onion, celery, green pepper for 5 minutes in melted butter. Add all remaining ingredients together in casserole. Bake at 350°F. for 1 hour.

Lillian Dusseault

SAUSAGE CASSEROLE

6 slices white bread
2 pounds hot bulk sausage
12 eggs
2 cups milk
2 cups very sharp Cheddar cheese,
  shredded

1 teaspoon dry mustard
1 5.3-ounce can evaporated milk
1 10¾-ounce can cream of
  mushroom soup

Trim bread and cut into small pieces; layer in bottom of a buttered 13x9-inch casserole. Cook and drain sausage; beat eggs by hand and add sausage, milk, cheese and mustard. Pour over bread, cover and refrigerate overnight. Next day mix evaporated milk and soup together and pour over casserole. Bake at 300°F. for 1½ hours or until firm in the center. Serves 10-12.

Carol Crisp (Mrs. Don)

ITALIAN SAUSAGE

3 pounds ground pork butt
1 pound lean ground beef
Hot pepper to taste
Salt to taste

8 ounces Romano cheese
1 teaspoon anise
1 teaspoon fennel seeds
½ cup red wine

Mix all ingredients well and stuff into sausage skins or shape into patties and fry.

Somethin's Cookin' Cooking School

VEAL CUTLETS IN MUSHROOM AND CREAM SAUCE

Mushroom Cream Sauce

¼ cup chopped onion
¼ cup melted clarified butter
2 tablespoons all-purpose flour
½ cup chicken broth
Salt and pepper to taste
1 tablespoon lemon juice

Dash of hot pepper sauce
¼ cup Chablis wine
½ cup light cream
¼ cup thinly sliced mushrooms
¼ cup sour cream

Cook onion in butter until limp, add flour and cook a little longer but do not brown. Stir in chicken broth, salt and pepper, lemon juice, hot pepper sauce, wine and cream. Cook about 15 minutes over low heat. Add mushrooms and simmer a few more minutes. Remove from heat and stir in sour cream; set aside.

Veal

2 pounds veal cutlets, ¼-inch
  thick
1 cup lemon juice
All-purpose flour
Salt and pepper to taste
¼ cup melted clarified butter

¼ cup vegetable oil
1 cup sliced mushrooms
Mushroom Cream Sauce
½ cup light cream
1 ounce Chablis wine

Marinate veal in lemon juice for a few minutes. Pat dry. Dredge in flour and season with salt and pepper. Sauté in butter and oil until lightly brown on each side. Remove to a platter and keep warm. In the same pan sauté mushrooms. Next, add the mushroom cream sauce to the pan, along with the ½ cup cream and the Chablis. When heated through pour sauce over veal and serve with noodles.

Lida Lewis (Mrs. James)

VEAL PARMESAN

½ cup chopped onion
Butter
2 veal cutlets
15 ounces tomato sauce
2 teaspoons Italian seasoning
1 teaspoon garlic salt

1 teaspoon oregano
1 tablespoon parsley
Dash garlic powder to taste
2 slices mozzarella cheese
½ cup parmesan cheese
3 ounces noodles

Brown onion in butter; remove onion and brown veal. Remove veal. Clean skillet and combine tomato sauce and seasonings. Simmer 15 minutes. Place veal in pan, cover with cheeses, spoon sauce over veal and cook slowly until cheese melts.

Anda Gagnet (Mrs. Ted)

VEAL MARSALA

½ cup all-purpose flour
Salt and pepper
2 pounds thin veal scallopini
6 tablespoons clarified butter

½ pound fresh mushrooms, sliced
½ cup Marsala wine
¼ cup chicken broth

Combine flour, salt and pepper; coat veal on both sides. Heat butter in a large heavy skillet and brown veal quickly on both sides. Remove to platter and keep warm. Add mushrooms to pan and cook until limp. Add wine and broth and cook over high heat for a few minutes to reduce the liquid a bit. Pour over veal and serve. Serves 6.

Lida Lewis (Mrs. James)

VEAL STEW MILANESE

2 pounds veal, cut into 1½-inch
  cubes
¼ cup olive or vegetable oil
1 large onion, diced
1 large carrot, diced
1 large rib celery, diced
1 garlic clove, crushed
⅓ cup white wine

1 15-ounce can tomatoes
2 teaspoons salt
½ teaspoon basil
½ teaspoon coarsely ground pepper
1 bay leaf
1 beef bouillon cube
1 tablespoon chopped parsley
1½ teaspoons grated lemon rind

Brown meat in hot oil in skillet or Dutch oven, then remove meat. Brown onion, carrot, celery and garlic. Stir in wine, tomatoes with liquid and seasonings. Break up tomatoes as your stir. Return veal to pan; bring to a boil. Reduce heat and simmer for 1¼ hours. May be thickened if desired by adding cornstarch in a little wine at end of cooking time. Serve alone or over rice or noodles.

Vicki Wenick (Mrs. Louis M.)

VEGETABLES

Sand Dollars—Living on sand bars only a few yards from our beaches, sand dollars are often washed ashore to be found by visitors.

VEGETABLES

ASPARAGUS-PEANUT CASSEROLE

1 29-ounce can asparagus spears,
drained
1 10¾-ounce can cream of
mushroom soup
½ cup roasted peanuts, with or
without salt

1 cup shredded Cheddar cheese
Dash of salt and pepper
¼ cup butter or margarine

Layer asparagus, soup, peanuts and cheese in casserole; season each layer with salt
and pepper. Dot with butter. Bake at 350°F. for 30 minutes. Serves 4-6.

Martha Ann Horn (Mrs. Joe)

ASPARAGUS DELIGHT

2 15-ounce cans asparagus spears,
drained
½ cup butter, melted

2 tablespoons lemon juice
½ cup grated Parmesan cheese
Paprika

Place drained asparagus in a 13x9-inch glass ovenproof dish. Drizzle with butter
and lemon juice. Sprinkle with cheese and paprika. Bake at 400°F. for 10
minutes. Serves 10-12.

Wanda Patterson (Mrs. James R.)

SWISS ASPARAGUS

½ cup butter
¾ cup all-purpose flour
6 cups milk
2 teaspoons salt
1 teaspoon pepper

½ teaspoon celery salt
1⅓ cups diced Cheddar cheese
3 15-ounce cans asparagus
1 cup toasted breadcrumbs

Melt butter in a large saucepan; add flour, mix well. Add milk and cook, stirring
constantly, until smooth and creamy. Add seasonings and cheese. Stir and cook 2
minutes or until cheese melts. Place asparagus in casserole with sauce; top with
toasted crumbs. Bake at 350°F. about 25 minutes or until bubbly. Serves 8-10.

Helen Kruse (Mrs. Foster)

ARTICHOKE AND RICOTTA PIE

2 9-ounce packages frozen
  artichoke hearts
½ cup water
½ teaspoon salt
½ cup minced scallions
2 tablespoons olive oil
1 pound ricotta cheese

1 cup shredded Gruyere cheese
¾ cup grated Parmesan cheese
½ cup sour cream
4 eggs
1 cup vegetable oil
18 phyllo sheets

In a covered pan, cook the artichoke hearts in salted water for 5 minutes or until tender. Drain and set aside. Sauté the scallions in olive oil until softened. In a bowl beat together all the cheeses, sour cream and eggs. Fold in the scallions and the reserved artichokes and season to taste. Brush a 10-inch springform pan with oil and line it with 5 sheets of phyllo, brushing each with oil. Overlap sheets and allow excess to hang over the edge. Add half the cheese mixture and top with 5 more sheets of phyllo, again brushing each with oil. Add the remaining cheese mixture and top with remaining phyllo sheets, each brushed with oil. Roll up the overhanging ends toward the pan. (It would be like a reverse curl.) Pierce the top with a fork in several places. Bake at 400°F. for 35-45 minutes or until golden. Cool 10 minutes; remove side of pan. Serve at room temperature. Serves 6-8.

Calliope Bryant (Mrs. Rowlett)

CRUNCH TOP BROCCOLI BAKE

2 tablespoons butter or margarine
2 tablespoons all-purpose flour
1 teaspoon salt
½ teaspoon sugar
¼ teaspoon pepper
½ teaspoon grated onion

1 cup sour cream
3 cups fresh broccoli flowerets or
  2 10-ounce packages frozen
1½ cups mozzarella cheese, shredded
Cheddar cheese croutons   ·

Heat butter until melted in small saucepan. Stir in flour, salt, sugar, pepper and onion. Add sour cream and stir until smooth. Cook, stirring constantly, until mixture comes just to a boil. Fold in broccoli and pour into greased 1½-quart baking dish. Toss cheese and cheese croutons together and sprinkle over broccoli. Bake at 350°F. for 20 minutes or until bubbly. Serves 6.

Isabel Hall (Mrs. Kent)

CREAMY BROCCOLI MOLD

3 tablespoons butter
1 bunch spring onions (white parts only), finely chopped
3 tablespoons all-purpose flour
1 chicken bouillon cube
¼ cup boiling water
1 8-ounce carton sour cream
3 eggs, beaten
¾ cup finely shredded Swiss cheese

½ cup toasted slivered almonds
¼ teaspoon salt
¼ teaspoon nutmeg
⅛ teaspoon pepper
1 10-ounce package frozen chopped broccoli, cooked and drained
Parsley, slivered almonds, pimento strips for garnish

In a saucepan melt butter over low heat; add onions and simmer until softened. Remove from heat; gradually add flour, stirring to mix. Add bouillon dissolved in boiling water to sour cream and mix evenly with flour. Cook over low heat, stirring constantly until thickened. Remove from heat and allow to cool. In mixing bowl combine sour cream mixture, eggs, cheese, almonds and seasonings. Add broccoli and mix evenly. Pour into lightly greased 1-quart ring mold. Place mold in a pan filled with water. Bake at 350°F. for 1 hour or until firm. Remove mold from water bath and turn out onto serving platter. Fill center with parsley and sprinkle with chopped parsley, almonds and pimento. Serves 4-6.

Microwave Directions

In a 4-cup microwave measure melt butter for 45 seconds on Full Power. Add onions and cook for 2 minutes. Gradually add flour and mix. Add bouillon and sour cream, mixing evenly. Cook for 3-4 minutes on 70% power, stirring after 2 minutes; let cool. In bowl combine sour cream mixture, eggs, cheese, almonds and seasonings. Add broccoli and mix; pour into mold. Cook for 10-11 minutes on 50% power, rotating dish ¼ turn after 5 minutes. Let stand 3-4 minutes to cool. Loosen outside and center areas with a knife and turn out onto serving platter. Fill center with parsley and sprinkle with chopped parsley, almonds and pimento.

Carol Jean Wheeler
Atlanta, Georgia

MARIE'S PARTY CABBAGE

1 large cabbage, cut into 8 wedges
Water
½ cup finely chopped green pepper
½ cup chopped green onions
4 tablespoons butter or margarine
1 cup all-purpose flour

½ teaspoon salt
½ teaspoon white pepper
1½ cups milk
½ cup mayonnaise
¾ cup shredded Cheddar cheese
3 tablespoons chili sauce

Cook cabbage wedges in small amount of boiling salted water for about 10 minutes; drain well. Place wedges in a 13x9x2-inch baking dish. Cook green pepper and onions in butter until tender. Blend in flour, salt and pepper. Add milk all at once and cook until thick. Pour over cabbage. Bake, uncovered, at 375°F. for 20 minutes. Combine mayonnaise, cheese and chili sauce. Spoon over top; bake 5 minutes longer. Serves 8.

Jane Keller (Mrs. Joe)

BRUSSELS SPROUTS IN LEMON SAUCE

2 10-ounce packages frozen
  brussels sprouts
¼ cup butter or margarine
⅔ cup mayonnaise
2 tablespoons lemon juice

½ teaspoon celery salt
2 tablespoons grated Parmesan
  cheese
¼ cup sliced almonds, toasted

Cook brussels sprouts according to package directions, omitting salt; drain. Place sprouts in a shallow 2-quart casserole and keep warm. Melt butter in a saucepan; add mayonnaise, lemon juice and celery salt. Beat with a wire whisk until smooth; cook over medium heat until hot, stirring constantly (do not boil). Pour sauce over sprouts; sprinkle with cheese and almonds. Serves 6.

Patty Segler (Mrs. Jack)

LO MEIN (SOFT NOODLES)

1 pound hot or mild bulk sausage
1 large onion, cut into rings
1 green pepper, cut into thin
  strips

1 medium cabbage, coarsely
  shredded
1 8-ounce package cooked egg
  noodles

Fry sausage and drain well. Add onions, green pepper and cabbage; fry until limp; toss with cooked noodles. Serve with green salad and hot French bread.

Yvi Fernandez (Mrs. Robert)

234

CELERY AND CARROTS-PARSLEY CREAM

2 cups celery slices, in 2-inch
   pieces
1 carrot, thinly sliced
½ teaspoon rosemary leaves,
   crushed
2 teaspoons chicken bouillon
   granules
½ cup hot water

2 tablespoons butter
1½ teaspoons arrowroot
Dash of pepper
1 tablespoon instant minced
   onions
1 cup milk
½ teaspoon parsley flakes

Combine celery, carrot and rosemary in a saucepan. Mix bouillon granules and water and pour over vegetables. Cover and simmer over low heat about 10 minutes. Drain and keep warm. Melt butter, stir in arrowroot, pepper, onions and milk. Cook over medium heat, stirring constantly, until sauce thickens. Stir in parsley, then pour over vegetables, mixing gently.

Hilda Bingham Beck
Gulf Breeze, Florida

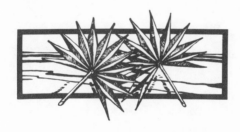

CARROT-CHEESE RING

2 cups cooked carrots, mashed
½ cup butter or margarine
2 cups shredded Cheddar cheese
2 eggs, beaten

½ cup milk
1 teaspoon salt
½ teaspoon pepper
Hot cooked vegetables for center

To hot cooked carrots add butter. Combine other ingredients, add to carrots and mix well. Pour into well-greased ring mold. Set in pan of hot water. Bake at 350°F. for 40-45 minutes. Cool slightly then turn out onto serving dish. Fill center with drained hot, cooked vegetables such as peas, brussels sprouts or broccoli. Serves 8.

Margaret Merriam (Mrs. Lauren, Jr.)

HERB-SEASONED CAULIFLOWER

1 head cauliflower
1 teaspoon salt
¼ teaspoon pepper
¾ cup herbed-seasoned stuffing
  mix

¾ cup butter or margarine,
  melted
1½ cups shredded Swiss cheese
¾ cup freshly grated Parmesan
  cheese

Steam cauliflower, season with salt and pepper. Place in large casserole. Combine stuffing mix and butter; add to cheeses and sprinkle over top of cauliflower. Bake at 400°F. for 15 minutes or until bubbly.

Anda Gagnet (Mrs. Ted)

FAR EAST CELERY

1 stalk celery, cut into 1-inch
  pieces (about 4 cups)
Water
1 6-ounce can water chestnuts,
  drained and thinly sliced
1 10¾-ounce can cream of
  chicken soup

¼ cup diced pimento
½ cup soft breadcrumbs
¼ cup toasted slivered almonds
2 tablespoons melted butter

Cook celery in small amount of boiling salted water until tender-crisp, about 8 minutes; drain. Mix celery, water chestnuts, soup and pimento in 1½-2 quart casserole. Toss breadcrumbs with almonds and butter; sprinkle over casserole. Bake at 350°F. for 35 minutes. Serves 6-8.

Lillie Brewton (Mrs. Harvey)

CORN PUDDING

1 cup evaporated milk
2 eggs
2 tablespoons sugar
1 tablespoon all-purpose flour

2 tablespoons butter or margarine
1 teaspoon salt
1 20-ounce can cream style corn

In a mixing bowl combine milk, eggs, sugar, flour, butter and salt; mix with electric mixer. Add cream style corn and mix by hand. Bake uncovered in a greased 12x8x2-inch baking dish at 350°F. for 1 hour. Serves 6.

Linda Grantham, (Mrs. Gregory)

FRIED CORN

4 slices bacon
3 cups fresh corn, cut from cob
1¼ cups water
1 tablespoon sugar

1 teaspoon salt
1 tablespoon cornstarch
2 tablespoons cold water

Fry bacon until crisp; drain, crumble and set aside. Drain all but 2 tablespoons drippings from skillet; add corn, water, sugar and salt. Bring to a boil over medium heat; cover and simmer 20-25 minutes. Combine cornstarch and 2 tablespoons cold water, stirring until smooth. Stir into corn mixture and boil for 1 minute, stirring constantly. Top with crumbled bacon before serving. Serves 4-5.

Ella Russ (Mrs. Carl S.)

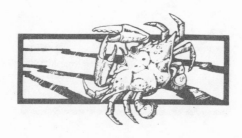

JALAPEÑO-CORN SOUFFLE

1 cup cold water
½ cup corn meal
1 tablespoon butter
1 teaspoon sugar
¾ teaspoon salt
⅛ teaspoon pepper
½ cup milk

½ cup shredded sharp Cheddar
  cheese
½ cup cooked corn
2 teaspoons finely chopped
  jalapeño pepper (more to taste)
2 eggs, separated
⅛ teaspoon cream of tartar

Combine water, corn meal, butter, sugar, salt and pepper in a saucepan. Cook and stir until thick; remove from heat and stir in milk, cheese, corn and jalapeño pepper. Beat egg yolks until lemon colored; stir in corn mixture. Beat egg whites and cream of tartar to stiff peaks; fold into corn mixture. Turn into an ungreased 1-quart souffle dish. Bake at 325°F. for 50-55 minutes. Serve with chili spooned over it if desired. Serves 4.

ONION-CORN CASSEROLE

¼ cup butter or margarine
1 large sweet onion, sliced
1½ cups corn muffin mix
1 egg
⅓ cup milk
1 cup cream style corn

¼ teaspoon hot pepper sauce
1 cup sour cream
¼ teaspoon salt
¼ teaspoon dill weed
1 cup shredded sharp Cheddar
cheese, divided

Melt butter in skillet; add sliced onion and sauté until soft. In a bowl combine corn muffin mix, egg, milk, corn and hot pepper sauce; place in greased 9-inch square pan. Add sour cream, salt, dill weed and half the shredded cheese to the sautéed onion. Spread over batter in pan. Sprinkle with remaining cheese. Bake at 425°F. for 30 minutes. Cut into squares and serve warm. Serves 9.

Bette Vetland (Mrs. Ted)

SCALLOPED CORN

10 ears (approximately) fresh
corn (3 cups kernels)
4 eggs, slightly beaten
1 teaspoon salt
¼ teaspoon pepper
1 cup plus 2 tablespoons heavy
cream

1 cup fresh breadcrumbs
2½ tablespoons butter or
margarine, melted
Paprika

Scrape corn with knife to remove all the milk until you have 3 cups corn. Mix corn with eggs, salt, pepper and cream. Pour into lightly buttered 1½-quart shallow baking dish. Sprinkle with breadcrumbs that have been tossed with melted butter. Sprinkle with paprika. Bake at 325°F. for 40 minutes or until knife inserted in center comes out clean. Serves 6-8.

Elizabeth Nixon (Mrs. Ray B.)

BARBECUED BLACK-EYED PEAS

1 cup dried black-eyed peas
1½ cups boiling water
1 teaspoon salt
¼ pound lean ground beef

½ medium onion, chopped
½ cup barbecue sauce
1 tablespoon prepared mustard
3 tablespoons brown sugar

Cook peas in boiling water with salt until barely tender. Pour off half the liquid. Brown beef and onions and add to peas. Stir in barbecue sauce, mustard and sugar. Pour into 1½-quart casserole. Bake at 200°F. for 1-1½ hours. Serves 4-6.

Chuck Braud

RATATOUILLE

½ pound eggplant
½ pound zucchini
2 teaspoons salt
7 tablespoons olive oil, divided
   (no substitutions)
½ pound onions, thinly sliced

2 green peppers, sliced
2 garlic cloves, mashed
Salt and pepper to taste
1 pound firm ripe tomatoes
3 tablespoons parsley flakes

Peel eggplant and cut lengthwise in slices about ½-inch thick and 1-inch wide. Scrub zucchini, cut off ends and slice same as eggplant. Put in a bowl and toss with salt. Let stand at least 30 minutes to remove moisture. (The longer the time, the more moisture removed.) Dry each slice in a paper towel. Sauté in 4 tablespoons olive oil until soft. Remove to side dish. In same skillet add remaining olive oil if needed to sauté onions and peppers until tender but not brown, about 10 minutes. Add garlic. Peel and seed tomatoes; layer over onions and peppers in skillet. Cook, covered, over low heat until tomatoes render their juices. Uncover and baste with juices, raise temperature and boil until juice is almost evaporated. In a 2½-quart casserole place ⅓ tomato mixture, sprinkle with 1 tablespoon parsley. Layer over with half the eggplant-zucchini mixture. Add another third of tomato mixture, sprinkle with 1 tablespoon parsley. Layer remaining eggplant-zucchini mixture. Cover with remaining ⅓ of tomato mixture and remaining 1 tablespoon parsley. Season with salt and pepper as desired. Cover and simmer over very low heat for 10 minutes. Uncover, tip casserole and baste mixture with its own juices. Correct seasoning with salt and pepper as needed. Raise heat and cook, uncovered, for 15 minutes or more, basting several times. Be careful not to scorch bottom; set aside. Reheat very carefully at serving time. Better made a day ahead. Serves 8.

Henryetta Groce
Charlotte, North Carolina

EGGPLANT CASSEROLE

2 large eggplants, peeled and
  sliced
Salt and pepper, to taste
Vegetable oil
¼ cup finely chopped onion
¼ cup finely chopped green
  pepper

½ cup finely chopped celery
1 10¾-ounce can cream of
  mushroom soup, undiluted
1 10¾-ounce can tomato soup,
  undiluted
¾ cup shredded Cheddar cheese

Season eggplant with salt and pepper and brown in hot oil. In large casserole dish place a layer of eggplant, onion, green pepper and celery. Repeat layers until all is used. Pour both cans of soup over top of casserole and spread evenly. With a fork make indentations throughout. Sprinkle cheese over top. Bake at 300°F. for 30 minutes.

Carolyn Fleming (Mrs. Robert)

SPICY VEGETABLE RELISH

1 head cauliflower broken into
  small flowerets
2 stalks celery, sliced in ½-inch
  lengths
6 ripe red peppers, coarsely
  diced
2 jumbo onions, coarsely diced
12 garlic cloves, finely minced
1½ pounds jalapeño peppers,
  drained, trimmed, seeded and
  coarsely diced
1 15-ounce can pitted ripe
  olives, sliced

1 18-ounce jar green olives
1½ cups olive oil
1½ cups vegetable oil
1½ cups wine vinegar
3 tablespoons salt
3 tablespoons crushed red
  peppers
1 tablespoon celery salt
1½ tablespoons pepper

Mix all ingredients together thoroughly. Divide into glass containers, seal and refrigerate. Turn jars frequently. Allow at least 2 weeks for full flavor to develop. Will keep refrigerated for several months. Good on salads, submarine sandwiches, anything! Makes 1½ gallons.

Melissa Sale (Mrs. Douglas)

LOUISE'S STUFFED VIDALIA ONIONS

6 large Vidalia onions, peeled
Water
½ cup butter or margarine
1 cup chopped pitted ripe
  olives
1 cup soft breadcrumbs
¾ cup shredded sharp Cheddar
  cheese

2 tablespoons chopped fresh
  parsley
¼ teaspoon salt
¼ teaspoon poultry seasoning
Dash of pepper
Paprika

Cut ¼-inch slice from top and bottom of each onion; reserve slices. Place onions in a Dutch oven, cover with water and bring to a boil over medium high heat. Reduce heat and simmer 20 minutes or until tender. Drain and cool. Chop reserved onion slices, sauté in butter until tender. Add remaining ingredients. Scoop out center portion of onions. Fill each onion with olive mixture, sprinkle with paprika. Place onions in a 13x9x2-inch baking dish and bake, covered, at 350°F. for 5 minutes.

Renate Marshall (Mrs. David)
Dothan, Alabama

GREEN BEAN CASSEROLE

3 16-ounce cans French style
  green beans
½ pound fresh mushrooms, sliced
1 large onion, chopped
½ cup butter or margarine
¼ cup all-purpose flour
2 cups light cream
¾ pound sharp Cheddar cheese,
  shredded

⅛ teaspoon hot pepper sauce
2 teaspoons soy sauce
Salt and pepper to taste
1 tablespoon Worcestershire sauce
1 8-ounce can water chestnuts,
  sliced
15 round buttery crackers, crumbled

Cook beans for 1 hour; drain well and set aside. Cook mushrooms and onion in butter until well done but not brown. Add flour, stirring to blend well, then add cream and cook until thick. Add cheese, stirring until smooth; add all seasoning. Mix in beans and water chestnuts; pour into large casserole and sprinkle top with cracker crumbs. Bake at 350°F. for 30 minutes or until bubbly. Serves 16.

Mary Hawkins (Mrs. W.O.)
Eufaula, Alabama

GARLIC POTATO STRIPS

4 baking potatoes
4 tablespoons butter

1 garlic clove, minced
Salt

Quarter potatoes lengthwise and peel if desired. Boil for 10 minutes; drain. Melt butter in baking pan. Add garlic and potato strips, turning to coat with butter and garlic. Sprinkle with salt. Bake at 350°F. for 45 minutes, turning several times during baking. Serves 4-6.

Anne Hull

POTATOES IN A SKILLET

6 medium potatoes, peeled and
  cut into ¼-inch slices
1 large onion, sliced
1 large green pepper, sliced
2 large tomatoes, sliced

1 cup water
2-3 slices bacon
1¼ teaspoons salt
⅛ teaspoon pepper

In a large skillet layer vegetables in order listed; add remaining ingredients. Cover and simmer 45 minutes or until potatoes are tender. Run under broiler to crisp bacon before serving. Serves 6-8.

Louise Fishel (Mrs. John)

STEAK POTATOES

6 potatoes (preferably red)
1 pound bacon
1 8-ounce package sharp Cheddar
  cheese, shredded

½ cup butter or margarine,
  melted

Cook whole potatoes until tender; drain, cool and cut into large cubes. Fry bacon, cool and crumble. In lightly greased 13x9x2-inch pan place potatoes. Sprinkle with cheese then bacon bits; pour butter over top. Bake at 350°F. for 20-25 minutes. Pass sour cream if desired. Serves 8.

Laura Darnell (Mrs. Douglas)

CALIFORNIA CASSEROLE

¼ cup butter or margarine
1 cup chopped onion
4 cups freshly cooked rice
2 cups sour cream
1 cup creamy cottage cheese
1 large bay leaf, crumbled

½ teaspoon salt
½ teaspoon pepper
3 4-ounce cans green chilies,
   drained and chopped
2 cups shredded sharp Cheddar
   cheese

In large skillet melt butter; sauté onion until golden. Remove from heat, stir in hot rice, sour cream, cottage cheese, bay leaf, salt and pepper; toss lightly but well. Layer half rice mixture in bottom of lightly greased 2-2½ quart baking dish. Next add half the chilies, sprinkle with half the shredded cheese. Repeat layers ending with cheese. Bake, uncovered, at 375°F. for 25 minutes. Serves 8.

Norma McCarthy (Mrs. Eugene)
Mary Reno (Mrs. R. R.)

RICE MILANESE

¼ cup finely chopped onion
1 garlic clove, chopped
½ pound fresh mushrooms, sliced
¼ cup butter
1 cup raw rice

3 cups chicken broth
½ cup Marsala wine or dry red
   wine
¼ teaspoon saffron
Grated Parmesan cheese

Brown onion, garlic and mushrooms in butter. Add rice, broth, wine and saffron. Bring to a boil; cover and cook over low heat 20-30 minutes or until rice is tender. Sprinkle each serving with cheese. Serves 6.

Vera Bruce (Mrs. M. H., III)
Pleasant Grove, Alabama

ORANGE RICE

1 cup orange juice
1 cup water
1 teaspoon salt

1 tablespoon grated orange rind
1 cup raw rice

Mix orange juice and water in saucepan and bring to a boil. Add salt, orange rind and rice; cook over medium heat about 30 minutes until done. Very nice with shrimp curry.

Louise Smith (Mrs. Thomas E.)

APPLE AND CHEESE STUFFED SQUASH

1 acorn squash, cut in half
and seeded
1 medium red delicious apple,
chopped
1 tablespoon chopped onion

⅔ cup cottage cheese
½ cup shredded Cheddar cheese
2 tablespoons plain yogurt
½ rounded teaspoon cinnamon

Place squash halves, cut side down, on baking sheet. Bake at 350°F. about 1 hour until tender. Cook apple and onion in small non-stick skillet about 5 minutes until soft. Combine with remaining ingredients. When squash is done, remove from oven and leave oven on. Scoop out squash pulp leaving shells intact. Mash about 1 cup of pulp, saving remaining squash for another use. Add squash to apple-cheese mixture; mix well. Stuff each shell with half of mixture and return to oven for 20 minutes. Cut each half in half to serve. Serves 4.

Dot Ennis (Mrs. Buford)

GARDEN STUFFED YELLOW SQUASH BOATS

8-10 medium yellow squash
Water
½ green pepper, chopped
1 medium tomato, chopped
2 slices bacon, fried crisp
and crumbled

½ cup shredded Cheddar cheese
½ teaspoon salt
Dash of pepper
Butter or margarine

Wash squash and simmer in water 8 minutes or until just tender; drain and cool slightly. Cut a thin slice from top of each squash. Combine remaining ingredients except butter; mix well and spoon into squash shells. Dot each with a pat of butter and bake at 400°F. for 20 minutes. May be made ahead of time. Serves 8-10.

Mrs. Robert T. Gray III
Houston, Texas

POTATO PIE

1 pound cottage cheese, pressed
   through a sieve
2 cups unseasoned mashed potatoes
½ cup sour cream
2 eggs

2 teaspoons salt
⅛ teaspoon cayenne pepper
½ cup green onions, thinly sliced
3 tablespoons Parmesan cheese
1 10-inch unbaked pastry shell

Place sieved cottage cheese into a medium-sized mixing bowl. Add mashed potatoes. Beat until well blended. Add sour cream, eggs, salt and cayenne pepper. Beat until thoroughly mixed. Stir in green onions. Spoon mixture into pastry shell. Sprinkle top with cheese. Bake at 450°F. for 50 minutes or until golden brown on top. Yield: 6 to 8 servings.

Note: This can be served hot the first day and cold the next. Instant mashed potatoes will work perfectly well in this dish.

Bette Vetland (Mrs. Ted)

BOURBON SWEET POTATOES

4-5 baked sweet potatoes
1 cup sugar
3 eggs, beaten
½ cup butter or margarine,
   melted

1 5.3-ounce can evaporated
   milk
1 teaspoon vanilla extract
1 ounce bourbon

Mash sweet potatoes and mix well with other ingredients; pour into 13x9x2-inch baking dish. Sprinkle topping over casserole and bake at 350°F. for 40 minutes.

Topping

½ cup butter
1 cup firmly packed brown sugar

1 cup chopped pecans
1 cup all-purpose flour

Melt butter, add sugar, stirring until melted. Mix well with pecans and flour; crumble on top of potatoes.

Lorean Allen (Mrs. K. P., Jr.)
Brandon, Mississippi

ORANGE CANDIED YAMS

2¼ cups water, divided
2 cups sugar
¼ teaspoon yellow food coloring
1 small orange, seeded and finely
  chopped in food processor
½ cup butter or margarine
½ cup firmly packed light brown
  sugar
½ teaspoon cinnamon

½ teaspoon nutmeg
½ teaspoon lemon juice
½ teaspoon salt
½ teaspoon vanilla extract
4 tablespoons cornstarch
Sweet potatoes (baked or boiled),
  peeled and sliced (1 medium
  per person)

Combine 2 cups water, sugar, food coloring and chopped orange. Bring to a boil, stirring to dissolve sugar; boil for 5 minutes. Add remaining ingredients except remaining ¼ cup water, cornstarch and sweet potatoes. Cook until butter is melted. Dissolve cornstarch in water and add to sauce. Boil until thick and syrupy, about 20 minutes. Pour over sweet potatoes in a casserole dish and bake at 350°F. for 30 minutes or until bubbly.

Note: Add sauce to taste and refrigerate leftovers.

Rosamond Coleman (Mrs. William H.)

INDIAN RICE PILAF

¼ cup sugar
2 tablespoons water
3 cups chicken broth
1 cup diced carrots
½ cup golden raisins
3 tablespoons butter

1½ cups long-grain rice
½ teaspoon salt
¼ teaspoon nutmeg
¼ teaspoon cinnamon
¼ teaspoon cardamon
Freshly grated nutmeg

Simmer sugar and water, uncovered, in medium saucepan until golden; add broth and cook 2 more minutes. Remove from heat. In a covered 2-quart saucepan sauté carrots and raisins in butter for 8 minutes; add rice and stir to coat rice with butter. Add broth and remaining ingredients. Bring to a boil, reduce heat to simmer, cover and cook 25-30 minutes. Place in a serving dish and sprinkle with freshly grated nutmeg. Great with pork. Serves 6.

Sue Harris (Mrs. Casper)

SQUASH DELUXE

2 pounds yellow squash
1½ medium onions, finely chopped
  and divided
Seasoned salt
Pepper
2 eggs, beaten
2 tablespoons sour cream

1 16-ounce package round,
  buttery crackers, rolled fine
  and divided
½ cup butter or margarine, melted
1 8-ounce package slivered
  almonds

Cook squash and 1 chopped onion until tender; drain, mash and add seasoned salt and pepper to taste. Mix in eggs, sour cream and ½ the cracker crumbs. Place in a casserole and top with melted butter and remaining onion which has been sautéed. Sprinkle almonds over onion and top with remaining crushed crackers; stir until all butter is absorbed. Bake at 350°F. 25-30 minutes.

PARTY PEAS

3 tablespoons butter or margarine
1 10-ounce package frozen
  sweet peas
2 cups shredded lettuce

1 teaspoon salt
Pinch of tarragon, basil or mint
¼ cup chopped onion
¼ teaspoon pepper

Heat butter in pan and add frozen peas. Cover and cook slowly until peas are defrosted; do not add water. When completely thawed, add lettuce and seasonings. Mix lightly and cover tightly; steam 4 minutes, no longer. Serve immediately.

Nancy Wyatt (Mrs. Terrence)

QUICK CREAMED SPINACH

1 10-ounce package frozen
  chopped spinach
1 tablespoon mayonnaise

2 tablespoons melted butter
Parmesan cheese

Cook spinach according to package directions; drain well. Mix mayonnaise and butter together and fold into spinach. Top with Parmesan cheese. Serves 2-3.

Calliope Bryant (Mrs. Rowlett)

SPINACH IN WHOLE WHEAT SESAME CRÊPES

1 10-ounce package frozen
  chopped spinach
3 green onions with tops,
  chopped
1 cup fresh mushrooms, sliced
1 tablespoon butter or margarine
1 3-ounce package cream cheese,
  softened

2 heaping tablespoons mayonnaise
2 heaping tablespoons sour cream
4 heaping tablespoons cottage
  cheese
2½ tablespoons grated Parmesan
  cheese

Cook spinach gently and drain. Sauté onions and mushrooms in butter. Stir together cream cheese, mayonnaise, sour cream, cottage cheese and Parmesan cheese. Beat gently until well blended. Add onions and mushrooms to sauce. Add half of sauce to spinach; reserve other half and set aside. Make crêpes.

Whole Wheat Sesame Crêpes

1⅓ cups skim milk
2 eggs
½ teaspoon sea salt

2 tablespoons safflower oil
1 cup whole wheat flour
½ cup hulled white sesame seeds

Combine milk, eggs, sea salt and oil. Add flour and sesame seeds to work bowl of food processor. Process until finely ground, 2-3 minutes. With machine running, add liquid and process until well-blended. Refrigerate batter at least 1 hour. Bake crêpes over medium heat. The edges will be crisp and slightly lacy.

Filled Crêpes

Spoon 2-3 tablespoons spinach filling on each crêpe. Roll and place in an oiled baking dish. Pour reserved sauce down center of crêpes. Cover with foil, making slits in top to let steam escape. Bake at 325°F for 15-25 minutes. Makes 8 large filled crêpes.

Holly Suber (Mrs. Stephen)

SPINACH PIE

1 cup olive oil
1 cup chopped onions
1 10-ounce package frozen
  chopped spinach, thawed
½ cup chopped parsley
½ cup chopped dill or 1 teaspoon
  dried dill

1 pound cottage cheese
Salt and pepper to taste
4 eggs
1 double crust pastry shell
Melted butter

In a skillet heat olive oil; brown chopped onions. Add spinach, parsley, dill, cottage cheese, salt and pepper to taste and eggs; mix well. Place bottom pastry in a greased pie plate; add the filling and cover with top pastry. Brush with melted butter. Bake at 375°F. for 40-45 minutes until golden brown. Remove from oven, cool and cut.

Note: The above recipe can be used with yellow squash instead of spinach.

Clio Pettis (Mrs. Hercules)

CRUSTY BAKED SPINACH

1 1-pound package phyllo sheets
½ cup butter, melted
2 bunches fresh spinach
¾ cup heavy cream

1 egg, beaten
Freshly grated nutmeg to taste
Salt and pepper

Brush a phyllo sheet with melted butter, place another sheet on top, brush with butter; continue until 6 sheets are used. Line a greased 13x9-inch baking pan with the buttered phyllo sheets. Wash fresh spinach, remove tough stalks, drain and coarsely chop. Place in mixing bowl; add cream, egg, nutmeg, salt and pepper to taste. Sprinkle thin layer of spinach mixture on phyllo. Brush another phyllo sheet with butter, top with 2 more sheets, brushing each with butter. Place 3-layer stack of phyllo on top of spinach. Top with more spinach mixture. Continue alternating spinach and 3-layer phyllo until spinach is used. Top with 3-layer phyllo and brush with butter. Bake at 350°F. about 25 minutes until set and golden brown.

Shirley Corriher
Somethin's Cookin' Cooking School

ZUCCHINI STUFFED LOVE APPLE

4 small zucchini
2 tablespoons unsalted butter
1 tablespoon freshly grated
 Parmesan cheese
1 tablespoon heavy cream
4 small tomatoes
1 fresh leaf of basil or ¼ teaspoon ground basil divided
 between the 4 tomatoes

Seasoned salt-to taste
Freshly ground pepper-to taste
Grated Parmesan cheese
Butter or margarine

Grate zucchini, skin and all, in a food processor; wrap in paper towels to drain. Sauté grated zucchini in butter until tender. Add 1 tablespoon Parmesan and cream; set aside. Scoop out center of each tomato and pat inside dry with paper towel. Sprinkle inside of each tomato lightly with seasoned salt, basil and pepper. Fill with zucchini mixture; top with grated Parmesan and a pat of butter. Bake at 350°F. for 20 minutes or until browned on top.

Dee Redding (Mrs. Ben)

GREEN TOMATOES

4-6 green tomatoes
Salt
Pepper
1 cup shredded hoop cheese
1 8-ounce package herb seasoned
 stuffing mix

½ cup butter
Curry powder
Paprika

Slice tomatoes into ½-inch slices or peel and cut into small pieces; season with salt and pepper to taste. Place tomatoes in bottom of an oblong casserole. Top with shredded cheese and stuffing mix. Dot with butter and sprinkle with curry powder and paprika to taste. Bake at 325°F. for 20-30 minutes. Run under broiler to brown. (For ripe tomatoes, omit baking just broil.) May add crumbled, cooked and drained sausage to stuffing mix (omit curry) for a delicious variation.

Note: The success of this recipe is dependent upon good acidic tomatoes, prefer-ably from North Carolina.

Tina Kelly (Mrs. Ray)

DESSERTS
CAKES, PIES & TEA TIME

Bay Magnolia—The flowering tree with the "bay leaves" grows in the wetlands of Bay County.

DESSERTS

CHOCOLATE MOUSSE CAKE

Filling

1½ pounds semisweet chocolate	½ cup Tia Maria
½ cup strong brewed coffee	2 tablespoons sugar
3 eggs, separated	½ cup heavy cream, whipped

Melt chocolate with coffee in top of a double boiler. When chocolate is completely melted, remove pan from heat. Beat egg yolks until pale yellow and stir into chocolate. Gradually stir in Tia Maria; cool. In a separate bowl beat egg whites gradually adding sugar until whites are stiff. Whip cream. Gently fold whipped cream into cooled chocolate mixture and then fold in egg whites.

Cake

1 23-ounce package brownie mix	2 tablespoons water
	3 eggs

Beat ingredients together at medium speed of electric mixer until batter is smooth. Grease and line with waxed paper a 15x10x1-inch jellyroll pan. Grease and flour paper, shaking off any excess flour. Spread batter evenly in jellroll pan. Bake for 10-12 minutes at 350°F. or until cake tests done. Turn cake onto a rack and peel off paper. Lightly oil a 9-inch springform pan and line with cooled cake. Cut rounds of cake to fit both top and bottom of pan and strip for sides. Place smaller round in bottom of pan. Wrap strip around inside of pan. (You may have to piece one section of side to cover completely.) Spoon chilled filling mixture into mold. Fit larger round of cake on top of mold. Chill for 3-4 hours or until firm. Unmold and cover with glaze.

Chocolate Glaze

½ pound semisweet chocolate	⅓ cup water

Melt chocolate in water and stir until smooth. Spread over top of mousse-cake and drizzle down sides; chill again. Serve in slender slices.

Mimi Bozarth (Mrs. John P.)

CHOCOLATE HAZELNUT TERRINE

12 ounces semisweet chocolate
1¾ cups sugar, divided
½ cup water
1½ cups unsalted butter, softened
2 cups cocoa
3 egg yolks
2 eggs

⅓ cup hazelnut liqueur
1 teaspoon vanilla extract
2½ cups hazelnuts, toasted, skinned
and chopped, divided
2 cups heavy cream
Cocoa

Melt chocolate in top of a double boiler; let cool. Bring 1½ cups sugar and water to a boil; let cool. Butter a 9x5x3-inch loaf pan. Line with buttered waxed paper. Beat butter and cocoa in mixer until very smooth. Add yolks, eggs, chocolate and sugar-water, beating well after each addition. Blend in liqueur, vanilla and 2 cups hazelnuts. Pour into loaf pan and chill overnight. When ready to serve, dip loaf pan in warm water and loosen terrine with knife. Remove waxed paper and decorate with remaining hazelnuts. Whip cream adding remaining ¼ cup sugar. Slice terrine into thin slices, top with whipped cream and sprinkle with a little cocoa. This is very, very rich. Freezes well. Serves 14-16.

Marsha Lewis (Mrs. E. Clay, III)

WHITE CHOCOLATE MOUSSE
...served at the White House...

6 ounces white chocolate
⅓ cup warm milk
2 egg whites at room temperature

1 cup heavy cream
Dash of lemon juice
Dark chocolate curls

Melt chocolate in top of double boiler over gently simmering water; stir and add warm milk. Stir until smooth. Cool to room temperature. Beat egg whites until peaks form. Use rubber spatula and fold into chocolate until incorporated. Whip cream until stiff and fold in. Add lemon juice. Spoon into bowl, glasses or your choice of serving dish. Refrigerate until ready to use. When ready to serve, sprinkle with a little of the dark chocolate. May be made the day before; cover tightly with foil or plastic wrap.

Gay Sudduth (Mrs. Rowe)

CHOCOLATE KIRSCH MOLD

⅔ cup semisweet chocolate
  morsels
1 cup butter, divided
4 egg yolks
½ cup sugar

Finely grated rind of 1 orange
⅔ cup Kirsch, divided
About 3 dozen ladyfingers, whole
Whipped cream

Combine chocolate with half the butter in a small saucepan. Melt over low heat, stirring occasionally; then beat until smooth and well-blended. Remove from heat. Beat egg yolks with sugar in a bowl over hot water until thick, creamy and pale. Beat in chocolate mixture; then add remaining butter in small pieces and beat vigorously until smooth. (If mixture is lumpy, strain it through a fine sieve.) Beat in orange rind and half the Kirsch. Dilute remaining Kirsch with ⅓ cup water in a shallow dish. Line bottom of a buttered 1½-quart charlotte mold with a layer of ladyfingers, dipping each one quickly in diluted Kirsch before placing it. Spoon a layer of chocolate cream over ladyfingers. Continue to alternate layers of ladyfingers soaked in Kirsch and chocolate cream until mold is full, ending with a layer of ladyfingers. Cover mold with foil and chill in the refrigerator overnight or until firmly set. When ready to serve, dip mold into very hot water for about 10 seconds only to loosen it and carefully turn out onto a serving dish. Decorate with swirls of piped whipped cream and serve. Serves 8.

Marie Bazemore (Mrs. Eugene J.)

STRAWBERRIES WITH WHITE CHOCOLATE

2 pints fresh strawberries (the
  best you can find)

1 pound ultra white chocolate
  with paraffin

Arrange the strawberries in your prettiest crystal or silver bowl lined with a linen napkin in a color to match your table. Melt chocolate in the top of a double boiler over very low heat. (Be absolutely sure that the steam does not get into the chocolate or it will become grainy.) Dip the strawberries into the chocolate to cover. May also use cantaloupe balls, cherries or pretzels for dipping.

The Boars Head Restaurant

CHOCOLATE TRUFFLES

Basic Dough

12 ounces bittersweet chocolate
4 egg yolks

¼ cup plus 2 tablespoons
unsalted butter, softened

1st Flavor

1 tablespoon rum

1 tablespoon instant coffee

2nd Flavor

½ cup ground nuts

2 tablespoons brandy

3rd Flavor

Grated rind of 1 orange

1½ tablespoons Grand Marnier

Melt chocolate over boiling water and stir until smooth. Add egg yolks and whisk in. The mixture will curdle. Add butter, whisk in and divide the mixture into 3 small bowls. Add one flavoring mixture to each bowl and whisk into the chocolate mixture. Whisk until mixture smooths out. (Add 1 tablespoon hot water to each bowl and continue to whisk if mixture has not smoothed out.) Cover bowls and chill. When chilled roll 1 teaspoonful of a flavor into a smooth ball and return to chill again. Continue until all of the three flavors have been made into balls keeping flavors separated. Roll rum and coffee-flavored balls in unsweetened cocoa powder. Sprinkle grand marnier-flavored balls with grated chocolate and roll to coat. Roll brandy-flavored balls in finely chopped nuts. Store finished truffles in air tight containers in the refrigerator. Truffles will keep up to 2 weeks.

Something's Cookin' Cooking School

FIG COBBLER

5-6 cups peeled fresh figs
¾ cup sugar
3 tablespoons all-purpose flour

Nutmeg and/or cinnamon to taste
Butter or margarine
1 8-inch pie pastry

Combine figs, sugar, flour, nutmeg and/or cinnamon; mix well. Spoon into an 8-inch square baking pan; dot with butter. Roll pastry to ¼-inch thickness on a lightly floured surface; cut into ½-inch strips. Arrange strips in lattice fashion over fig mixture. Bake at 375°F. for 45 minutes or until golden brown. Serves 6.

Jimmie Elchos (Mrs. Ted)

APPLE DESSERT

1 18½-ounce package yellow
cake mix
½ cup butter or margarine
3 apples, peeled and sliced
Cinnamon
Sugar

1 cup sour cream
1 egg
1 teaspoon vanilla extract
1 teaspoon cinnamon
⅓ cup firmly packed brown
sugar

Combine cake mix and butter. Spread all but 1½ cups into a 13x9-inch pan. Place sliced apples over top. Sprinkle with cinnamon and sugar. Combine sour cream, egg and vanilla; spread over apples. Add 1 teaspoon cinnamon and brown sugar to reserved cake mix; spread over the top. Bake at 350°F. for 25-30 minutes.

Nancy Harris (Mrs. David)

FRUIT TART FOR FOOD PROCESSOR

Crust

2¼ cups all-purpose flour
Pinch of salt
¾ cup powdered sugar

¾ cup butter, chilled
2 small egg yolks

Using steel blade of food processor, process flour, salt and sugar together briefly. Add butter, 1 tablespoon at a time, processing after each addition just enough to cut in. Add egg yolks and process just until mixture holds together. With your fingers, press dough into a 12-inch false bottom tart pan and place in freezer at least 10 minutes or until needed. Bake at 400°F. for 15-20 minutes. Save any leftover dough for another use.

Filling

12 ounces cream cheese
½ cup sugar
3½ tablespoons Grand Marnier,
divided

3 tablespoons butter, softened
Fresh fruit in any combination
¼ cup red currant jelly

With steel blade, process cream cheese, sugar and 1½ tablespoons Grand Marnier until smooth. Spread evenly in cooled tart shell. Arrange fruit on top of filling. Glaze fruit with jelly and remaining Grand Marnier.

Genie Lloyd (Mrs. Rayford)

FRESH FRUIT TRIFLE

1 14-ounce can sweetened
condensed milk
1½ cups cold water
2 teaspoons grated lemon rind
1 3¼-ounce package vanilla
instant pudding mix

2 cups heavy cream, whipped
4 cups pound cake cubes
1 pound ripe, fresh peaches,
peeled and chopped
2 cups fresh or frozen blueberries, rinsed and drained

In a large bowl combine condensed milk, water and lemon rind; mix well. Add pudding mix and beat until well blended. Chill for 5 minutes. Fold in whipped cream. Spoon 2 cups pudding mixture into a 4-quart glass serving bowl. Top with half the cake cubes, peaches, half the remaining pudding mixture, the remaining cake cubes then the blueberries. Add the remaining pudding mixture and spread to 1 inch of the bowl's edge. Chill several hours. Serves 10-12.

Ann McElheney (Mrs. Lorie E.)

MOM'S APPLE STRUDEL

1 package phyllo pastry
¾ cup melted butter, divided
1 8-ounce carton sour cream

3 large apples, peeled and sliced
½ cup raisins
½ cup sugar

Place phyllo pastry on flat surface on aluminum foil. Brush dough with half the butter; spread sour cream on dough. Place apple slices on top of sour cream. Add raisins, sugar and roll together in shallow baking pan using aluminum foil as a guide; discard foil. Baste top of strudel with remaining butter during baking at 350°F. for 45 minutes.

Renate Marshall (Mrs. David)
Dothan, Alabama

GOLDEN PEARS

6 pears
2 cups apricot nectar
1 cup sugar

1 teaspoon grated lemon rind
¼ cup lemon juice
¼ cup sherry

Peel pears; place in a bowl of a salted water. Combine apricot nectar, sugar, lemon rind and juice in a deep saucepan. Bring to a boil; simmer 5 minutes. Add sherry and place pears in syrup. Cook, covered, until fork tender. Chill pears; serve with vanilla ice cream with Galliano added.

Barbara Palmer (Mrs. Don)

TOASTED ALMOND SOUFFLÉ

2 tablespoons butter
3 tablespoons all-purpose flour
Dash of salt
½ cup light cream
¾ teaspoon finely grated
  orange rind

¼ cup orange juice
3 eggs, separated
¼ teaspoon finely chopped
  toasted almonds
3 tablespoons sugar
Strawberry-Orange Sauce

In a saucepan melt butter; stir in flour and salt. Add cream all at once. Cook and stir until bubbly, cook 1 minute more. (Mixture will be very thick.) Remove from heat; stir in orange rind and juice; mix well. In a small bowl beat egg yolks on high speed of electric mixer about 5 minutes or until thick and lemon-colored. Gradually blend the orange mixture into the beaten egg yolks. Gently stir in chopped toasted almonds. (Wash beaters thoroughly.) In a large bowl beat egg whites to soft peaks; gradually add sugar, beating to stiff peaks. Fold the orange almond mixture into egg whites. Turn into ungreased 1½-quart souffle dish. Bake at 325°F. 40 minutes or until golden and knife inserted near center comes out clean. Serve the souffle immediately with Strawberry-Orange Sauce. Serves 4.

Strawberry-Orange Sauce

3 tablespoons sugar
1 teaspoon cornstarch
Dash of salt

½ cup orange juice
2 teaspoons butter
1 cup fresh strawberries, halved

In a medium saucepan combine sugar, cornstarch and salt. Stir in the orange juice; cook and stir until mixture is thickened and bubbly. Cook and stir 1-2 minutes more. Remove from heat; stir in the butter until melted. Stir in the strawberries. Cover surface of sauce with clear plastic wrap or waxed paper. Let stand at room temperature until serving time. Makes 1¼ cups sauce.

Ann Aldrich Logue

ANATOLE BROSÉ
Whiskey Cream

2 cups heavy cream
1 cup honey

½ cup scotch whiskey

Beat cream until it holds stiff peaks. Combine honey with scotch and fold into cream. Divide among 8 sherbet or parfait glasses. Cover with foil and chill overnight.

John Henry Sherman, Jr.

DOUBLE LEMON CREPES

½ cup butter
2 teaspoons grated lemon rind
½ cup lemon juice
⅛ teaspoon salt

1½ cups sugar
3 eggs
3 egg yolks, beaten
2 cups heavy cream, whipped

In medium saucepan melt butter; add lemon rind, lemon juice, salt and sugar. Stir in beaten eggs and yolks. Cook over very low heat, beating constantly, with a whisk until thick; cool, then add to whipped cream. Fill crepes, fold over, top with remaining sauce and additional whipped cream. Top with fresh strawberries or other fruit if desired. Makes 15 crepes.

Lemon Crepe Batter

2 tablespoons clarified butter
½ cup cold water
¼ cup milk
2 eggs
2 egg yolks

¾ cup all-purpose flour
1 tablespoon sugar
1 teaspoon grated lemon rind
¼ teaspoon salt

In medium bowl combine clarified butter with remaining ingredients; blend until smooth. Heat crepe pan over medium high heat. Pour in 2-3 tablespoons of batter. Tilt in all directions, swirling batter so it covers pan. Cook crepe until browned, turn and brown other side for a few seconds. Remove from pan and stack between waxed paper.

Louise Cogburn (Mrs. Robert A.)

POTS DE CRÈME MARNIER

2 cups heavy cream
4 egg yolks
5 tablespoons sugar
⅛ teaspoon salt

1 tablespoon grated orange rind
2 tablespoon Grand Marnier
Candied Violets (optional)

Place cream in saucepan and bring almost to a boil. Beat egg yolks, sugar and salt until light and lemon colored. Gradually add cream to egg yolks, stirring with a wire whisk. Place saucepan over low heat (in double boiler) and stir with wooden spoon until the custard thickens and coats spoon. Immediately set it in a basin of cold water to stop the cooking action. Stir in grated orange rind and Grand Marnier. Pour into creme pots; chill thoroughly. Garnish each, if desired with violets.

Candied Violets

Violets
Egg whites

Superfine sugar

Brush individual violets with egg whites and dip in sugar; dry. Violet leaves may be brushed with egg whites also.

Ann Aldrich Logue

ANGEL CAKE ROYALE

1 envelope gelatin
½ cup cold water
6 eggs, separated
1½ cups sugar, divided
1½ teaspoons grated lemon rind
¾ cup lemon juice

1 angel food cake, broken into
  pieces (about 6 cups)
2 cups heavy cream, whipped
Fresh strawberries or twisted
  lemon slices for garnish

Soften gelatin in cold water. Combine egg yolks, ¾ cup sugar, lemon rind and juice. Cook over hot, not boiling, water, stirring constantly until mixture coats a spoon. Remove from heat; add gelatin and stir to dissolve. Chill until partially set, about 30 minutes. Beat egg whites until stiff, adding remaining sugar. Fold into custard. Tear cake into pieces and alternate layers of cake and custard in a greased tube pan. Refrigerate to set. Run knife around edge of pan and turn cake onto platter; frost with whipped cream. Garnish with fresh strawberries or twisted lemon slices.

Jan Fensom (Mrs. James B.)

BRANDY SOUFFLÉ

5 eggs, separated
¾ cup sugar
¼ cup brandy
¼ cup sherry
¼ cup Benedictine

2 tablespoons lemon juice
3 envelopes unflavored gelatin
½ cup water
2 cups heavy cream, whipped and
  divided

Wrap a collar of greased aluminum foil around the top of a lightly greased and sugared 1½-quart souffle dish. Beat egg yolks until light and lemon colored. Gradually add sugar, brandy, sherry, Benedictine and lemon juice; beat until well-blended. Soften gelatin in water; place over low heat, stirring until dissolved. Add to egg mixture. Beat egg whites until stiff but not dry; fold into gelatin mixture along with whipped cream. Pour mixture into souffle dish; chill overnight or until firm. Remove foil collar before serving. Serves 12.

Hannelore Holland (Mrs. William E.)

SOUFFLÉ AU GRAND MARNIER

1 cup fresh milk
4 eggs, separated
⅝ cup powdered sugar
⅓ cup whole wheat flour

2 tablespoons butter
  (no substitutes)
¼ cup Grand Marnier
Powdered sugar

Bring milk to a boil in saucepan. In large saucepan mix egg yolks and sugar until smooth. Add flour and mix thoroughly. Pour boiling milk over this mixture, mix briskly with whisk and continue to beat as you bring it to a boil over high heat. Remove from heat immediately when boiling begins. Melt in butter and Grand Marnier; set mixture aside. Butter inside of a souffle dish and sprinkle with powdered sugar; set aside. Whip egg whites until stiff. Fold gently into Grand Marnier mixture with wooden spoon. Place in souffle dish and quickly into preheated oven at 350°F. for 15 minutes or until souffle is dark gold. Sprinkle with powdered sugar and serve immediately. A devil to fix, but sinfully delicious!

Nina Godwin (Mrs. Mark T.)

VANILLA CREAM PUDDING

1 cup sugar	4 egg yolks, slightly beaten
¼ cup cornstarch	4 teaspoons butter or margarine
½ teaspoon salt	2 teaspoons vanilla extract
4 cups milk	Dash of cinnamon (optional)

Mix sugar, cornstarch and salt in large saucepan. Gradually stir in milk and beaten egg yolks. With a wire whisk beat all ingredients until well-blended. Cook over medium heat, stirring constantly, until mixture thickens and boils. Boil 1 minute, remove from heat and add butter and vanilla; blend well and cook ½ minute longer. Remove from heat and cool. Pour into individual dessert dishes and sprinkle top of pudding with cinnamon. Serves 8-10.

Variations: Slice bananas and layer bottom of dessert dish, pour vanilla pudding. Encircle edge of dessert dish with vanilla wafers and sprinkle top with cinnamon. Serve cool. Slice pound cake and layer in bottom of a glass bowl; top with pineapple slices. Pour vanilla pudding and sprinkle top with cinnamon; serve chilled.

Dottie San Juan (Mrs. Edward F.)

NEW ORLEANS BREAD PUDDING
WITH WHISKEY SAUCE

1 1-pound loaf French bread	2 cups sugar
4 cups light cream	2 tablespoons vanilla extract
3 eggs, beaten	3 tablespoons butter

Break bread into small pieces and place in a large shallow bowl. Add cream and let stand 10 minutes. Mix well with hands. Add eggs, sugar and vanilla. Melt butter in a 13x9-inch pan. Spoon pudding mixture into pan. Bake at 325°F. for 40-45 minutes or until firm. Cool, cut into squares and serve with whiskey sauce. Serves 15.

Whiskey Sauce

1 cup butter	2 eggs, beaten
2 cups sugar	¼-½ cup whiskey

Cream butter and sugar together; place in a saucepan and cook, stirring constantly, about 10 minutes. Stir in a small amount of hot mixture into eggs; stir eggs into hot mixture. Cook an additional 3 minutes, stirring constantly; let cool. Stir in whiskey to taste. When ready to serve, pour hot sauce over squares. Makes 2 cups.

Ruth Lark (Mrs. William E.)

BUTTER CRUMB CRÈME WITH LEMON SAUCE

½ cup butter
¼ cup firmly packed brown sugar
1 cup sifted all-purpose flour

½ cup chopped pecans
1 gallon vanilla ice cream
Marschino cherries

Combine first 4 ingredients and mix with hands or pastry blender. Spread flat in a 9x11x2½-inch pan. Bake 15 minutes at 400°F. Stir once or twice or it will burn. Remove from oven; reserve ¾ cup for topping. Immediately press rest of mixture on bottom of pan. Cool and fill with vanilla ice cream. Serve in squares topped with lemon sauce. Sprinkle reserved crumbs on top of sauce; garnish each with a cherry. Serves 12.

Lemon Sauce

½ cup butter or margarine
Juice of 3 lemons
Grated rind of 1 lemon

1½ cups sugar
¼ teaspoon salt
4 eggs, beaten

Melt butter in top of double boiler. Add juice, lemon rind, sugar and salt. Add eggs and cook, stirring constantly with a wire whisk, until mixture is thick and glossy; cool.

Patty Segler (Mrs. Jack)

FROZEN AMARETTO PARFAITS

1 package macaroon cookies
6 egg yolks
2 eggs
¾ cup sugar
¾ cup Amaretto liqueur

2 cups heavy cream, whipped
Crushed macaroons
Additional whipped cream
Toasted almonds

Crumble macaroons coarsely and toast at 300°F. for 20 minutes until brown and crunchy but not too hard. Stir occasionally during baking; set aside. In a large bowl, combine egg yolks, eggs and sugar. Beat on high speed of electric mixer until thick and fluffy and sugar is dissolved, about 6 minutes. Continue beating and gradually add liqueur. By hand fold in whipped cream and ¾ of macaroon crumbs. Gently spoon ½ mixture into parfait glasses. Layer a thin layer of crumbs and spoon remaining souffle. Freeze 4-6 hours (cover with foil if longer). To serve top with whipped cream and toasted almonds. Serves 4-6.

Louise Cogburn (Mrs. Robert A.)

EXPRESSO TORTE

4 teaspoons instant coffee powder
1 tablespoon hot water
4 eggs, separated
½ cup sugar, divided

1 cup heavy cream
3 tablespoons coffee-flavored
   liqueur
Almonds

Dissolve coffee powder in hot water and set aside. Beat egg whites until stiff; then gradually add half the sugar, beating until whites hold distinct, short glossy peaks. Fold in coffee liquid and set aside. Beat yolks with remaining sugar until thick and lemon colored; set aside. Whip cream until stiff and blend in liqueur. Thoroughly fold whites, yolks and cream together. Pour into springform pan lined with graham cracker crust. Cover and freeze until firm, at least 8 hours. Remove pan sides, set torte in serving dish, top with almonds and cut in wedges. Serves 12-16.

Crust

1 cup finely crushed graham
   crackers
2 tablespoons melted butter

3 tablespoons sugar
¼ cup finely chopped almonds or
   walnuts

Blend graham crackers with butter, sugar and nuts. Pat evenly over bottom of a 9-inch springform pan.

Fotula Slaughter (Mrs. Jim)

CANTALOUPE SHERBET

1 large cantaloupe
Juice of 1 lemon

1½ cups simple syrup
½ cup heavy cream

Puree the cantaloupe and lemon juice in a blender. Combine puree, cooled syrup and cream in a bowl in freezer. Freeze overnight or until hard. Re-blend mixture in a food processor and place back in freezer. May be made with other fresh fruit of your choice.

Simple Syrup

1 cup sugar

1½ cups water

Combine sugar and water over medium heat; stir for 5 minutes until sugar dissolves and slightly thickens; cool.

The Boars Head Restaurant

PINEAPPLE SHERBET

1½ quarts milk
1 13-ounce can evaporated milk
3 cups sugar

1 20-ounce can crushed pineapple with juice
1 cup lemon juice

Combine ingredients well and freeze in ice cream freezer.

Mrs. John Robert Smith
Port St. Joe, Florida

GRANDMOTHER'S LEMON VELVET ICE CREAM

1 cup lemon juice, strained
4 cups sugar

1 quart heavy cream
Light cream

Soak sugar in lemon juice overnight until sugar dissolves. In ice cream freezer pour in 1 quart heavy cream. Add lemon mixture. Finish filling container with light cream; freeze according to manufacturer's directions.

Bettina Youd (Mrs. Richard)

ORANGE SAUCE FOR ICE CREAM

¼ cup sugar
1 tablespoon cornstarch
½ teaspoon ground ginger

1 11-ounce can mandarin oranges
2 teaspoons butter
1 quart vanilla ice cream

Combine sugar, cornstarch and ginger in a saucepan; blend well. Drain juice from oranges into saucepan and mix. Cook over low heat until thickened, stirring constantly. Add mandarin oranges and butter. Serve warm over ice cream.

Amy Armstrong (Mrs. Larry)

SHIRLEY'S SPECIAL HOT FUDGE SAUCE

6 tablespoons butter or margarine
2 ounces unsweetened chocolate
⅔ cup evaporated milk

2 cups powdered sugar
1 teaspoon vanilla extract

Place butter and chocolate in top of a double boiler and melt over hot water. Add milk and sugar and blend until smooth with wire whisk. Cover and cook 10 minutes over simmering water; add vanilla and sauce is ready to serve. Keeps well in refrigerator for several weeks.

Variation: For Chocolate Fondue: substitute 2 tablespoons (more or less to taste) liqueur (Cointreau, creame de cocoa or brandy). Keep warm in chafing dish or fondue pot for dipping pieces of angel food cake, maraschino cherries, marshmallows or well-drained pieces of fresh fruit.

Shirley Penewitt (Mrs. Paul S.)

CRÈME DE MENTHE SAUCE

½ cup crushed pineapple
1 cup sugar
½ cup light corn syrup

1 cup water
Dash of salt
2 ounces Creme de Menthe Liqueur

In a saucepan combine all ingredients except liqueur and boil for 10 minutes until pineapple is clear in color. Remove from heat; add liqueur and chill. Serve over vanilla ice cream. Store in refrigerator.

Susan Siragusa (Mrs. Robert)

FLAMING MINCEMEAT SAUCE

½ cup sugar
½ cup water
¼ cup cherries
1 cup mincemeat

¼ cup nuts
Sugar cubes
Lemon extract

Combine sugar and water in a saucepan and boil for 5 minutes; remove from heat and add cherries, mincemeat and nuts. Spoon over ice cream. Top with sugar cube dipped in lemon extract; light cube.

Margaret Downer (Mrs. K. C.)

CAKES & ICINGS

BANANA CAKE

2 large ripe bananas
1 18½-ounce package banana
  cake mix
1 3¾-ounce package banana cream
  flavor instant pudding mix

½ cup vegetable oil
4 eggs
1 teaspoon vanilla extract
½ cup water

Peel bananas, scrape off strings and mash well. Blend all ingredients in bowl with electric mixer; beat 3 minutes. Spoon into greased and floured tube pan. Bake at 350°F. for 45-55 minutes or until done. Cool right side up 10 minutes; remove from pan. Freezes well.

Glaze

½ cup butter or margarine
1 cup powdered sugar

About 2 tablespoons pineapple
  juice

Melt butter, blend in powdered sugar until smooth; add juice until runny. Drizzle over warm cake.

Nan Mathis (Mrs. Alex)

APPLE FILLED CAKE

3 cups all-purpose flour
1¼ cups sugar, divided
1 teaspoon baking powder
1 teaspoon soda
1 cup butter or margarine
2 eggs

1 cup sour cream
1 teaspoon vanilla extract
1 21-ounce can apple pie
  filling
1 tablespoon cinnamon

Sift flour, 1 cup sugar, baking powder and soda together in a bowl. Cut in butter. Make a well in center and add eggs; blend well. Add sour cream and vanilla; mix by hand until blended. Put ½ batter into a greased 13x9x2-inch glass ovenproof dish. Spread with apple pie filling. Cover with remaining batter using a wet knife to spread batter over filling. Sprinkle with remaining sugar and cinnamon mixture. Bake at 350°F. 40-50 minutes.

Jean Cardinale (Mrs. Richard)

BLACK FOREST CAKE

4 ounces semisweet chocolate
½ cup butter, softened
½ cup sugar
4 eggs

¾ cup ground almonds
½ cup all-purpose flour
½ cup cornstarch
2 teaspoons baking powder

Melt chocolate in top of a double boiler or in a saucepan over direct low heat. Cream butter and sugar until fluffy, about 5 minutes. Beat in eggs, 1 at a time. Stir in almonds and chocolate. Sift together flour, cornstarch and baking powder. Fold (do not stir) into batter. Pour into 3 (8 or 9-inch) greased cake pans. Bake at 350°F. for 20 minutes. Test for doneness; cool completely.

Filling

4 cups heavy cream
Sugar to taste
1 teaspoon vanilla extract

2 1-pound cans pitted cherries, drained
½ cup cherry brandy

Whip cream until stiff adding sugar to taste; add vanilla. Drain cherries very well on paper towels. Sprinkle each cake layer with ⅓ of the cherry brandy. Spread 2 layers with whipped cream topped with half the drained cherries on each layer. Spread top and sides of cake with remaining cream. Pipe rosettes around top of cake. Place a cherry in the center of each rosette. Put remaining cherries in the center of the top of the cake. Keep refrigerated.

Mary Lane Smallwood (Mrs. Henry)

JANE'S APPLESAUCE TORTE

1 18¼-ounce package spice cake mix
1 cup fine graham cracker crumbs
1 cup applesauce

1 12-ounce container frozen non-dariy whipped topping, thawed and divided
½ cup finely chopped walnuts

Prepare cake mix according to package directions adding graham cracker crumbs before mixing. Bake as directed in 2 round (8 or 9-inch) greased, floured and waxed paper-lined pans. Split cooled layers to form 4 thin layers. Combine applesauce and 1 cup whipped topping; spread between layers. Frost top and sides with remaining whipped topping. Sprinkle with walnuts. Chill at least 1 hour before serving; keep refrigerated. Serves 16.

Laura Darnell (Mrs. Douglas)

"BETTER THAN EVER CAKE"

½ cup butterscotch flavored
  morsels
1 cup semisweet chocolate morsels
½ 4-ounce package German sweet
  chocolate, grated
1 3¾-ounce package vanilla
  instant pudding mix

1 18½-ounce package yellow
  cake mix
4 eggs
½ cup water
1 cup chopped nuts
½ cup vegetable oil
1 cup sour cream

In a large mixing bowl combine all ingredients; mix well. Pour into a greased and floured bundt pan or 13x9x2-inch pan. Bake at 350°F. for 1 hour. May frost with cream cheese frosting.

Brenda Miller (Mrs. Darwin)

BRAZIL NUT CAKE

3 cups Brazil nuts (2 pounds in
  shell)
1 pound pitted dates
1 8-ounce bottle maraschino
  cherries
¾ cup sifted all-purpose flour

¾ cup sugar
½ teaspoon baking powder
½ teaspoon salt
3 eggs
1 teaspoon vanilla extract

Cut nuts in medium pieces; quarter dates; drain cherries. Combine nuts and fruit in a bowl. Mix and sift all dry ingredients over fruit. Beat eggs until foamy and add vanilla. Combine with fruit mixture. Bake in waxed paper-lined, well-greased and floured 9x5x3-inch loaf pan at 300°F. for 1 hour. Reduce heat if cakes brown too quickly. (Let stand a few days before slicing.)

Marjorie Shoemaker (Mrs. John H.)
Hueytown, Alabama

EASY APRICOT BRANDY CAKE

3 cups sugar
1 cup butter
6 eggs
3 cups all-purpose flour
½ teaspoon salt
¼ teaspoon soda

1 cup sour cream
½ teaspoon rum extract
¼ teaspoon almond extract
½ teaspoon lemon extract
1 teaspooon vanilla extract
½ cup apricot brandy

Cream sugar and butter; add remaining ingredients, beating well. Turn into a well-greased 10-inch tube pan. Bake at 325°F. for 1½ hours.

Renaté Marshall (Mrs. David)

CHEESE CAKE

Crust

1 6-ounce package zwieback,
  finely crushed

½ cup butter or margarine, melted
1 tablespoon sugar

Mix all ingredients and press onto sides and bottom of tube cake pan.

Filling

3 8-ounce packages cream cheese,
  softened
¾ cup plus 2⅔ tablespoons
  sugar, divided

3 eggs
1 tablespoon lemon juice
2 cups sour cream

Combine cream cheese, ¾ cup plus 1 tablespoon sugar, eggs and lemon juice; mix well and pour into crust. Bake at 350°F. for 20 minutes. Mix sour cream and remaining sugar and pour slowly over baked cake. Return to oven and bake 5 minutes more. Cool and refrigerate. Serve thoroughly chilled. Freezes well. Serves 6-8.

Gloria Russo (Mrs. Frank)
Genelle Wynn (Mrs. William)

TERRIFIC CHEESE CAKE

Crust

1½ cups cinnamon graham cracker
  crumbs
½ cup melted butter or margarine

¼ cup ground pecans
¼ cup sugar

Mix all ingredients; put into greased springform pan and pat thin.

Filling

3 8-ounce packages cream cheese,
  softened
4 eggs

1 cup sugar
½ teaspoon lemon juice
1 teaspoon vanilla extract

Mix cream cheese on high speed of electric mixer. Beat with eggs, 1 at a time, sugar, lemon juice and vanilla. Beat until smooth. Pour into prepared crust. Bake at 350°F. for 40-50 minutes; chill.

Glaze

1 21-ounce can cherry pie filling
  or your own fresh strawberry
  glaze

Glaze only when cake is thoroughly chilled. Serve very cold.

Jean Ann Fleege (Mrs. Robert)
Pensacola, Florida

CHEWY CHOCOLATE CHIP CAKE

½ cup butter or margarine
2 cups sugar
3 eggs, beaten
2 cups self-rising flour
1 12-ounce package semisweet
  chocolate morsels

1 3½-ounce can coconut
2 cups chopped pecans
1 teaspoon vanilla

Combine all ingredients and pour into a greased 13x9x2-inch pan. Bake at 350°F. for 35-45 minutes.

Carolyn Easterling (Mrs. Tullis)

ORANGE CHEDDAR CHEESE CAKE

Crust

1½ cups crushed cookie wafers 3 tablespoons melted butter
1 teaspoon grated orange rind

Mix crumbs, orange rind and butter; pat into bottom of a greased 10-inch springform pan. Bake at 350°F. for 8 minutes.

Filling

4 8-ounce packages cream cheese, ¼ cup orange flavored liqueur
  softened   or ½ cup beer
1 cup finely shredded sharp   ½ cup heavy cream
  Cheddar cheese   ½ teaspoon grated orange rind
¼ cup all-purpose flour   ½ teaspoon grated lemon rind
1½ cups sugar   ½ teaspoon vanilla extract
5 large eggs

Whip cream cheese until fluffy; blend in Cheddar. Mix flour with sugar and add gradually to cheese. Add eggs, 1 at a time, beating until smooth. Mix in liqueur and cream. Add rinds and vanilla; mix well. Turn into prepared crust and bake at 350°F. for 1¼ hours. Test center for firmness. Cool, then chill. Serve with Orange Sauce.

Orange Sauce

1 cup sugar   Juice of ½ lemon
5 tablespoons all-purpose flour   3 egg yolks
Pinch of salt   1 teaspoon butter
Grated rind of 1 orange   1 cup heavy cream, whipped
½ cup fresh orange juice

In a heavy saucepan mix together sugar, flour and salt. Add rind, juices and egg yolks. Cook over low heat, stirring until thick and smooth. Add butter and cool. Fold in whipped cream. Makes about 2½ cups.

Martha Middlemas (Mrs. Warren, Jr.)

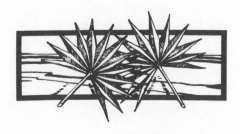

ZUCCHINI CHOCOLATE CAKE

½ cup sour milk or buttermilk
½ cup vegetable oil
½ cup butter or margarine,
  softened
2 eggs
1 teaspoon vanilla extract
2½ cups all-purpose flour
½ teaspoon baking powder

1¾ cups sugar
4 tablespoons cocoa
1 teaspoon cinnamon
2 cups shredded zucchini
1 6-ounce package semisweet
  chocolate morsels
½ cup nuts (optional)

Beat together milk, oil, butter, eggs and vanilla. Add dry ingredients zucchini and chocolate morsels. Pour into a greased and floured bundt pan. Bake at 350°F. for 45 minutes.

Brenda Miller (Mrs. Darwin)

CHAMPAGNE CAKE

1 18½-ounce package butter
  cake mix
1 15½-ounce can crushed pineapple
  with juice
1 3¾-ounce package vanilla
  instant pudding mix

1 8-ounce package cream cheese,
  softened
1 12-ounce container frozen
  non-dairy whipped topping
1 3½-ounce can coconut
Maraschino cherries for garnish

Prepare cake mix according to package directions in a 13x9x2-inch pan. Drain pineapple and pour juice over cake then top with pineapple. Prepare pudding mix according to package directions; mix with cream cheese and spread over pineapple. Top with whipped topping and sprinkle with coconut. Garnish with cherries. Keep cake refrigerated.

Ann Digsby (Mrs. Paul)

SAUERKRAUT SURPRISE CAKE

½ cup butter
1½ cups sugar
3 eggs
1 teaspoon vanilla extract
2 cups sifted all-purpose flour
1 teaspoon baking powder

1 teaspoon soda
¼ teaspoon salt
½ cup cocoa
1 cup water
1 8-ounce can sauerkraut, drained,
    rinsed and finely snipped

In a large mixing bowl cream butter and sugar until light. Beat in eggs, 1 at a time; add vanilla. Sift together flour, baking powder, soda, salt and cocoa; add to creamed mixture alternately with water, beating after addition. Stir in sauerkraut. Turn into greased and floured 13x9x2-inch baking pan. Bake at 350°F. for 35-40 minutes; cool in pan. Frost and cut into squares to serve.

Sour Cream-Chocolate Frosting

1 6-ounce package semisweet
    chocolate morsels
¼ cup butter
½ cup sour cream

1 teaspoon vanilla extract
¼ teaspoon salt
2½-2¾ cups powdered sugar,
    sifted

Melt chocolate pieces and butter over low heat. Remove from heat; blend in sour cream, vanilla and salt. Gradually add powdered sugar to make spreading consistency; beat well.

Jenny Doster (Mrs. Henry)

EASY LEMON CAKE

1 18½-ounce package yellow
    cake mix with pudding
1 14-ounce can sweetened
    condensed milk
1 6-ounce frozen lemonade
    concentrate

1 8-ounce container frozen
    non-dairy whipped topping,
    thawed

Prepare cake mix according to package directions and bake in either 2 9-inch layer cake pans or a bundt pan. Split cake baked in bundt pan before frosting. Cool cake. Combine milk, lemonade and whipped topping; mix well and spread on cooled cake. Refrigerate cake at least 24 hours before serving. Will keep at least a week in refrigerator.

Mary Catherine Jinks (Mrs. C. L., Jr.)

GRAHAM CRACKER CAKE

Cake

1 cup butter
2 cups sugar
5 eggs
¾ cup milk
1 pound graham cracker crumbs

2 teaspoons vanilla extract
2 teaspoons baking powder
1 cup chopped pecans
1 cup coconut

Cream butter and sugar. Add eggs 1 at a time, beating well after each. Add remaining ingredients; mix well. Bake in 4 greased and waxed paper-lined round cake pans at 325°F. for about 30 minutes.

Filling

1 20-ounce can crushed pineapple,
  partially drained
1 cup sugar
½ cup lemon juice

3 tablespoons all-purpose flour
¼ cup butter or margarine,
  melted

Combine all in a heavy saucepan; cook until thick. Spread on 3 cake layers.

Frosting

½ cup butter
2 3-ounce packages cream cheese,
  softened
1 16-ounce package powdered
  sugar

2 teaspoons vanilla extract
3 dashes salt
½ cup chopped pecans

Cream butter and cream cheese; add powdered sugar, vanilla and salt; mix well. Frost top and sides of cake; sprinkle with chopped pecans.

Mrs. C. W. Snell
Marge Walters (Mrs. W. B.)

ELEGANT LEMON CAKE ROLL

4 eggs, separated
¼ cup sugar, divided
1 teaspoon lemon extract
1 tablespoon vegetable oil

⅔ cup sifted cake flour
1 teaspoon baking powder
¼ teaspoon salt
Powdered sugar

Beat egg yolks until light and lemon colored, gradually add ¼ cup sugar, beating constantly. Stir in lemon extract and oil; set aside. Beat egg whites until foamy; gradually add remaining ½ cup sugar, beating until stiff but not dry. Fold yolk mixture into whites. Combine flour, baking powder and salt; fold into egg mixture. Grease a 15x10x1-inch jelly roll pan and line with waxed paper; grease and flour waxed paper. Spread batter evenly in pan. Bake at 375°F. for 10 minutes. Sift powdered sugar in a 15x10-inch rectangle on a linen towel. When cake is done, immediately loosen from sides of pan and turn out onto sugared towel; peel off waxed paper. Starting at narrow end, roll up cake and towel together; cool on wire rack, seam side down. Unroll cake, spread with half Cream Lemon Filling and reroll. Place on serving plate, seam side down; spread remaining filling on all sides. Sprinkle colored coconut over cake roll. Refrigerate 1-2 hours before serving. Serves 8-10.

Creamy Lemon Filling

1 14-ounce can sweetened
   condensed milk
⅓ cup lemon juice
5 drops yellow food coloring

1 4-ounce container frozen
   non-dairy whipped topping,
   thawed

Combine milk, lemon juice and food coloring; mix well. Fold in whipped topping.

Colored Coconut

½ cup coconut
½ teaspoon water

1-2 drops yellow food coloring

Combine all in a plastic bag, close securely and shake well. Sprinkle over cake roll.

Louise Fishel (Mrs. John)

OATMEAL CAKE

1¼ cups boiling water
1 cup oats
½ cup butter or margarine
1 cup firmly packed brown sugar
1 cup sugar
2 eggs, well-beaten

1 teaspoon vanilla extract
1⅓ cups sifted all-purpose
   flour
1 teaspoon soda
½ teaspoon salt
1 teaspoon cinnamon

Pour boiling water over oats and let stand 20 minutes. Cream butter and sugars; mix with oats mixture. Add remaining ingredients. Pour into a greased 13x9x2-inch pan and bake at 350°F. for 30-50 minutes.

Topping

1 cup firmly packed brown sugar
¼ cup butter or margarine
½ cup light cream or evaporated
   milk

1 cup chopped pecans
1 cup coconut

Mix all together and spread on warm cake. Put under broiler and brown about 5 minutes.

Lillian Cooper (Mrs. Michael)

JACK SEGLER'S PEAR CAKE

2 cups sugar
3 eggs, well-beaten
1½ cups vegetable oil
3 cups all-purpose flour
1 teaspoon soda

1 teaspoon salt
1 teaspoon vanilla extract
2 teaspoons cinnamon
4 cups thinly sliced pears,
   drained

Combine sugar, eggs and oil; beat well. Combine flour, soda and salt; add to sugar mixture, 1 cup at a time, mixing well after each addition. Stir in vanilla, cinnamon and pears. Spoon batter into a well-greased 10-inch bundt or tube pan. Bake at 350°F. for 1 hour or until done. Remove from pan and allow to cool; top with Powdered Sugar Glaze. Makes one 10-inch cake.

Powdered Sugar Glaze

1¼ cups sifted powdered sugar

2-4 tablespoons milk

Combine ingredients, blending until smooth. Makes about ½ cup.

Jack Segler
Lorena Surber (Mrs. Emmett)

FUDGE MOCHA CAKE

1 cup unsweetened cocoa
1 teaspoon instant coffee granules
2 cups boiling water
2¾ cups sifted all-purpose
   flour (sift before measuring)
2 teaspoons soda

½ teaspoon salt
½ teaspoon baking powder
1 cup butter, softened
2½ cups sugar
4 eggs
1½ teaspoons vanilla extract

In a medium bowl combine cocoa, coffee granules and boiling water, mixing with a wire whisk until smooth. Cool completely. Sift flour, soda, salt and baking powder together. In a large bowl with electric mixer at high speed, beat butter with sugar, eggs and vanilla until light and fluffy, about 5 minutes, scraping bowl occasionally. At low speed beat in flour mixture alternately with cocoa mixture, beginning and ending with flour mixture; do not overbeat. Divide evenly in 3 greased and lightly floured 9-inch cake pans, smoothing top with spatula. Bake at 350°F. for 25-30 minutes until surface springs back when gently pressed with finger. Loosen sides gently with knife and cool 5 minutes in pans; then turn out onto racks to cool completely.

Filling

1 cup heavy cream, chilled
¼ cup powdered sugar, unsifted

1 teaspoon vanilla extract

Whip cream with sugar and vanilla until thick; set aside.

Frosting

1 6-ounce package semisweet
   chocolate morsels
½ cup light cream

1 cup butter
1 teaspoon instant coffee granules
2½ cups powdered sugar, unsifted

Combine chocolate morsels, cream, butter and coffee granules in saucepan. Cook over medium heat until smooth. Remove from heat and blend in powdered sugar. Turn into a bowl and place over ice; beat until frosting holds its shape.

To assemble: On cake plate place 1 cake layer and top with filling. Place the second layer top side down and spread with remainder of filling. Place third layer top side up. Frost sides of cake first and then the top. Refrigerate at least 1 hour before serving. Very rich-equally good without coffee granules.

Martha Kampbell (Mrs. Harold)

IRISH WHISKEY CHOCOLATE CAKE

4 squares unsweetened chocolate
½ cup butter or margarine
2 cups sugar
2 eggs
2 cups all-purpose flour

2 teaspoons baking powder
1¼ cups milk
¼ cup Irish whiskey
2 teaspoons vanilla extract
1 cup chopped walnuts or pecans

Melt chocolate and allow to cool. Cream butter and sugar. Beat eggs slightly and add to the creamed mixture; stir in cooled chocolate. Sift dry ingredients together and add to butter mixture alternately with milk and whiskey. Blend in vanilla and nuts. Bake in 2 9-inch greased and floured cake pans at 350°F. for 30 minutes. After cake has cooled, remove from pans and slice horizontally with sharp knife. Spread frosting between layers and on top and sides of cake.

Frosting

2 cups heavy cream
⅓ cup cocoa
1 cup powdered sugar

1 teaspoon vanilla extract
¼ cup Irish whiskey
½ cup chopped walnuts

Whip cream with cocoa until soft peaks form. Slowly add sugar, vanilla and whiskey; blend well. Frost cake and sprinkle with chopped nuts.

Melissa Sale (Mrs. Douglas)

MOCHA BUTTER FROSTING

6 tablespoons butter
¼ cup cocoa
1 1-pound package powdered
  sugar, sifted
1½ teaspoon vanilla extract

½ teaspoon instant coffee powder
  dissolved in small amount
  of water or very strong
  brewed black coffee
¼ cup light cream (or less if
  using brewed coffee)

Cream together butter and cocoa in a mixing bowl. Add sugar, vanilla, coffee and enough cream for spreading consistency.

Linda Johnson (Mrs. Greg)

FROST ON THE PUMPKIN CAKE

2 cups sugar
1 cup vegetable oil
4 eggs
2 cups all-purpose flour
2 teaspoons soda
1 teaspoon baking powder

½ teaspoon salt
2 teaspoons ground cinnamon
1 16-ounce can (2 cups) cooked
　mashed pumpkin
½ cup chopped nuts

Combine sugar, oil and eggs in large mixing bowl; mix well. Combine dry ingredients and add to oil mixture, beating well. Stir in pumpkin thoroughly. Pour batter into 2 9-inch greased and floured cake pans or a 13x9x2-inch oblong pan. Bake at 350°F. for 35-40 minutes. Cool cake thoroughly before frosting. Spread frosting on cake and sprinkle with nuts. Refrigerate cake to harden frosting. Makes 1 2-layer cake or 1 oblong sheet cake.

Cream Cheese Frosting

¼ cup butter or margarine,
　softened
1 8-ounce package cream cheese,
　softened

1 16-ounce package powdered
　sugar
2 teaspoons vanilla extract

In a mixing bowl combine all ingredients mixing until smooth and creamy.

Elaine Pilcher (Mrs. M. R.)

LIBBIE'S CAKE FILLING

1 cup crushed pineapple
1 cup sugar
1 cup prepared cake batter

1 teapoon butter flavored
　extract
1 teaspoon vanilla extract

In a medium saucepan combine pineapple and sugar. Bring to a fast boil. Add cake batter and flavorings; cook over medium heat until thick, stirring constantly; cool. Makes filling for 3 9-inch layer cake.

Note: Makes an ordinary white or yellow frosted cake a special treat.

Libbie Comerford (Mrs. Joe)

WHITE CHOCOLATE CAKE

¼ cup white chocolate (4 pieces
   block size or 30 white chocolate
   kisses)
½ cup boiling water
½ cup butter or margarine
½ cup shortening
2 cups sugar

5 eggs, separated
2 cups sifted all-purpose flour
1 teaspoon soda
1 cup buttermilk
1 teaspoon vanilla extract
1 4-ounce can flaked coconut
1 cup chopped nuts

In a small bowl combine chocolate and boiling water, stir to melt chocolate; set aside to cool. In a separate bowl cream butter and shortening until fluffy. Add sugar gradually, beating well. Add yolks, 1 at a time, beating well after each addition. Add chocolate to mixture. Combine flour and soda and add to creamed mixture alternately with buttermilk. Stir in vanilla. Add coconut and nuts; gently fold in beaten egg whites. Pour into 3 greased and floured 8-inch cake pans or one 13x9x2-inch pan. Bake at 350°F. for 25-30 minutes (45-50 minutes for larger pan) or until cake tests done. Let cool in pans for 10 mintues. Let cake cool completely before frosting.

Frosting

1 8-ounce package cream cheese,
   softened
¼ cup butter or margarine,
   softened

1 16-ounce package powdered
   sugar, sifted
1 teaspoon vanilla extract
Coconut and nuts (optional)

Combine all ingredients in a mixing bowl. Beat until smooth and of spreading consistency.

Ros Coleman (Mrs. William H.)

CHOCOLATE POUND CAKE FROSTING

9 tablespoons evaporated milk
½ cup butter
1 16-ounce package powdered
   sugar

½ cup cocoa
1 teaspoon vanilla extract
½ teaspoon almond extract

In a saucepan bring milk and butter to a slight boil and mix in sugar and cocoa; add flavorings. Cream well; spread on cooled chocolate pound cake.

Claudia Shumaker (Mrs. Bob)

SWEET POTATO CAKE
Original recipe

2 cups self-rising flour
2 cups sugar
½ teaspoon soda
½ teaspoon salt
2 teaspoons cinnamon
1½ teaspoons pumpkin pie spice

1 teaspoon vanilla extract
4 eggs
1 cup vegetable oil
1 18-ounce can sweet potatoes,
    drained and mashed
1 cup chopped nuts

Beat all ingredients at low speed of mixer for 30 seconds, scraping bowl constantly. Beat on medium speed 3 minutes, scraping bowl occasionally. Bake in a greased and floured bundt pan at 350°F. for 60-70 minutes or until wooden pick inserted near center comes out clean. Cool 10 minutes in pan; remove from pan. Cool completely; pour glaze over cake.

Glaze

6 tablespoons butter
¼ cup evaporated milk

⅓ cup firmly packed brown sugar
1 cup powdered sugar

Combine butter, milk and brown sugar in a saucepan; bring to a boil. Beat in powdered sugar. Drizzle over cool cake.

Becky Donohue (Mrs. Jim)
Tallahassee, Florida

DUSTY CREAM CHEESE FROSTING

1 3-ounce package cream cheese
½ teaspoon vanilla extract
1 cup powdered sugar

3 tablespoons cocoa
1 teaspoon milk or cream
    (may need more)

Soften cream cheese and blend in vanilla. Sift sugar and cocoa together and gradually add to cream cheese; blend thoroughly. If too stiff to spread, add milk or cream 1 teaspoon at a time until desired consistency is reached.

Carol Crisp (Mrs. Donald)

PUMPKIN ROLL

3 eggs
1 cup sugar
⅔ cup cooked pumpkin
1 teaspoon lemon juice
¾ cup all-purpose flour
1 teaspoon baking powder

½ teaspoon salt
1 teaspoon cinnamon
½ teaspoon allspice
¼ teaspoon nutmeg
1 cup chopped pecans

Beat eggs 5 minutes at high speed, gradually add sugar, then pumpkin mixed with lemon juice. Sift flour, baking powder, salt and spices together; add to egg mixture. Spread in greased and floured 15x10x1-inch pan. Top with chopped nuts, pressing gently into the batter. Bake at 350°F. for 15 minutes or just until set. Remove from oven, loosen edges and turn onto a towel that has been sprinkled generously with powdered sugar. Roll towel and cake up together jelly-roll style and let cool. Unroll and fill, roll again and wrap in foil. Keeps refrigerated for several days.

Filling

1 cup powdered sugar
2 3-ounce packages cream
  cheese, softened

4 teaspoons butter or margarine
Vanilla extract to taste

Combine ingredients, beat until smooth. Spread over cake.

Nellie Laird Johnson

POUND CAKE

1 cup butter or margarine,
  softened
½ cup shortening
1 teaspoon vanilla extract
2½ cups sugar
5 eggs, separated

3½ cups all-purpose flour
  (sift before measuring)
1 teaspoon baking powder
¼ teaspoon salt
1 cup light cream

In a large mixing bowl cream butter, shortening, vanilla and sugar until light; add egg yolks 1 at a time, beating well after each addition. Sift flour, baking powder and salt together. Add flour and light cream alternately to creamed mixture. Beat egg whites until stiff. Fold into cake mixture. Pour batter into a greased and floured 10-inch tube pan. Bake at 325°F. for 1¼ hours or until done. Let cool slightly in pan; remove from pan and cool completely. Serves 12-16.

Sara Scoggins (Mrs. Richard)
Cornelia, Georgia

COCONUT CHIFFON CAKE

2 cups sifted cake flour
1⅓ cups sifted sugar
2½ teaspoon sifted baking
   powder
1 teaspoon sifted salt
½ cup vegetable oil
6 eggs, separated

⅔ cup lukewarm water
2 teaspoons vanilla extract
2 tablespoons coconut extract
½ teaspoon cream of tartar
Pinch of salt
2 4-ounce cans flaked coconut,
   divided

Preheat oven to 325°F. In a large mixing bowl sift flour, sugar, baking powder and salt together. Make a well in center and add oil, egg yolks, water and flavorings. Beat by hand until ingredients are smooth; do not overbeat. Beat egg whites (at room temperature) with cream of tartar and pinch of salt until whites are stiff, not dry. Fold whites into flour mixture, adding 1 can coconut as you fold. Pour batter into an ungreased tube pan and bake at 325°F. for 50-60 minutes. (Do not leave cake sitting while oven heats). Test cake for doneness—cake will spring back when pressed lightly with fingertips when it is done. Remove cake from oven and invert over the neck of a bottle; cool completely, at least 2 hours. When cool, frost cake and press remaining coconut into frosting.

Frosting

4 cups powdered sugar
¼ cup melted butter
1 teaspoon vanilla extract

1 teaspoon coconut extract
About ¼ cup heavy cream

Sift powdered sugar into a bowl. Beat in butter, flavorings and enough heavy cream to make frosting spreadable; use immediately.

Pat Kierman (Mrs. D. E.)
Mabel Godwin (Mrs. J. D.)

CRUSTY POUND CAKE

8 eggs
1½ cups vegetable oil
2¾ cups sugar
3 cups sifted all-purpose flour

Pinch of salt
4 teaspoons flavored extracts
   (3 vanilla, 1 lemon)

Combine ingredients in order listed. Pour into a greased and floured 10-inch tube pan. Bake at 325°F. for 1½ hours.

Laura Landgraf (Mrs. Fred Jr.)

MAMA TOO'S LEMON CHEESE CAKE

2½ cups cake flour
⅛ teaspoon salt
2½ teaspoons baking powder
1 cup butter

2 cups sugar
1 cup milk
5 egg whites
1 teaspoon vanilla extract

Sift flour, salt and baking powder together 3 times; set aside. Cream butter and sugar together until quite fluffy. Add flour mixture alternately with milk to the creamed mixture, beginning and ending with flour and beating slowly only until flour disappears. Fold in stiffly beaten egg whites and vanilla. Pour batter into 3 greased and floured cake pans. Bake at 350°F. for 25 minutes. Put cake together with filling and cover sides and top with 7-minute frosting if desired.

Filling

½ cup butter
1½ cups sugar

5 egg yolks
Juice and rind of 2 lemons

Cream butter and sugar until fluffy. Add egg yolks and beat well. Add lemon juice and grated lemon rind. Cook over boiling water until thickened, stirring occasionally. Filling begins to cling to the side of the pan when it is done. Cool and spread on cooled cake layers.

Gretchen Vann (Mrs. Leroy)

SEVEN MINUTE FROSTING

2 egg whites, at room temperature
1¾ cups sugar
¼ cup light corn syrup
6 tablespoons water, at room
    temperature

¼ teaspoon cream of tartar
1 teaspoon vanilla extract

Combine all ingredients except vanilla in saucepan; cook over very low heat for 7 minutes, beating constantly. (Use electric mixer if available.) Remove from heat and add vanilla.

Elizabeth Crocker
Shreveport, Louisiana

MELINDA'S BIRTHDAY CAKE

1 6-ounce package semisweet
   chocolate morsels
½ cup graham cracker crumbs
⅓ cup plus ½ cup butter, divided
½ cup chopped pecans
2 cups all-purpose flour
1 teaspoon salt

1 teaspoon soda
1¾ cups sugar, divided
2 eggs
1 teaspoon vanilla extract
1¼ cups buttermilk
2 cups heavy cream

Melt ⅓ cup chocolate morsels; set aside. Combine graham cracker crumbs and ⅓ cup melted butter; stir in nuts and remaining chocolate morsels; set aside. Combine flour with salt and soda. Cream remaining butter; add 1½ cups sugar gradually. Add eggs 1 at a time and beat well. Blend in melted chocolate and vanilla. At low speed of mixer add dry ingredients alternately with buttermilk. Pour into 2 9-inch greased and floured pans. Sprinkle with crumb mixture. Bake at 375°F. for 30-45 minutes. Allow cake to cool. Beat cream with remaining ¼ cup sugar until stiff. Place 1 cake layer, crumb side up, on serving plate, top with whipped cream. Place second layer on top, crumb side up. Frost only the sides; chill. Better if made a day ahead.

Fran Mozley (Mrs. Hugh)

ORANGE-PINEAPPLE DELIGHT CAKE

1 18½-ounce package butter
   recipe golden cake mix
¾ cup vegetable oil

4 eggs
1 11-ounce can mandarin oranges,
   juice reserved

In large mixing bowl blend cake mix, oil and eggs. Fold in mandarin oranges, beating well. Pour into 3 greased and floured 9-inch cake pans; bake at 375°F. for 15-20 minutes or until done. Cool cake in pans 10 minutes; remove from pans and frost when completely cooled.

Frosting

1 20-ounce can crushed pineapple,
   undrained
1 10½-ounce package cheese cake
   filling mix
1 heaping tablespoon sugar

1 8-ounce carton sour cream
1 8-ounce container frozen
   non-dairy whipped topping,
   thawed

Combine pineapple, cheese cake filling, sugar and sour cream; mix well. Fold in whipped topping; frost cake and refrigerate.

Anda Gagnet (Mrs. Ted)

SPICE AND RUM RAISIN CAKE
WITH BUTTERMILK FROSTING

3 eggs, beaten
1 cup vegetable oil
1½ cups sugar
2 cups self-rising flour
1 teaspoon ground allspice
1 teaspoon ground cinnamon

1 teaspoon nutmeg
1 cup milk
1 teaspoon rum
1 cup raisins, soaked in rum
    and chopped
1 teaspoon vanilla extract

Combine eggs, oil and sugar in a bowl. In a separate bowl combine dry ingredients; add to egg mixture alternately with the milk, beating well after each addition. Stir in raisins and vanilla. Bake in tube pan at 350°F. for 45-50 minutes or until pick inserted in center comes out clean.

Buttermilk Frosting

1 cup firmly packed brown sugar
½ teaspoon soda
2 tablespoons butter

1 tablespoon dark corn syrup
½ cup buttermilk
1 tablespoon rum

Combine all ingredients except rum in a saucepan. Cook, stirring constantly, to the soft-ball stage (approximately 235°F.) for about 5 minutes. Remove from heat, add rum and beat well. Frosting should be consistency of a glaze (not hard). Pour over raisin cake.

Gerry Sale (Mrs. Tom)

LEMON EXTRACT FRUIT CAKE

2 cups butter or margarine
2 cups sugar
6 eggs
4 cups sifted all-purpose flour
1½ teaspoons baking powder
1½ teaspoons salt

3 ounces lemon extract
½ pound candied cherries
½ pound candied pineapple
½ pound golden raisins (soaked
    overnight in white wine)
1 pound chopped nuts

In a large bowl cream butter and sugar. Add eggs, 1 at a time, beating after addition. Alternately add dry ingredients and lemon extract to creamed mixture: mix in fruit and nuts. Pour into 2 greased, floured and waxed paper-lined loaf pans. Bake at 300°F. for 1½-2 hours.

Dorothy Logue Durham

PIES

PÂTÉ BRISÉE FOR FOOD PROCESSOR

For Quiche

1 ¼ cups all-purpose flour
¼ teaspoon salt

½ cup butter
3 tablespoons ice water

For Pie Pastry

1 ¼ cups all-purpose flour
¼ teaspoon salt

½ cup shortening
3 tablespoons ice water

Combine flour and salt in food processor. Freeze butter or shortening for approximately 20 minutes or until hard. Cut butter or shortening into 5 pieces. Add to flour. Pulse until mixture resembles corn meal. With machine running, add ice water until pastry almost forms a ball. Shape dough into a ball, dust with flour, wrap in plastic wrap, and chill for 1 hour. Roll out on floured surface.

Martha Middlemas (Mrs. Warren, Jr.)

CREAM CHEESE PIE PASTRY

½ 8-ounce package cream
  cheese
¾ cup unsalted butter

2 ¼ cups all-purpose flour
¼ teaspoon salt

In a bowl mix all ingredients with your hands. It should take no longer than 3-5 minutes. Divide dough and wrap with plastic wrap and refrigerate 30 minutes. Roll out between 2 extra-wide pieces of plastic wrap, adjusting as needed. Place in pie pans. This freezes very well before it's rolled out or in pans. Makes 2 9-inch pastry shells.

Marsha Lewis (Mrs. E. Clay, III)

CLASSIC PUFF PASTRY

3 cups all-purpose flour
Pinch of salt
1 cup ice water

6 tablespoons plus 1½ cups
unsalted butter, well-chilled,
divided

Combine flour and salt in large bowl and blend well. Add 6 tablespoons butter and incorporate into flour with your hands until mixture resembles corn flakes. Add ice water and mix well. Knead dough until it is slightly smooth. Wrap dough well in aluminum foil and chill in refrigerator for 15 minutes. Meanwhile knead remaining butter with your hands until it becomes a pliable ball. Set butter aside. Lightly flour a large work surface and a cold rolling pin (preferably marble). Roll dough into large square ¼-inch thick. Place butter in center and fold sides of dough over butter as if folding an envelope. Flour the dough, transfer to a plastic bag and refrigerate for 30 minutes. Lightly flour work surface. Roll dough into an 18x8-inch rectangle, do not roll completely to edges or butter may escape. Fold dough into ⅓s as if you were folding a business letter, making sure that edges match up perfectly. This completes the first turn. Cover and refrigerate dough 1 hour or freeze 30 minutes. Repeat procedure 4 times for a total of 5 turns. Following the fifth turn, wrap and refrigerate the dough for 2 hours. Puff pastry dough may be kept in refrigerator 3 days or frozen up to 6 months. Makes about 2 pounds of pastry or 1 dozen patty shells.

Hannelore Holland (Mrs. William E.)

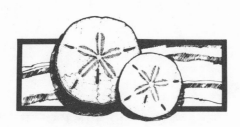

MERINGUE PIE SHELL

2 egg whites
½ cup sugar

⅛ teaspoon cream of tartar
1 teaspoon vanilla extract

Beat egg whites until foamy. Add sugar and cream of tartar gradually; add vanilla. Spread egg whites in buttered bottom of a glass dish. Bake at 300°F. for 1 hour. When done, open oven door and cool completely.

Dot Ennis (Mrs. Buford)

SWEETENED CONDENSED MILK

1 cup powdered milk
⅔ cup sugar

3 tablespoons melted butter
⅓ cup boiling water

Process all ingredients in a food processor or blender. Use this recipe any time sweetened condensed milk is called for.

Kathleen Vance (Mrs. Charles)

PEANUT BUTTER PIE
A super rich pie

Crust

1 cup Graham cracker crumbs
¼ cup butter, melted

¼ cup light brown sugar, firmly packed

Combine all and press into a deep dish pie dish or a 9-inch spring form pan.

Filling

2 cups creamy peanut butter
2 cups sugar
2 8-ounce packages cream cheese

2 tablespoons butter, melted
2 teaspoons vanilla
1½ cups whipping cream, whipped

Beat together all but whipped cream. Then, fold whipped cream into cream cheese mixture. Place in crust.

Glaze

4 ounce semisweet chocolate

3 tablespoons and 2 teaspoons hot coffee

Melt together over double boiler or in microwave. Spread over filling. Chill 6 hours, or until firm.

Powell Ennis

GRANDMOTHER HOBBS' LEMON PIE

1 cup water
1 tablespoon butter
1 cup sugar
¼ cup cornstarch

2 eggs, well-beaten
Juice and grated rind of 2 lemons
1 9-inch baked pastry shell

In top of a double boiler or in a saucepan over low heat cook together water, butter, sugar and cornstarch until of custard consistency. Pour small amount of custard into eggs, mix well and place back into boiler; cook for 2 minutes, stirring constantly. Stir in lemon juice and rind. Pour into pastry shell; top with meringue.

Ruthie Hauser (Mrs. Michael R.)

PINEAPPLE SOUR CREAM PIE

¾ cup sugar
¼ cup all-purpose flour
½ teaspoon salt
1 20-ounce can crushed pineapple,
   undrained

1 cup sour cream
1 tablespoon lemon juice
2 egg yolks, slightly beaten
1 9-inch baked pastry shell

In saucepan combine sugar, flour and salt. Stir in next 3 ingredients. Cook and stir until mixture thickens and bring to a boil; cook 2 minutes. Stir small amount of hot mixture into egg yolks; return to hot mixture, stirring constantly. Cook and stir 2 minutes. Spoon into cooled pastry shell. Allow to cool and top with whipped cream before serving.

Whipped Cream

1 cup heavy cream
2 teaspoons sugar

½ teaspoon vanilla extract

Whip cream with sugar and vanilla. Spread over pie.

Yvi Fernandez (Mrs. Robert)

STRAWBERRY TART

1 8-ounce package cream cheese,
  softened
½ cup sugar
2 tablespoons lemon juice
1 teaspoon grated lemon rind

2 tablespoons heavy cream
1 baked tart shell or pastry
  shell
Fresh ripe strawberries

Mix the cream cheese, sugar, lemon juice and rind and cream until very light and fluffy (like whipped cream). Line the tart shell with the cheese mixture, fill with fresh whole ripe strawberries and cover with glaze.

Strawberry Glaze

3 cups strawberries
1 cup sugar

3 tablespoons cornstarch

Mash berries with the sugar and let stand 30 minutes. Mix with the cornstarch and cook until thick and clear, stirring constantly. Strain and cool. Pour over the berries and refrigerate. Top with whipped cream if desired.

Gay Sudduth (Mrs. Rowe)

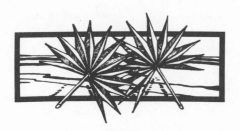

JAPANESE FRUIT PIE

½ cup butter, melted
½ cup margarine, melted
4 eggs, unbeaten
2 cups sugar
1 cup nuts

1 cup coconut
1 6-ounce package semisweet
  chocolate morsels
1 teaspoon vanilla extract
2 9-inch unbaked pastry shells

Combine all ingredients for filling of pie; mix well. Pour into unbaked pastry shells and bake at 350°F. for 45 minutes. Makes 2 9-inch pies or 10-12 smaller snack pies.

Note: Called Japanese Fruit Pie because raisins were originally used instead of chocolate morsels.

LEMON-BLUEBERRY PIE

Lemon Filling

1½ cups sugar
3 tablespoons cornstarch
3 tablespoons all-purpose flour
Dash of salt
1½ cups hot water

3 eggs, slightly beaten
½ teaspoon grated lemon rind
2 tablespoons butter
⅓ cup lemon juice

Mix sugar, cornstarch, flour and salt in a saucepan. Blend in water; bring to a quick boil over high heat, stirring constantly. Reduce to medium heat; cook for about 8 minutes. Remove from heat. Add some of hot liquid to eggs then add back to rest of hot mixture. Bring to a boil, stirring constantly. Reduce to low heat for 4 minutes; remove from heat. Add lemon rind and butter; gradually stir in lemon juice. Allow to cool.

Blueberry Topping

1 cup fresh blueberries
½ cup sugar

2 tablespoons all-purpose flour

Mix blueberries, sugar and flour; cook over medium heat until thick; cool.

1 9-inch graham cracker crust

When cool, pour lemon filling into graham cracker crust; top with blueberry topping and chill for several hours before serving.

Brenda Veal (Mrs. James)
Sweatmore Ranch

VINEGAR PIE

½ cup butter, melted and cooled
1½ cups sugar
2 tablespoons all-purpose flour
1½ tablespoons vanilla extract

2 tablespoons vinegar (apple
  cider or white)
3 eggs, beaten
1 9-inch unbaked pastry shell

Combine the butter and sugar. Add flour, vanilla, vinegar and eggs; pour into unbaked pastry shell and bake for 45 minutes at 375°F.

Gerry Sale (Mrs. Tom, Jr.)

WHITE CHRISTMAS PIE

1 tablespoon unflavored gelatin
¼ cup cold water
1 cup sugar, divided
¼ cup all-purpose flour
½ teaspoon salt
1½ cups milk
¾ teaspoon vanilla extract

¼ teaspoon almond extract
½ cup heavy cream, whipped
3 egg whites
¼ teaspoon cream of tartar
1 cup moist shredded coconut
1 9-inch baked pastry shell

Soften gelatin in cold water; set aside. In a saucepan mix together ½ cup sugar, flour and salt; gradually stir in milk. Cook over low heat, stirring until mixture boils. Boil for 1 minute; add gelatin; chill. When partially set, beat with rotary beater until smooth. Add flavorings. Fold whipped cream into mixture. Make a meringue of the egg whites beaten with cream of tartar and remaining ½ cup sugar. Fold the flavored mixture gently into the meringue. Fold in coconut, reserving a small amount to sprinkle on top of pie. Pile into pastry shell, sprinkle with coconut and chill in refrigerator.

Kathryn Olivier (Mrs. Jules)

BUTTERMILK PIE

3 eggs, beaten
1½ cups sugar
½ cup buttermilk
2 tablespoons all-purpose flour

1 teaspoon vanilla extract
½ cup melted butter or margarine
1 9-inch pastry shell

Mix all ingredients in order listed. Pour into pastry shell. Bake at 300°F. for 1-1½ hours or until set.

Gwen Fulford (Mrs. Aubrey)

Variation: Add ⅔ of a 14-ounce bag of coconut to mixture. Sprinkle remaining coconut over pie before baking.

Laura Hauser McCain (Mrs. Allen)

PRALINE SURPRISE PIE

⅓ cup firmly packed brown sugar
⅓ cup butter, melted
½ cup chopped nuts
1 9-inch unbaked pastry shell

1 5⅝-ounce package instant
  vanilla pudding mix
Milk
1 4-ounce container frozen
  non-dairy whipped topping

Combine sugar, butter and nuts and spread in pastry shell. Bake at 450°F. for 10 minutes; cool. Prepare pudding according to package directions using a little less milk. Take out 1 cup pudding. Spread remainder over nut layer in pastry shell. Mix reserved pudding with whipped topping and spread on top of pie.

Mary Anne Christo

MISS MAGGIE'S PUMPKIN PIE

2 eggs, beaten
1 cup pumpkin
1 tablespoon melted butter
1 cup sugar
1 scant teaspoon salt
1 cup evaporated milk
2 teaspoons cinnamon
1 teaspoon ginger

Dash of cloves
Dash of allspice
Dash of mace
Grated lemon rind (optional)
½ teaspoon vanilla extract
  (optional)
1 10-inch partially baked deep
  dish pastry shell

Combine pie ingredients in order given; blend well. Pour into partially baked pastry shell and bake at 450°F. for 10 minutes; reduce heat to 350°F. for 35 minutes or until a knife inserted in center comes out almost clean. Remove from oven; cool completely. Spread topping over pie.

Topping

½ cup coarsely chopped pecans
½ cup firmly packed brown sugar

2 tablespoons butter, softened

Combine ingredients and spread over pie. Broil 5 inches from heat until it bubbles.

Mary Louise Moyer (Mrs. Walter)
Pensacola, Florida

HOLIDAY FRUIT PIE

1 16-ounce can cherries,
drained and juice reserved
1 20-ounce can crushed pineapple, drained and juice
reserved
Water
½ cup sugar

¼ cup all-purpose flour
1 6-ounce package cherry
flavored gelatin
5 large bananas, sliced
1 cup chopped pecans
3 9-inch baked pastry shells
Whipped cream or favorite topping

Drain cherries and pineapple into a 2-cup measure. Finish filling with water and add sugar and flour; bring to a boil and cook until thick. Stir in gelatin, stirring until dissolved. Add pineapple, cherries, bananas and pecans. Pour into pastry shells and cool. Top with whipped cream or your favorite topping.

Helen McGee

FROSTED DAIQUIRI PIE

1 envelope unflavored gelatin
1 cup sugar, divided
½ teaspoon salt
3 eggs, separated
¼ cup cold water
½ cup fresh lime or lemon juice

1 teaspoon grated lime or lemon
rind
Few drops green food coloring
⅓ cup light rum
1 9-inch baked pastry shell
Whipped cream

In top of a double boiler combine gelatin with ⅔ cup sugar, salt, egg yolks, water and lime juice. With rotary beater beat until blended. Cook over boiling water, stirring until mixture coats a spoon. Remove from heat; add rind and food coloring to a pale green tint. Cool mixture; stir in rum. Refrigerate mixture until slightly thicker than unbeaten egg whites. In large bowl beat egg whites until they form soft peaks; add remaining ⅓ cup sugar, 1 tablespoon at a time, beating until stiff. Fold in gelatin mixture. Turn mixture into baked pastry shell; refrigerate several hours. Top with whipped cream before serving.

Bette Vetland (Mrs. Ted)

SUPER CHOCOLATE PIE

1⅓ cups semisweet chocolate   1 cup sugar, divided
   morsels   8 eggs, separated
1 cup butter or margarine,   1 teaspoon vanilla extract
   melted   ¼ teaspoon cream of tartar

In a food processor with steel blade process chocolate morsels until well chopped. With machine running, add melted butter. Process until chocolate is completely melted. Add ½ cup sugar, egg yolks and vanilla; process until smooth and thick. Beat egg whites with cream of tartar until stiff peaks form, then add remaining ½ cup sugar and beat until smooth and glossy. Add half the chocolate mixture to the egg whites. Fold in carefully and add remaining half, folding until no chocolate streaks remain. Pour mixture into a 10-inch glass pie pan until it reaches ½-inch below the edge of pan. Reserve remaining batter (about 3 cups). Bake at 325°F. for 35 minutes. Cool shell completely; it will fall some. Add filling when cool.

Filling

1 cup sour cream   3 tablespoons powdered sugar
3 cups reserved chocolate batter   1 teaspoon vanilla extract
1 cup heavy cream, whipped   Shaved chocolate

Combine sour cream with reserved chocolate mixture and mix well. Add filling to cooled pie shell; refrigerate before serving. Whip cream with powdered sugar and vanilla; pipe around edges of pie and garnish with shaved chocolate.

Ruth Lark (Mrs. William E.)

CHOCOLATE CHESS PECAN PIE

1½ cups sugar   3½ tablespoons cocoa
2 eggs   1 teaspoon vanilla extract
1 5.3-ounce can evaporated milk   1 cup chopped or broken pecans
½ cup butter or margarine, melted   1 9-inch unbaked pastry shell

Mix together first 7 ingredients and pour into pastry shell. Bake at 325°F. for 45-50 minutes. Cool and serve topped with whipped cream.

Whipped Cream

1 cup heavy cream   1 teaspoon vanilla extract
2 teaspoons sugar

Beat cream, gradually adding sugar and vanilla until fluffy. Serve on top of pie.

Jann Daughdrill (Mrs. Bill)

298

SHANG-HAI PIE
Traditionally served at Shang-Hai card games.

2 eggs, at room temperature
1 cup sugar
½ cup all-purpose flour
½ cup butter, melted and cooled
1 cup chocolate morsels

1 tablespoon bourbon
1 tablespoon vanilla extract
1 cup chopped nuts
1 9-inch unbaked pastry shell
Whipped cream

Beat eggs, gradually add sugar, flour and butter. Stir in chocolate morsels, bourbon, vanilla and nuts; pour into pastry shell. Bake at 350°F. about 40 minutes until golden. Top with whipped cream.

Helen Ingram

FRENCH SILK CHOCOLATE PIE

Crust

1⅓ cups crushed vanilla
   wafers

6½ tablespoons melted butter
1½ tablespoons sugar

Combine crumbs, butter and sugar. Line the bottom and ½-inch up the sides of a 9-inch pie plate. Bake at 350°F. for 7 minutes; cool.

Filling

¾ cup butter, at room
   temperature
1 cup plus 2 tablespoons superfine
   sugar

1½ squares unsweetened chocolate,
   melted
1½ teaspoons vanilla extract
3 eggs

Beat butter until creamy with electric mixer. Add sugar gradually, continue beating, then add melted chocolate and vanilla. Add 2 eggs and beat 3 minutes. Add remaining egg and beat 3 minutes. Pour into cooled crust and refrigerate.

Topping

1 cup heavy cream
1 tablespoon sugar

¼ teaspoon vanilla extract
⅓ cup toasted sliced almonds

Whip cream until peaks form, add sugar and vanilla and mix thoroughly with cream. When pie is chilled, add cream; sprinkle with toasted almonds.

Gay Sudduth (Mrs. Rowe)

CHOCOLATE DELIGHT

Crust

4 egg whites, at room temperature
¼ teaspoon cream of tartar
1 cup sugar

⅛ teaspoon salt
½ teaspoon vanilla extract
½ cup finely chopped pecans

Beat egg whites with cream of tartar and salt until foamy. Continue beating, adding sugar gradually until very stiff, glossy peaks are formed. Fold in vanilla and nuts. Spread over bottom and sides of a well-greased 9-inch pie plate and a well-greased 8-inch pie plate. Bake at 275°F. for 50 minutes. Turn off heat and allow to cool in oven.

Filling

1 12-ounce package semisweet
chocolate morsels
4 egg yolks
½ cup hot water

½ teaspoon cinnamon
½ cup sugar
2 cups heavy cream

Melt chocolate morsels over hot, not boiling, water. Blend egg yolks, beaten with hot water, into melted chocolate until smooth. Spread 3 tablespoons chocolate mixture over each cooled meringue. Chill remaining chocolate mixture until it begins to thicken, about 20 minutes. Whip cream until it begins to thicken, gradually adding cinnamon and sugar. Continue whipping until thick. Spread half of whipped cream over chocolate in pie shells. Fold chilled chocolate mixture into remaining whipped cream. Spread over whipped cream in each pie shell. Chill at least 4 hours before serving. Yield: 2 pies.

Joan Morrow (Mrs. John)

SOUTHERN PECAN PIE

2 tablespoons butter or
margarine, softened
1½ cups firmly packed dark
brown sugar
1½ cups light corn syrup
5 eggs

1½ teaspoons vanilla extract
¼ teaspoon salt
1½ cups pecan pieces
1 10-inch unbaked deep dish
pastry shell

Cream butter and sugar; add syrup, eggs, vanilla and salt. Beat well; stir in pecans. Pour into pastry shell and bake at 325°F. for 1 hour or until set.

Nell Ennis (Mrs. Powell)

TEA TIME

RUTH KORBER'S OATMEAL COOKIES

1 cup butter
1 cup powdered sugar
1½ cups all-purpose flour
1 cup old-fashioned oats

½ teaspoon soda
2 teaspoons vanilla extract
Chocolate sprinkles

Cream butter and sugar, add all other ingredients except chocolate; mix well. Roll dough in waxed paper into cylinder-shape the size desired. Then place dough in another sheet of waxed paper covered with chocolate sprinkles; roll until coated and refrigerate overnight. Slice thin and bake at 350°F. for 25-30 minutes. These are a light, buttery tea cookie-not at all like the usual oatmeal cookie.

Rosilin Mead
Louisa Salinas (Mrs. Bob)
Bettina Youd (Mrs. Richard)

MARGARET'S PERSIMMON COOKIES

1 teaspoon soda
1 cup persimmon pulp
½ cup shortening
1 cup sugar
1 egg, beaten
2 cups all-purpose flour

½ teaspoon salt
½ teaspoon cloves
½ teaspoon cinnamon
½ teaspoon nutmeg
1 cup raisins
1 cup black walnuts

Stir soda into persimmon pulp. Cream shortening and sugar; add egg and pulp. Sift dry ingredients; add to creamed mixture. Add raisins and nuts. Drop by teaspoon onto greased cookie sheet. Bake at 350°F. for 10-12 minutes.

Note: Mash persimmon through colander to obtain pulp.

June Greenwell (Mrs. Mark)
Mt. Dora, Florida

TURTLE SQUARES

1 14-ounce package caramels
1 cup evaporated milk, divided
1 18½-ounce package German
   chocolate cake mix

¾ cup butter or margarine
1 cup pecans
1 cup milk chocolate morsels

Melt caramels with ¼ cup evaporated milk; set aside. Beat together dry cake mix, remaining ¾ cup evaporated milk and butter; beat well. Bake half the cake batter in a greased 13x9-inch dish at 350°F. for 15 minutes. Spread caramel mixture on top; add pecans and chocolate morsels. Spread with remaining batter and bake 15-20 minutes longer. Test with toothpick or baking straw for doneness.

Mae Morris (Mrs. Rodney)

COOKIE OWLS

⅔ cup shortening
1 cup firmly packed brown sugar
1 egg
1 teaspoon vanilla extract
1 cup crunchy peanut butter
1⅓ cups all-purpose flour
1 teaspoon baking powder

½ teaspoon salt
1 cup quick or old-fashioned
   oats, uncooked
1 ounce no melt chocolate
1 6-ounce package semisweet
   chocolate morsels
Whole cashews

Beat shortening and sugar until creamy. Add egg, vanilla, peanut butter and blend. Sift together flour, baking powder and salt; add to creamed mixture and blend. Stir in oats. Divide dough in half. Shape one half to form an 8-inch roll; add chocolate to remaining half of dough. Roll chocolate dough on waxed paper to form an 8-inch square. Place rolled dough on chocolate dough and wrap chocolate dough around roll; pinch seam together. Cover with plastic wrap and chill at least 1 hour. (If refrigerated several hours, let stand at room temperature 10 minutes before slicing.) Cut into ¼-inch slices. For each owl face, pinch chocolate dough to form 2 ears, use 2 chocolate morsels for eyes and a cashew for a beak. Place on ungreased cookie sheet and bake at 350°F. for 12-15 minutes.

Note: If desired make small hole in cookie with skewer before baking; after cookies bake, thread ribbon through to hang on tree. These have become a Halloween tradition at our house.

Jane Keller (Mrs. Joe M.)

CHEESE CAKE SQUARES

Crust

⅓ cup butter or margarine
⅓ cup firmly packed light
  brown sugar

1 cup all-purpose flour
½ cup chopped pecans

Cream butter and sugar in a small mixing bowl. Add flour and nuts to make a crumb mixture. Press into bottom of a greased 9-inch square pan and bake at 350°F. for 10-12 minutes.

Filling

¼ cup sugar
1 8-ounce package and 1
  3-ounce package cream
  cheese, softened

1 egg
2 tablespoons milk
½ teaspoon vanilla extract

Blend sugar with cream cheese until smooth. Add egg, milk and vanilla. Beat well and spread over crust. Bake at 350°F. for 25 minutes.

Topping

1 cup sour cream   ¼ cup sugar

Combine sour cream and sugar; spread over top of baked filling and return to oven for 5 minutes more. Makes 16 2-inch squares.

Karen Green (Mrs. Hubert)

CORINNE'S COOKIES

1 cup all-purpose flour
½ teaspoon soda
½ teaspoon baking powder
¼ teaspoon salt
½ cup sugar
½ cup firmly packed brown sugar
½ cup butter

1 egg
1 tablespoon cold water
1 teaspoon vanilla extract
1½ cups rolled oats
¼ cup nuts
½ cup coconut

Mix dry ingredients; add sugars, butter and egg and beat until creamy. Add water and vanilla, blend well then stir in oats, nuts and coconut. Bake on ungreased cookie sheet for 15 minutes at 350°F.

Corinne DeRuiter (Mrs. James)

MINIATURE CHEESE CAKES

2 8-ounce packages cream cheese   Butter or margarine
¾ cup sugar   Graham cracker crumbs
3 eggs, separated

Beat together cream cheese, sugar and egg yolks until fluffy. Beat egg whites until stiff and fold into mixture; set aside. Butter 48 miniature muffin cups; sprinkle with graham cracker crumbs (dump out excess). Fill tins with mixture and bake at 350°F. for 15-20 minutes until set. Place about ½ teaspoon of cooked topping on each cake. May top each cake with favorite pie filling or fruit.

Topping

¾ cup sour cream   2 tablespoons sugar

Mix sour cream and sugar and put in baking dish. Cook mixture in 450°F. oven for 5 minutes.

Carol Crisp (Mrs. Donald)

CHESS PIE SQUARES

1½ cups all-purpose flour   1 cup chopped nuts
1¼ cups firmly packed brown   2 tablespoons milk
   sugar, divided   1 tablespoon all-purpose flour
1 cup butter or margarine,   1 tablespoon corn meal
   divided   2 eggs
½ cup sugar   Juice of 1 lemon

Combine 1½ cups flour and ¼ cup brown sugar. Cut in ½ cup butter, using mixer on low speed. Press into a 13x9x2-inch pan. Bake at 375°F. for 10 minutes. Combine remaining ingredients and pour over crust. Bake 20 minutes longer or until browned. Cool and cut into squares to serve.

Nell Ennis (Mrs. Powell)

CREAM CHEESE COOKIES

Pastry

4 ounces cream cheese
½ cup butter
1 egg
1 teaspoon sugar

Pinch of salt
1 cup all-purpose flour
Melted butter or margarine

Blend all ingredients except butter and refrigerate overnight. Roll pastry very thin on a floured board; spread with filling mixture. Roll up once basting top with melted butter. Bake at 350°F. 20-30 minutes until golden brown. When cool, cut slices diagonally, about 3-inches long.

Filling

½ cup jelly or preserves
¼ cup raisins

¼ cup chopped nuts
Dash of cinnamon (optional)

Combine all ingredients and spread over pastry.

Susan Siragusa (Mrs. Robert)
Susan Brancato (Mrs. Joseph)

DANISH PUFF

2 cups all-purpose flour,
  divided
1 cup butter or margarine,
  divided

2 tablespoons plus 1 cup water,
  divided
1 teaspoon almond extract
3 eggs

Measure 1 cup flour in bowl; cut in ½ cup butter, sprinkle with 2 tablespoons water; mix with fork. Round into a ball; divide in half. Pat into 2 strips 12x3-inches; place 3-inches apart on ungreased baking sheet. In a saucepan mix remaining ½ cup butter and 1 cup water and bring to a boil. Remove from heat, add flavoring. Beat in remaining 1 cup flour, stirring quickly to prevent lumping. When smooth, add 1 egg at a time, beating well after each addition until smooth. Divide in half and spread one half evenly over each piece of pastry. Bake at 350°F. about 1 hour (puff has a tendency to shrink while cooling, leaving a custard-like portion in center). Frost with powdered sugar frosting and sprinkle with chopped nuts. Serves 8-12.

Renee Adams

BRAZIL NUT STICKS

2 eggs
2 cups firmly packed light
   brown sugar
1 pound shelled Brazil nuts
   (2 pounds unshelled)

2 cups all-purpose flour
½ teaspoon baking powder
1 teaspoon vanilla extract
Powdered sugar

Beat eggs until light; add sugar and beat again. Grind nuts coarsely; add to flour and baking powder. Stir flour mixture into eggs and sugar, add vanilla and beat until thoroughly mixed. Let stand 1-2 hours in refrigerator. Mold into bars 2-inches long, ¼-inch wide and ½-¾ inch thick. Bake at 325°F. for 25-30 minutes. Roll in powdered sugar when cool. Let soften for 3 weeks in a covered tin before serving. If cookies fail to soften, put a piece of soft white bread in tin overnight.

Note: To shell Brazil nuts, freeze and crack frozen; don't remove brown skin. This recipe has been in my family 50 years-a Christmas favorite!

Anda Gagnet (Mrs. Ted)

MELTING MOMENTS

1 cup butter or margarine,
   softened
½ cup powdered sugar

1¼ cups unsifted all-purpose
   flour
¾ cup cornstarch

In a large mixing bowl cream butter and sugar until light and fluffy. Beat in flour and cornstarch until well mixed. Wrap and refrigerate dough at least 2 hours or overnight. Roll dough into 1-inch balls. Place on ungreased cookie sheet; bake at 325°F. for 10 minutes or until firm but golden. Cool slightly and remove from pan; cool completely. Top cookies with glaze; let dry. Makes about 3½ dozen.

Glaze

1½ cups powdered sugar, sifted   3 tablespoons orange or lemon juice

In a small bowl mix sugar and juice. Frost cookies.

Sara Scoggins (Mrs. Richard)
Cornelia, Georgia

JANE'S CHOCOLATE COOKIES

½ cup corn oil
4 squares unsweetened chocolate, melted
2 cups sugar
4 eggs
2 teaspoons vanilla extract

2 cups sifted all-purpose flour
2 teaspoons baking powder
½ teaspoon salt
1 cup chopped pecans
1 cup powdered sugar

Mix corn oil, melted chocolate and sugar. Blend in 1 egg at a time until well-mixed. Add vanilla; sift and stir together flour, baking powder and salt; add to mixture. Stir in pecans. Chill dough for several hours. Drop a teaspoon of dough into sifted powdered sugar and roll into a small ball. Place balls of dough about 2-inches apart on a greased baking sheet. Bake at 350°F. for 10-12 minutes; cool on a rack. Makes about 6 dozen cookies.

Martha Brock (Mrs. Lester)

KOURAMBIEDES
Greek Wedding Cookies

2 cups butter (sweet or clarified), at room temperature
½ cup sugar
1 egg yolk
1 ounce cognac or whiskey
1 teaspoon vanilla extract

½ teaspoon baking powder
1 cup coarsely chopped almonds, roasted
2 cups sifted all-purpose flour
2-3 16-ounce packages powdered sugar

Place butter in mixing bowl and beat about 30 minutes. Add sugar and egg yolk; continue to beat for 30 minutes. Add liquor, vanilla and baking powder. Place mixture in larger bowl and add almonds. Add flour until mixture is firm enough to shape by hand. Pinch off pieces of dough; shape round as a silver dollar or in a "U" shape. Bake on greased cookie sheet at 250°F. about 25 minutes or until golden brown. Run under broiler for 1-2 seconds. Sift powdered sugar liberally over each cookie, covering it, while it is hot. Let cool. Sift again with powdered sugar. Makes 40-45 cookies.

Evdokia Vallas (Mrs. Tony)

RUSSIAN ROCKS

½ cup butter
1½ cups sugar
3 eggs, well-beaten
½ teaspoon baking powder
½ teaspoon cinnamon
½ teaspoon nutmeg
½ teaspoon cloves
½ cup blackberry wine

½ teaspoon lemon extract
½ teaspoon vanilla extract
3 cups all-purpose flour
½ teaspoon salt
½ pound candied pineapple
1 pound candied cherries
2 pounds chopped dates
4 cups nut halves

Cream butter and sugar; add eggs. Mix spices and baking powder in warm wine; add to creamed mixture. Add flavorings. Sift flour and salt over fruit and nuts; mix well. Add creamed mixture and mix well. Drop by spoonfuls onto greased cookie sheet. Bake at 350°F. for 15 minutes. While baking, baste cookies with wine. Wrap cookies well in cheese cloth and aluminum foil. Place in covered container with apple to help maintain moistness. Dribble wine over cookies every few days. Makes about 100 cookies.

Debbie Lane

BENNE SEED COOKIES

½ cup benne seeds (sesame seed)
1 cup sugar
½ cup butter
1¼ cups flour
1 teaspoon baking powder

½ teaspoon salt
½ teaspoon baking soda
1 egg
1 teaspoon vanilla

Sauté seeds in a non-stick skillet over a low heat; watching carefully as they will burn easily. Set aside. Cream sugar and butter until light and fluffy. Combine dry ingredients; add to butter sugar mixture and mix well using a fork. Stir in egg, vanilla and seeds. Mix until all ingredients are well blended. Drop by teaspoonfuls onto an ungreased baking sheet. Bake for 8 to 10 minutes or until lightly browned. Cool slightly on the baking sheet then remove from sheet and cool completely. Yield: 3 dozen.

Note: Benne seeds may be purchased by the pound at a health food store.

Dedee Higby (Mrs. Lynn C.)

DATE AND NUT BARS

¼ cup vegetable oil
1 cup firmly packed brown sugar
2 eggs
½ teaspoon vanilla extract
¾ cup sifted all-purpose flour

¼ teaspoon baking powder
¼ teaspoon salt
½ cup chopped nuts
1 cup chopped dates
Powdered sugar

Mix oil and sugar; add eggs and vanilla and beat well. Sift dry ingredients together; add to egg mixture. Stir in nuts and dates. Place in an oiled 8 or 9-inch square pan. Bake at 350°F. for 30-35 minutes. Cut into bars and roll in powdered sugar while still warm. Makes about 32 (1x2-inch) bars.

Ann Bane (Mrs. Curtis)

AUNT MARCY'S APRICOT SQUARES

2 cups butter
2 cups sugar
4 egg yolks

4 cups all-purpose flour
1 cup chopped pecans
1 cup apricot preserves

Cream butter until light and fluffy; gradually add sugar and beat until creamy. Add egg yolks; beat well. Gradually add flour then fold in nuts. Press half the batter into the bottom of 2 8-inch square, greased pans. Spread with preserves; cover with remaining batter. Bake at 325°F. for 1 hour until light brown.

Susan Blue (Mrs. Robert, Jr.)

TOFFEE SQUARES WITH CHOCOLATE TOPPING

1 cup butter, softened
1 cup firmly packed light
  brown sugar
1 egg yolk
1 teaspoon vanilla extract

2 cups sifted all-purpose flour
6 ounces semisweet chocolate
  (or more for thicker
  topping)
1 cup chopped walnuts

In a large mixing bowl cream butter and sugar; beat in the egg yolk and vanilla. Stir in the flour. Spread thinly in a 13x9-inch pan; bake at 350°F. for 15-20 mintues. Remove from oven. In the top of a double boiler melt chocolate; spread on cookie surface while still warm. Sprinkle with chopped walnuts; cut into squares when cool. Makes 40 squares.

Marsha Benton (Mrs. John J., Jr.)

FRUIT CAKE BARS

2 pounds pitted dates
½ pound candied cherries
½ pound candied pineapple, cut
  into bite-size pieces
1 pound pecan halves

1 cup all-purpose flour
1 cup sugar
2 teaspoons baking powder
4 eggs
2 teaspoons vanilla extract

Mix fruit, nuts and dry ingredients in a large bowl. Beat eggs and vanilla in a separate bowl; add to fruit mixture. Spread in a greased baking sheet at 300°F. for 1 hour. Cool and cut into bars. Delicious for holiday giving.

Note: If you prefer, substitute 1 pound cherries, 1 pound pineapple and 1 pound dates.

Faye Carroll (Mrs. John)
Kissimmee, Florida

GRANDMOTHER'S NUTTY BUTTER CHOCO BARS

½ cup butter or margarine,
  softened
½ cup firmly packed light
  brown sugar
1¼ cups all-purpose flour
¼ teaspoon salt

¾ cup creamy peanut butter
1 6-ounce package chocolate
  morsels
2 tablespoons light corn syrup
2 tablespoons water
1 cup chopped pecans

Combine butter and brown sugar; beat until creamy. Sift together flour and salt and blend with creamed mixture. Press evenly into bottom of a 13x9x2-inch pan and bake at 350°F. for 20 minutes. Spread peanut butter over crust while hot; then cool. Over hot water in top of a double boiler, melt chocolate, corn syrup and water, stirring occasionally. Stir in pecans and spread over peanut butter. Let stand until set; cut into 48 bars.

Anda Gagnet (Mrs. Ted)

FULL OF FRUIT BARS

1½ cups all-purpose flour
1 teaspoon salt
¾ teaspoon soda
1 teaspoon nutmeg
½ teaspoon cinnamon
¼ cup butter or margarine,
  softened
¾ cup sugar
2 eggs
1 teaspoon vanilla extract

1 8-ounce can crushed pineapple
  in juice, drained and 1 teaspoon
  juice reserved (for frosting)
1 cup finely chopped unpeeled
  apples
½ cup golden raisins
Cream Cheese Frosting (recipe
  below)
Pecan halves

Stir together flour, salt, soda and spices; set aside. In a large bowl cream butter, gradually add sugar; cream until well blended. Beat in eggs 1 at a time, then add vanilla. Stir in pineapple and flour mixture, then apples and raisins until well blended. Spread evenly in a greased 15x10x1-inch jelly-roll pan. Bake at 350°F. for 20 minutes or until pick inserted in center comes out clean. Remove from oven; cool on rack. Spread with frosting; cut into 64 bars. Garnish each bar with pecan half.

Cream Cheese Frosting

1 3-ounce package cream cheese,
  softened
2 tablespoons butter or margarine,
  softened

1 teaspoon pineapple juice
1 teaspoon milk
1 teaspoon grated lemon rind
2 cups powdered sugar

Mix cream cheese and butter until well blended. Beat in juice, milk and lemon rind. Gradually beat in powdered sugar until mixture is of spreading consistency.

Roberta Hudgins (Mrs. Al, III)

FORGOTTEN COOKIES

2 egg whites
⅔ cup sugar

1 teaspoon vanilla extract
½ cup chopped nuts

Beat egg whites until stiff, gradually adding sugar. Fold in vanilla and nuts. Drop by spoonful onto foil-lined cookie sheet. Preheat oven to 350°F.; turn heat off and place cookies in oven and forget them overnight.

Ann Kovaleski
Tallahassee, Florida

COCONUT DREAM BARS

Crust

½ cup butter   1½ cups all-purpose flour
½ cup firmly packed brown sugar

Cream butter and sugar; add flour. Press into 13x9x2-inch pan. Bake at 350°F. for 15 minutes. Cool.

Filling

3 eggs   ¼ teaspoon salt
1½ cups firmly packed brown   1 teaspoon vanilla extract
  sugar   1½ cups coconut
¼ cup all-purpose flour   1 cup chopped nuts
1 teaspoon baking powder

Beat eggs, add brown sugar and mix well. Add dry ingredients, vanilla and mix. Fold in coconut and nuts. Spread in baked crust. Bake at 350°F. for 15-20 minutes.

Faye Carrol (Mrs. John)
Kissimmee, Florida

JIFFY NUT BARS

1 cup butter   ½ teaspoon salt
1 cup sugar   2 cups all-purpose flour
1 egg, separated   ½-1 cup chopped nuts
½ teaspoon vanilla extract

Cream butter; add sugar and egg yolk; mix well. Add remaining ingredients except egg white and nuts. Softly pat dough into a buttered cookie sheet (with sides). Brush surface of dough with beaten egg white, draining off excess. Sprinkle with nuts. Bake at 325°F. approximately 25 minutes or until golden brown. Cut into bars with a sharp knife 3-4 minutes after removal from oven.

Barbara Coleman (Mrs. Frank)

BUTTERSCOTCH BARS

1 18½-ounce package yellow
 cake mix
½ cup vegetable oil
1 8-ounce carton sour cream
1 3¾-ounce package instant
 vanilla pudding mix

4 eggs
½ cup chopped nuts
1 6-ounce package butterscotch
 morsels

Mix all ingredients except nuts and butterscotch morsels with electric mixer in a medium bowl. Add nuts and butterscotch. Bake in a greased and floured waxed-paper lined 13x9x2-inch pan. Bake at 325°F. for 30-40 minutes. Remove from oven, cool 5-10 minutes and turn out (upside down) to cool. When cool, cut into bars. The butterscotch morsels make a crunchy topping.

Note: For variation, try instant butterscotch or butter pecan pudding mix.

Elynor Chalker
Dothan, Alabama

OATMEAL CHIP BAR COOKIES

1 cup unsifted all-purpose
 flour
1 cup quick cooking oats
¾ cup firmly packed light
 brown sugar
½ cup butter or margarine,
 softened

1 14-ounce can sweetened condensed milk
1 6-ounce package chocolate
 morsels or butterscotch morsels
1 cup chopped nuts (optional)

Mix together flour, oats, brown sugar and butter, reserving ½ cup of the mixture. Press the remainder in a thin layer over the bottom of a lightly greased 13x9x2-inch dish. Bake at 350°F. for 10 minutes. Pour condensed milk over this crust. Top evenly with morsels and nuts, if desired. Sprinkle reserved oat mixture over the top; press down firmly using the back of a spoon. Bake 25-30 minutes or until lightly brown. Cool thoroughly before cutting. Makes 36 bars.

Laurie Combs (Mrs. Samuel L.)

CRÈME DE MENTHE SQUARES

1¼ cups butter or margarine,
divided
½ cup cocoa
3½ cups sifted powdered sugar,
divided
1 egg, beaten

1 teaspoon vanilla extract
2 cups graham cracker crumbs
⅓ cup Creme de Menthe
1½ cups semisweet chocolate
morsels

In saucepan combine ½ cup butter and cocoa. Heat and stir until well blended. Remove from heat and add ½ cup powdered sugar, egg and vanilla. Stir in graham cracker crumbs; mix well. Press into the bottom of an ungreased 13x9x2-inch baking pan; set aside. Melt another ½ cup butter and mix with Creme de Menthe; beat in the remaining 3 cups powdered sugar at low speed of electric mixer until smooth. Spread over the chocolate layer; chill 1 hour. In small saucepan combine the remaining ¼ cup butter and chocolate morsels. Cook and stir over low heat until melted. Spread over mint layer; chill 1-2 hours. Cut into small squares. Store in refrigerator. Seal each piece in plastic wrap for gifts. Makes about 96 squares.

Karen Bassett (Mrs. Jeff)
Mabel Rhyne (Mrs. Bill)

CANADIAN COOKIES

¼ cup butter
1 cup all-purpose flour
2 eggs, well-beaten
1½ cups firmly packed dark brown
sugar

½ cup flaked coconut
¼ teaspoon baking powder
1 cup chopped nuts
½ teaspoon salt
1 teaspoon vanilla extract

Mix together butter and flour with fingers and spread in a greased 12x10-inch baking dish. Bake at 350°F. for 12-15 minutes; cool. Mix remaining ingredients together well; spread over baked layer and bake at 325-350°F. for 25 minutes longer. Cool; then spread with frosting and cut into small pieces.

Frosting

1½ cups powdered sugar
2 tablespoons butter, softened

2 tablespoons orange juice
1 teaspoon lemon juice

Combine ingredients well; spread on cake after it cools.

Theola Blackwell (Mrs. Jack A.)

CREAM CHEESE BROWNIES

Chocolate Mixture

8 ounce semisweet chocolate
  squares
6 tablespoons butter
4 eggs
1½ cups sugar
1 cup all-purpose flour

1 teaspoon baking powder
½ teaspoon salt
½ teaspoon almond extract
3 teaspoons vanilla extract
1 cup chopped nuts

Melt chocolate and butter; set aside to cool. Beat eggs until fluffy. Add sugar and beat until thick. Add flour and baking powder, beating well. Add remaining ingredients and cooled chocolate mixture.

Cream Cheese Mixture

1 8-ounce package cream cheese
¼ cup butter
½ cup sugar

2 eggs
2 tablespoons all-purpose flour
1 teaspoon vanilla extract

Cream butter and cream cheese until fluffy; add sugar. Add remaining ingredients and thoroughly blend together. (This works well in a food processor.) Put half the chocolate mixture into two 8-inch square buttered pans. Add all of cream cheese mixture and top with remaining chocolate mixture; swirl with a knife. Bake at 350°F. for 35 minutes. Better when refrigerated.

Ruth Lark (Mrs. William E.)

OLD FASHIONED BLONDE BROWNIES

1 cup butter
4 cups firmly packed light
  brown sugar
4 eggs

2 heaping cups all-purpose flour
2 teaspoons vanilla extract
2 cups nuts

Cream butter and sugar well. Add eggs 1 at a time, beating well after each addition. Add flour, vanilla, nuts and blend. Bake in a well-greased and floured 13x9-inch pan at 325°F. about 1 hour or until the brownies start to pull away from sides of pan. This recipe halves very well.

Pat Syfrett (Mrs. Frank)

CHOCOLATE COVERED CHERRIES

⅓ cup butter or margarine
2 cups marshmallow creme
Dash of salt
1 teaspoon almond extract
4 cups sifted powdered sugar
36 maraschino cherries, well-
  drained and dried with
  paper towels

1 12-ounce package semisweet
  chocolate morsels
1 block of paraffin

Cream butter; beat in marshmallow creme, salt and almond extract. Add powdered sugar gradually, mixing well after each addition. Turn out and knead until smooth, working in extra powdered sugar if mixture becomes too sticky; refrigerate 1 hour. Wrap each cherry in marshmallow mixture being sure it is completely covered; refrigerate. Melt chocolate and paraffin in top of a double boiler over hot, not boiling, water. Using toothpicks or stems of cherries, dip cherries into melted chocolate. Place on waxed paper. If using stemless cherries, close toothpick holes with dribble of hot chocolate. Refrigerate until chocolate hardens, then store. Fondant will not liquify until cherries are removed from refrigeration for a day or so.

Pam Whitelock (Mrs. Richard)

WHITE CHRISTMAS CANDY

2 cups sugar
½ cup sour cream
⅓ cup light corn syrup
2 tablespoons butter
¼ teaspoon salt

1 teaspoon vanilla extract
1 teaspoon rum or brandy extract
¼ cup candied cherries, quartered
1 cup coarsely chopped walnuts
Butter or margarine

Combine first 5 ingredients in a large saucepan; gradually bring to a boil, stirring until sugar is dissolved. Boil (do not stir) over medium heat to soft ball stage (236°F.) on candy thermometer. Remove from heat; let stand for 15 minutes (do not stir). Add flavorings and beat until it begins to lose its gloss. Add cherries and nuts and pour into a buttered 8-inch square pan. Let harden and cut into squares. Do not double.

Marsha Lewis (Mrs. E. Clay, III)

INDEX

INDEX

INDEX

INDEX

INDEX

INDEX

INDEX

PRINTS FROM *BEYOND THE BAY*

Lithographs of the original watercolors created by artist Paul Brent for *Beyond the Bay* can now be ordered. Each painting has been reproduced at its original size of 11" X 16" and is printed on high-quality heavy stock.

The prints can be ordered individually for $15.00 each, or for a special price of $100, you may purchase the entire set of eight. The titles of each painting can be found on the page behind each print within the cookbook, along with the short descriptive passage.

To order your prints from *Beyond the Bay* fill out the following order form or send the necessary information to:

Prints from *Beyond the Bay*
Art Zone
P.O. Box 12064 • Panama City, Florida 32401
Telephone: (904) 769-7384

	Price	Qty.	Total
Conch and Palmetto	15.00	_____	_____
Sand Dollar and Palmetto	15.00	_____	_____
Daylily	15.00	_____	_____
Magnolia	15.00	_____	_____
Sandpipers	15.00	_____	_____
Tern	15.00	_____	_____
Pelicans	15.00	_____	_____
Snapper and Grouper	15.00	_____	_____
Set of all eight prints	100.00	_____	_____
packing			1.00
postage			1.50
Florida resident 5% sales tax			_____
Total			_____

☐ Check or money order ☐ Mastercard or VISA

card number _____ expiration date_____

bank number _____
(Mastercard only)

Please allow 4 weeks for delivery

Name _____ date _____

Address _____

City _____ State _____ Zip _____

Bay Publications

Post Office Box 404   Panama City, Florida 32402   (904) 785-7870

Please send _____ copies of *Beyond the Bay* @ $13.95 each $ _____
Postage and Handling @ $ 1.55 each $ _____
Fl. residents add 5% sales tax @ $ .70 each $ _____
* Check here for gift wrap ☐   Total enclosed $ _____

Please send _____ copies of *Bay Leaves* @ $9.95 each $ _____
Postage & Handling @ $1.55 $ _____
Fl. residents add 5% sales tax @ $ .50 $ _____
* Check here for gift wrap ☐   Total enclosed $ _____

Please charge my VISA ☐   MASTER CARD ☐

Card number _____

Signature_____Exp. Date _____

Name _____

Address _____

City _____ State _____Zip_____

Bay Publications

Post Office Box 404   Panama City, Florida 32402   (904) 785-7870

Please send _____ copies of *Beyond the Bay* @ $13.95 each $ _____
Postage and Handling @ $ 1.55 each $ _____
Fl. residents add 5% sales tax @ $ .70 each $ _____
* Check here for gift wrap ☐   Total enclosed $ _____

Please send _____ copies of *Bay Leaves* @ $9.95 each $ _____
Postage & Handling @ $1.55 $ _____
Fl. residents add 5% sales tax @ $ .50 $ _____
* Check here for gift wrap ☐   Total enclosed $ _____

Please charge my VISA ☐   MASTER CARD ☐

Card number _____

Signature_____Exp. Date _____

Name _____

Address _____

City _____ State _____Zip_____

I would like to see *Beyond the Bay* and *Bay Leaves* sold in the following stores:

Store name _____

Address _____

City _____ State _____ Zip_____

Store name _____

Address _____

City _____ State _____ Zip_____

- -

I would like to see *Beyond the Bay* and *Bay Leaves* sold in the following stores:

Store name _____

Address _____

City _____ State _____ Zip_____

Store name _____

Address _____

City _____ State _____ Zip_____

Bay Publications

Post Office Box 404   Panama City, Florida 32402   (904) 785-7870

Please send _____ copies of *Beyond the Bay* @ $13.95 each $ _____
Postage and Handling @ $ 1.55 each $ _____
Fl. residents add 5% sales tax @ $ .70 each $ _____
* Check here for gift wrap ☐   Total enclosed $ _____

Please send _____ copies of *Bay Leaves* @ $9.95 each $ _____
Postage & Handling @ $1.55 $ _____
Fl. residents add 5% sales tax @ $ .50 $ _____
* Check here for gift wrap ☐   Total enclosed $ _____

Please charge my VISA ☐ MASTER CARD ☐

Card number _____

Signature_____Exp. Date _____

Name _____

Address _____

City _____ State _____Zip_____

Bay Publications

Post Office Box 404   Panama City, Florida 32402   (904) 785-7870

Please send _____ copies of *Beyond the Bay* @ $13.95 each $ _____
Postage and Handling @ $ 1.55 each $ _____
Fl. residents add 5% sales tax @ $ .70 each $ _____
* Check here for gift wrap ☐   Total enclosed $ _____

Please send _____ copies of *Bay Leaves* @ $9.95 each $ _____
Postage & Handling @ $1.55 $ _____
Fl. residents add 5% sales tax @ $ .50 $ _____
* Check here for gift wrap ☐   Total enclosed $ _____

Please charge my VISA ☐ MASTER CARD ☐

Card number _____

Signature_____Exp. Date _____

Name _____

Address _____

City _____ State _____Zip_____

Reorder Additional Copies

I would like to see *Beyond the Bay* and *Bay Leaves* sold in the following stores:

Store name _____

Address _____

City _____ State _____ Zip _____

Store name _____

Address _____

City _____ State _____ Zip _____

I would like to see *Beyond the Bay* and *Bay Leaves* sold in the following stores:

Store name _____

Address _____

City _____ State _____ Zip _____

Store name _____

Address _____

City _____ State _____ Zip _____